FEAR AS A WAY OF LIFE

FEAR AS A WAY OF LIFE

mayan widows in rural guatemala

Linda Green

COLUMBIA UNIVERSITY PRESS  NEW YORK

Columbia University Press
Publishers Since 1893
New York Chichester, West Sussex

A different version of chapter 3, titled "Fear as a Way of Life," appeared in *Cultural Anthropology* 9(2): 227–259, 1994, and as "Living in a State of Fear," in Carolyn Nordstrom and A. C. G. M. Robben, eds., *Fieldwork Under Fire* (Berkeley: University of California Press), pp. 105–128.
Chapter 7 appeared in a different version as "Shifting Boundaries: Mayan Widows and Evangelicos," in David Stoll and Virginia Burnett, eds., *Rethinking Protestantism in Latin America* (Philadelphia: Temple University Press, 1993), pp. 159–179.

Library of Congress Cataloging-in-Publication Data
Green, Linda.
Fear as a way of life : Mayan widows in rural Guatemala / Linda Green.
p. cm.
Includes bibliographical references.
ISBN 0-231-10032-9 (cloth). — ISBN 0-231-10033-7 (paper).
1. Cakchikel women—Wars. 2. Cakchikel women—Crimes against. 3. Cakchikel women —Social conditions. 4. War widows—Guatemala—Social conditions. 5. War widows—Guatemala—Economic conditions. 6. Guatemala—Politics and government. I. Title.
F1465.2.C3G74 1999
972.8105'3'082—DC21 98-52083

Casebound editions of Columbia University Press books are printed on permanent and durable acid-free paper.
Designed by Chang Jae Lee
Printed in the United States of America
c 10 9 8 7 6 5 4 3 2 1
p 10 9 8 7 6 5 4 3

In memory of my mother, Beatrice Green

For the widows of Xe'caj

and for Tan

contents

list of illustrations

acknowledgments

This book has been a long time in the making—a summer field trip to Guatemala in 1986 first inspired it—and I have incurred many debts, intellectual and otherwise. I am pleased now to have the opportunity to acknowledge publicly those to whom I am indebted.

The initial research and writing of the fieldwork in Guatemala were made possible by the generous financial support of the Institute of International Education Fulbright Fellowship, Foreign Language Area Studies Fellowship; the University of California, Berkeley, Chancellor's Fellowship; the Robert H. Lowe and Ronald L. Olson Funds of the Department of Anthropology at Berkeley; and summer travel grants from the Institute of Latin American Studies at Berkeley.

At Columbia University I am grateful for financial support I received for revisions to the manuscript: Council for Research in the Humanities and Social Sciences summer fellowships in 1994 and 1995, the Leonard Hastings Schoff Publication Fund of the University Seminars, and a summer travel grant from the Institute of Latin American and Iberian Studies in 1996.

At the University of California, Berkeley, I owe my greatest debt to my principal adviser and mentor, Nancy Scheper-Hughes, whose intelligence, wit, and political engagement have been guiding inspiration for my own work. My other advisers—Fred Dunn, Margarita Melville, Laura Nader, and Michael Watts—gave generous guidance and assistance every step of the way. Burton Benedict, Gerald Berreman, Meg Conkey, Aiwah Ong, and William Shack substantially furthered my intellectual growth while at Berkeley. I owe special thanks to Michael Watts, not only for his consistently astute comments but for his exemplary scholarship and teaching, a model to which I aspire.

I am grateful to my colleagues, both former and present, in the Departments of Anthropology and International and Public Affairs at Columbia for providing an intellectual atmosphere that aided me in completing this work. Several of my graduate students at Columbia, both former and present, deserve special mention: Andy Bickford, Alex Costley, Marcial Godoy-Antivia, Lance Lattig, Cynthia Pierce, and Tresa Thomas, as well as students in my undergraduate seminars, A Legacy of Power and Violence in Central America and Body and Society. Special thanks is due to my research assistant, Cynthia Pierce, for her help in the final push to get the bibliographic references in order.

Other colleagues in New York and beyond have been generous with their input and advice over the years, especially Mary Garcia Castro, Cynthia Enloe, Lesley Gill, Matt Gutmann, Jim Handy, Roger Lancaster, Antonio Lauria, Deborah Levenson-Estrada, George Lovell, Brinton Lykes, Marybeth Mills, June Nash, Katherine Newman, Carolyn Nordstrom, Victor Perera, Jim Quesada, Lesley Sharp, Gerald Sider, and the late Hernan Vidal. I am indebted to June Nash for the inspiration for the title.

As the manuscript took shape, several colleagues contributed important critiques on portions of it, especially Mary Garcia Castro, Roger Lancaster, June Nash, Lesley Sharp, Gerald Sider, and the late Hernan Vidal. Gerald Sider, in particular, read innumerable drafts and gave bountifully of his time, energy, and intellect. Oral presentations drawn from this work were given at the Cultural Pluralism seminar at Columbia University, CUNY Graduate Center, the New York Academy of Sciences, Rutgers University, Tufts University, the University of New Mexico, and conferences in Zagreb, Caracas, and Buenos Aires. To these many colleagues whose comments were crucial in subsequent revisions, my heartfelt thanks.

I had the good fortune to be part of the MS Writer's Group at Columbia these past four years, where Zita Nunes, Maggie Sale, Karen Van Dyke,

Priscilla Wald, Judith Weisenfeld, and Angela Zito offered unstinting comments and friendship. Likewise the regular members of the Cultural Pluralism Seminar at Columbia have provided unfailing support and incisive analyses, especially, Carol Charles, Lesley Gill, Antonio Lauria, Hannah Lessinger, Susan Lowes, Gerald Sider, and Janet Suskind.

Over the years, conversations with Guatemalan anthropologists, scholars, intellectuals, and writers have been instrumental in helping me try to make sense of this complicated country; among them, Tani Adams, Clara Arenas, Tom Barry, Laurel Bossen, Peggy Cain, Claire Creelman, Matt Creelman, Rachel Garst, Pat Goudvis, Jim Handy, Carol Hendrickson, Rachel Lausch, Deborah Levenson-Estrada, George Lovell, Chris Lutz, Brinton Lykes, Beatriz Manz, Marcie Mersky, Elissa Miller, Marilyn Moors, Liz Oglesby, Ben Paul, Victor Perera, Debra Preusch, Carol Smith, David Stoll, Frank Taylor, Kay Warren, John Watanabe, and Paula Worby.

Guatemalans who helped significantly with this project are, under the present circumstances, best left unnamed. Suffice it to say that my debt to them is enormous, and the biggest of all is to the widows of Xe'caj who opened their lives to me. The women among whom I worked and lived gave their time to me as a researcher, patiently answering my seemingly irrelevant questions. More important, however, they taught me about dignity, courage, and hope in the face of relentless adversity. Their friendships continue to enliven me. Without the generosity, friendship, and intellectual contribution of my field assistant, Sophia, as well as the support of her family, my understanding of Mayan culture would be sorely lacking.

At Columbia University Press, I am especially grateful to my editor, John Michel, for his humor, patience, and enthusiastic championing of this manuscript throughout its various stages; to Alexander Thorp, for guiding the manuscript through the production process; and to my manuscript editor, Sarah St. Onge, for making insightful suggestions and for saving me from some of my worst grammatical impulses.

Several dear friends have been pivotal in encouraging my efforts in this project from its inception, among them, Gail Lamont, Jeanne Roche, and Ann Tamminen. Last, my husband, Sebastian Quinac, has been a constant source of love, commentary, and inspiration. Without his generosity of spirit and sustained commitment to seeing this book to completion it would surely be less than it is. And during the last year and a half of writing our son, Juan Miguel, has given me new perspectives on this project and on life, for which I am truly grateful.

author's note

For reasons of safety, none of the photographs in this book features people from Xe'caj. The subjects of the photographs, however, are emblematic of the situations of many rural Mayan people throughout the altiplano.

six women from xe'caj

As is the case with most of us who conduct ethnographic studies, I came to know a few of my informants quite well. Although many women generously shared their experiences with me over the course of the fieldwork, it is the stories and lives of Marcelina, Elena, Eufemia, Alejandra, Juana, and Martina that have given shape to much of this book.

Doña Marcelina lives in Ri Bay, a small aldea of Xe'caj. Raised as a Catholic, she is now a member of the Prince of Peace evangelical church. At age thirty-four she was left with four adolescent children when her husband was killed on his way to work the milpa. Doña Marcelina speaks Kaqchikel and some Spanish; she never attended school. She was one of the participants in the weaving project.

Doña Elena, doña Marcelina's daughter, lives in the same compound as her mother in Ri Bay. She too was raised a Catholic and is now a member of the Prince of Peace evangelical church. She was seventeen, with two babies, when her husband was killed on the patio in front of her house. She attended two years of school but can neither read nor write, although she speaks both Kaqchikel and some Spanish. She participated in the weaving project intermittently and traveled to harvest coffee in Esquintla and Antigua.

Doña Eufemia also lives in Ri Bay. Raised as a Catholic, now she is ostensibly a member of the Price of Peace Church, although she does not participate in cultos. She was thirty-two, with four children, when her husband was disappeared near the aldea. She speaks Kaqchikel and some Spanish and never attended school. Like doña Elena, she participated in the weaving project for widows and occasionally traveled to harvest coffee in Esquintla and Antigua.

Doña Alejandra lives in one of the pueblos of Xe'caj, having moved there from an aldea when her husband was disappeared. She was forty at that time, with six sons. Raised in the Central American Mission Church, she is a member of El Grupo. Although she never attended school, she learned to read and write in Spanish and speaks both Spanish and Kaqchikel. A master weaver, she is often commissioned to make huipils by women from the pueblo and aldeas.

Doña Juana lives in Be'cal, an aldea of Xe'caj. She was raised as a Catholic. Forty years old in 1988, she lives with her mother, who is a widow. Although she never married, Juana participates in widows' projects—weaving, raising hens, and making soap—in her mother's stead. She never attended school and speaks only Kaqchikel.

Doña Martina also lives in Be'cal. She was raised a Catholic. Forty-five when her husband was disappeared, she was left with four children. Like doña Eufemia, she speaks Kaqchikel and some Spanish and never attended school. She participated in the weaving project as well as the hen-raising and soap-making projects.

part one

a legacy of violence

FEAR AS A WAY OF LIFE

FIGURE I.1

A widow and her son performing a ceremony at the gravesite of her husband. (*Jonathan Moller*)

1. in the aftermath of war: an introduction

Wars don't simply end
And wars don't end simply

—Cynthia Enloe, "Women After Wars: Puzzles and Warnings" (1996)

La Violencia

If you want to speak to widows, go to Xe'caj," the young man sitting across from me advised. His companion nodded in agreement. The year was 1987, and I was spending the summer in Guatemala exploring the possibilities of doing ethnographic fieldwork on the topic of Mayan widows, women whose husbands had been killed during the past decade of political violence that had wracked the country. I was traveling around the altiplano (the highlands),[1] looking for a research site, talking discreetly with people about *la violencia* (the violence). Even in 1987, three years after the counterinsurgency campaign had ostensibly ended, the civil war was referred to in public discourse simply as la violencia or *la situacion* (the situation), and public discussions about widows or orphans were nonexistent.[2] Conversations with strangers about the violence were rare and usually held in private.

The two young Mayan Indian men with whom I was speaking that July day were brothers, aged sixteen and seventeen, who had fled Xe'caj four years earlier after witnessing the brutal death of their father and mother at the hands of the Guatemalan military. Like many of their neighbors, these youths had fled to the mountains as the Guatemala military swept through the department of Chimaltenango intermittently from 1981 to 1983, killing, looting, and burning in a campaign now known infamously as "scorched earth." Raul and Manuel—cold, hungry, frightened—survived for several months by hiding in the shadows of the nearby mountains as soldiers scoured the area. Now the two boys were living some distance from their *pueblo* (town) with a priest who had offered them sanctuary.

"But if you do work in Xe'caj," they warned, "it will be difficult: the army is everywhere."

I returned to Guatemala a year later to begin the fieldwork for this book about the lives of some Mayan widows who live in Xe'caj. After my conversation with those young brothers, I had imagined Xe'caj as being too risky for a possible field site. Initially, my plan was to focus on the lives of women widowed by the violence, but my primary interest was to understand their economic survival strategies in the aftermath of war. If possible, I wanted to sidestep the areas that were still filled with tension, such as Xe'caj. I had originally assumed that the violence of the past and the military control of the present would serve only as a backdrop for my study. During my first few months of living in Guatemala, however, no longer seeing things as a tourist, I came to understand that violence and fear suffused people's everyday lives. Through a series of serendipitous events, I ultimately did work in Xe'caj, convinced by trusted Guatemalan friends that while it might not be emblematic, neither was its way of life unique among many of the towns and villages that dot the altiplano.

Although human rights organizations, such as Amnesty International and America's Watch, have painstakingly documented la violencia in Guatemala, the true extent of that violence remains unknown. Present estimates account for more than 100,000 people killed and another 40,000 people disappeared in the course of one of the longest-running insurgencies in Latin America.[3] During the 1980s alone, tens of thousands of refugees—men, women, and children—fled across the Mexican border, while another million people were internally displaced for various periods of time during the decade. Today there are an estimated 80,000 widows and 250,000 orphans—those who have lost at least one parent—in Guatemala. Such numbers can never reflect the true nature of the violence that took place; moreover, as one official working for PAVYH (a state-run Assistance Program for Widows and Orphans of the Violence) in Chimaltenango said to me soon after a 1988 massacre of twenty-two peasants in the nearby village of Aguacate, San Andreas Itzapa, "We are making new widows every day."[4]

Representations of military power were, and to some extent remain, readily visible and ubiquitous in the western highlands. Ranging from the large, fortressed *zona militars* (military bases) that dominate the provincial capitals to the smaller, less conspicuous army barracks—*destacamentos*—situated in so-called areas of conflict and down to the rough-hewn mud-and-scrap-wood civil militia posts that guarded the entrances to many villages, the America's Watch characterization of Guatemala as a "nation of prisoners" rang hauntingly true (1984).

By the mid-1990s, the military presence in the central highlands of the department of Chimaltenango was less obvious, with some of the smaller barracks in nearby towns having been dismantled. Still, the intermittent presence of soldiers and the constant vigilance of civil patrollers and military commissioners in many villages such as Xe'caj continued unabated.[5] What remains hidden even today, except to those near at hand, are the representational and material legacies of terror: the silences that permeate everyday life, the innumerable clandestine cemeteries that only now are being excavated, the blood on people's hands—both literally and figuratively—and the half secrets about what was done to whom and by whom.

On my first trip to Guatemala in the summer of 1986, I traveled around the highlands with two friends who gave me an accelerated course in the geography and history of la violencia. Our travels spanned almost the entire breadth of the Sierra de Cuchumatanes—one of the most spectacular mountain ranges in the western highlands—from the provincial capital of Coban in Alta Vera Paz, to the Ixil Triangle in Northern Quiche, to the small, remote town of Todos Santos in Huehuetenango. Yet the beauty of the land could not obscure the effects of the recent violent bloodshed. The passionate voice of the *commandante* (commander) of the military barracks in Nebaj who boasted of protecting and defending the people from the subversives by any means necessary mingled in my mind with the timid inquiry of a young boy in Todos Santos who wanted to know if we too had suffered from the violence; these memories continued to disturb me long after the trip ended.

One incident from the trip forcefully foreshadowed my subsequent understanding of how political violence operates. My friends and I had stopped for lunch in a small *cantina* (bar) in Salama, Baja Vera Paz. Afterward we strolled around the town square, buying handicrafts as souvenirs. As in so many towns we had visited in the past few weeks, the central square was dominated by a military barracks. On one of the compound walls was scrawled graffiti reading "The Army is here to defend the people of Guatemala, to guarantee peace and freedom." One of my companions decided to snap several photographs of this slogan and of the soldiers guarding the entrance to the barracks. A short while later, as we drove out of town on an old dirt road, we caught up with a military jeep that we had noticed leaving some minutes before us. Just as we were about to pass the jeep, the soldier on the passenger side extended his right arm and fired a shot into the adjacent field. Then—in slow motion, it seemed—he withdrew his arm and then extended it once again, this time only to flex his fingers. Needless to say, we stayed well behind the jeep, despite the whirlwind of dust it left in its wake, until it turned off the road in the next town. I puzzled over this event for some time. What did it mean? Was it a message, or was it only a coincidence? Maybe it was nothing? I did not realize until much later in my fieldwork how such acts of intimidation rely precisely on these ambiguities for their effectiveness. And it was only through the mundane rounds of daily living that I eventually gained a fuller understanding of the complexities of violence in rural Guatemala.

This book is a study of how the intricacies of violence are inextricably linked to the widows' survival in Xe'caj. Violence is not simply the historical background for this ethnography, as I had initially imagined it; it is implicated in the ways in which the women refashion social memory and cultural practices, both as a consequence of and in response to the fear that circumscribes their lives. Sociopolitical violence, as Antonio Gramsci (1971) observed in Italy of the early twentieth century, becomes deeply embedded within social institutions and cultural conceptions of power and identity; silences and secrecy may often speak more powerfully than words. This book explores the creative ways in which some of the widows have constructed alternative forms of community in the midst of their suffering, efforts that speak to the resiliency of the human spirit.

Analyses that explain the political violence and repression in Guatemala solely in terms of the blows and counterblows exchanged by the Guatemalan state and the guerrilla insurgency or those based on the well-documented wholesale massacres, mutilations, and political murder of unarmed civilians—characterized as genocide against the Mayan people—provide only partial accounts of the intricacies of that violence. What they overlook is how the political violence operated locally. The intellectual contributions of Michel Foucault (1977), Henri Lefebvre (1991), and Antonio Gramsci (1971) offer ways of understanding how structures of violence in complex societies come to be embedded in social institutions and cultural conceptions that may be reproduced locally and revealed in daily life. In Guatemala, violence and militarization shape the very character of daily interactions. Yet if one pays close attention to the quotidian—the humble, familiar, mundane aspects of everyday experience—one may discern not only the alienation and violence produced by modernity but also the possibilities for creativity that may emerge from these processes.

To do justice to the complexities that suffuse lived lives, particularly in my efforts to formulate abstractions from observations, this work draws extensively on the theoretical understandings of Raymond Williams (1977, 1983, 1989) and David Harvey (1988, 1996) with regard to dialectical ways of thinking. Their insights in turn are grounded in Marx's notion of dialectics. Harvey's distillation of basic theses about dialectics "emphasizes the understanding of processes, flows, fluxes, and relations over the analysis of elements, things, structures, and organized systems" (1996:49). Crucial to this study is an understanding of violence as a historical and political economic process and a recognition that notions of space and time are "not external to processes but are contingent and contained within them" (Harvey 1996:53). With these in mind, I engage the dilemmas posed by the concurrence of mutual betrayal and collective dignity among the Mayas in the most recent period of violence. In addition, the interactions between two axes of Mayan identity and culture, what Stuart Hall (1994:395) has referred to in the Caribbean context as "the vector of similarity and continuity" and "the vector of difference and rupture," are brought to the fore. Finally, intrinsic to a dialectical approach is an emphasis on the necessary connection between knowledge and engagement (Ollman 1993).

Lived Lives

Lived lives and a sense of value that attaches thereto are embedded in an environment actively molded and achieved through work, play, and a wide array of cultural practices.

—David Harvey, *Justice, Nature, and the Geography of Difference*, p. 34

The central focus of this book is the survival tactics of Mayan widows—women heading households alone in rural communities—in the aftermath of war and the ways in which hunger and fear, as well as culture and community, configure their lives. As I became more involved in the women's lives over the course of the fieldwork, however, I saw that to understand the choices they were making necessitated an exploration of how violence has marked their lives on a daily basis, not only in their memories of the tragic individual deaths of their husbands but in the way violence, both structural and political, operated locally. Recognizing the intricate links between the political violence and repression of the past decade and the long-term systemic violence connected with class and gender inequalities and ethnic oppression—the "violence of everyday life"—is crucial to this understanding.

In this book, I also examine the complex relationship between Mayan people and the Guatemalan state from the perspective of rural widows in the western highlands. In doing so I address one of the striking and perhaps unresolvable tensions in Mesoamerican ethnography: the simultaneous continuity and rupture of Mayan identity in Guatemala. Through an examination of the everyday survival tactics utilized by some Mayan widows in Xe'caj, this research explores the contradictions and complexities of violence in their lives and how these effects are mediated through culture, gender, and experience.

This study underscores how practical notions of ethnicity, cultural identity, and community remain powerful shapers of Mayan thinking and practice, even in the face of ongoing violence aimed at destroying the very countenance of that identity and loyalty. The ways in which the widows of Xe'caj situate and humanize themselves in the face of dehumanizing experiences can shape our understandings of suffering and history. In addition, the lives and stories of the women of Xe'caj provide a lens for viewing the less visible, taken-for-granted suffering of Mayan people perpetuated by Western development in conjunction with the Guatemalan state.

A gendered analysis in the Guatemalan context is crucial to explaining both the commonalities and the differences in the effects of structural and political violence on men's and women's lives and the importance of culture in their everyday lived experiences. The following exploration of the material conditions under which the widows operate, live their lives, and construct their histories, as well as the specific forms of subjectivity and consciousness through which they negotiate their material and affective relationships, contributes to our understanding of the mutual dependence of agency and structure, what Marx referred to as "praxis."

Blood on People's Hands

The devastation of communities, both people and places, was massive in the highlands of Guatemala: it went far beyond physical destruction and murder. In Xe'caj many women and children were forced to witness the brutal murders of their family members and neighbors. Others hid in the mountains nearby. The army used force to relocate those who remained behind to towns or makeshift camps where they could be more easily controlled. As has become commonplace in counterinsurgency warfare throughout the world in the latter half of this century, in Guatemala unarmed civilians were configured as the enemy and treated as such.

Jean Franco (1985) notes that attacks on civilian populations as part of counterinsurgency deployment also represent a war over meaning. She argues that assaults by repressive states in Latin America on priests, nuns, women, and children are not only violations against individuals but also transgressions on "sanctuary spaces." The spatial and symbolic boundaries of home, church, and family that offer some immunity from violence are ruptured through acts of state terror, their meaning resignified insofar as they no longer offer protection from repression. Their erstwhile meaning subtly shifts, a shift that Franco, borrowing from Deleuze and Guatarri (1977), calls the process of "deterritorialization."

In Guatemala in the aftermath of war not only have community spatial boundaries as sites of refuge been transgressed, but the community now embodies the very mechanisms of state terror under the aegis of military control. Army garrisons, civil militias (even though they have been now demobilized, as mandated by the peace accords), spies, forced recruitment of young boys into the military, and the subsequent return of soldiers to their natal villages create anxiety among community members. Silences imposed by the ongoing, entrenched impunity add another element of fear. In this investigation, I demonstrate how meanings attached to spaces and places in the widows' everyday lives have been reworked. Some of the widows of Xe'caj, for example, silenced by the ubiquitous presence of civil militias and local army garrisons in their community, now utilize the physical landscape and their own bodies as sites for remembering. Thus some of them have radically transformed the clandestine cemeteries where their loved ones were "disappeared" or even the physical pain and suffering embedded within their own bodies into a counterdiscourse and locus of struggle.

Without viewing the recent state violence directed against the civilian and mostly Mayan population of the altiplano in its historical context, it is easy to misread the counterinsurgency war as an instance of generals going momentarily mad or as overzealousness on the part of the beleaguered Guatemalan state in its attempt to rout out a communist insurgency, with the Mayas viewed as pawns inadvertently caught between the two armies (Stoll 1993). This ahistorical reasoning obscures precisely what I illuminate in this study, namely, the relationship between political violence and the deeply rooted and historically based structural violence of inequality and impunity that suffuses Guatemalan society, expressed through class, ethnicity, and gender divisions and experienced by Mayas as virulent racism.

The particularly brutal and insidious nature of the political violence and repression that took place in highland Guatemala during the counterinsurgency war from 1976 to 1985 and the continuing impunity for those acts are unprecedented, and the consequences profound. The delicate, intricate bonds that held communities together—if only tenuously during this century—have been severed by the microeffects of both structural violence and the militarization of daily life, which continues even though the local military commissioners and civil militias have been demobilized.

Any exploration of violence in highland Guatemala must address the difficult and tragic problems caused by what I have come to think of as "the blood on people's hands." It must consider the utter devastation of families and communities in a world where community members denounced their neighbors as subversives to the army (or, less often, as spies to the guerrillas) because of interfamilial feuding and where widows saw their husbands killed or disappeared by an army in which their own sons served as soldiers. It must acknowledge the horror of living side by side with the person responsible for the murder of your father, or of walking by the innumerable clandestine cemeteries that scar the local landscape, or of remaining silent and fearful in the face of the half secrets of who did what to whom. It must view these tragedies as something more than individual, albeit brutal, acts or stereotypical instances of Mayas as a backward, primitive, and violent people. It must understand how it was possible for the Guatemalan military to exploit effectively the cleavages, divisions, and animosities that have existed in, and between, some communities in the altiplano for centuries. To achieve such an analysis, a turn to history is essential, not grand narrative history but social history of specific relations that connects land, labor, and identity—the parameters of normal life—with the newly intensified violence.

In this study, I explore the implications of microsocial processes of structural and cultural changes that have taken place, their relation to political violence and militarization, and how fear has become a way of life in the altiplano. This requires an inquiry into how structural violence operated internally in communities and families and an examination of the linkages among subsistence, social relations, and suffering. In addition, Stuart Hall's (1994) notion of how "dominant regimes of representation" operate in the construction of the Other is useful in understanding the ways in which these processes are internalized so that individuals see and experience themselves as the Other. Within the marginalized communities themselves exist those elements of thinking and practice that represent the interests of the dominant center, what Raymond Williams has called "that most crucial form of imperialism" (1989:117), and this can at times create irresolvable tensions between resistance to and complicity with dominant social processes existing side by side (Harvey 1996).

A Silence on Suffering

Sociocultural anthropology, like most other disciplines in the social sciences, has undergone a sea change in the latter half of the twentieth century. Positivistic theories regarding "primitive" peoples and cultures have collapsed under postmodern scrutiny, undermining the long-entrenched beliefs about the Other that Johannes Fabian (1983) succinctly described as the denial of coevalness. The anthropological concept of cultural relativism, for example, which had provided the logical framework for understanding the seemingly undiscernable, irrational life ways of the Other, has been roundly criticized for its disregard of theory, history, and politics (Kessing 1987; Mohanty 1994) and its failure to address ethical questions (Scheper-Hughes 1992). In this book I offer a corollary critique—the conspicuous analytical silence on suffering.[6] I am referring to the suffering engendered by processes of domination in which, as Sider notes: "People are forced by circumstances utterly beyond their influence to try to cope with the sorts of economic changes that tear them from their history and their kin" (Sider 1989:14).

Representations of violence, whether political or structural, that are detached from the concrete and specific experiences of people and, in particular, from the complex consequences of suffering, have tended to reduce theorizing to an autonomous, disembodied activity, what Perry Anderson

(1976:44) has called in another context the "studied silence of Western Marxist intellectuals," with their retreat from the realities of political struggles. As Gerald Sider (1989:14) has eloquently pointed out, anthropologists have often failed to see the Other in understandable ways, to say what we have actually seen. There is a silence "at the center of the anthropological vision—our attempt to give voice to our sight—a profound void, a destructive silence: a silence about suffering."

In Guatemalan monographs, for example, North American ethnographers who conducted studies in the 1930s, 1940s, and 1950s were clearly aware that outside economic changes were affecting Mayan people's lives and livelihoods, as the work of Charles Wagley (1941) and Sol Tax (1953) aptly demonstrated. Wagley's observations about land inequality and wage labor in Santiago Chimaltenango in the late 1930s accurately predicted the intensification of land concentration in communities decades later that would leave only a small minority with sufficient land on which to subsist (Watanabe 1992). Yet the monographs produced from this period did not analytically account for the very palpable poverty and misery or the destructive influences of state power and pervasive racism on Mayan people's lives. One of the very real effects produced by the assault on subsistence was an intensified undermining of social and cultural life attached to that form of production.

Most of these monographs did document the importance of land to both milpa production and cultural traditions, the crucial relationship between growing corn and a Mayan worldview that premised survival on a collective enterprise between the living and the dead. As Ruth Bunzel succinctly articulated, for many Mayas "land is conceived of as belonging to the ancestors, one lives upon it by their grace" (1952:18). While the *cofradia* system—a Catholic cult of religious brotherhood originally introduced by the Spanish—captured the imagination of anthropologists during the decades of the mid-twentieth century, most of their work focused on symbolic cultural traditions, economic marginality, or individual prestige and failed to examine the contradictory social effects of the system's debilitation, and in some cases dissolution, as a powerful local institution. Yet the demise of cofradia power and authority not only undermined the community hegemony of Mayan elders but the hegemony of the ancestors as well (Brintnall 1979). This "death of the belief in death," as Nestor Garcia Canclini has put it (1993:100), internally weakened the ways in which communal and community life was reproduced. This belief in death worked as a survival strategy of sorts that both contributed to a degree of social stability while at the same time subordinated the village to structures of inequality. The breakdown of central community institutions, such as the cofradia, in the region of Chemaltenango between the mid-nineteenth and mid-twentieth centuries, along with the loss of ancestral land, must have produced widespread social and cultural suffering among the Mayas, as the material and symbolic bases by which for centuries they had conveyed their past through their present to their future was effectively destroyed.

There is a pressing need to interrogate the empirical realities of suffering and oppression in a way that "emphasizes the heterogeneity of experiences of injustice" both internal and external to local communities (Harvey 1996:349). At the intersection of violence, oppression, and suffering, it is possible to begin to formulate questions of social suffering in relation to the problems of history and cultural practices. In the following pages I explore the multiple ways in which some Mayas in the rural highlands have experienced suffering, not only the obvious suffering produced by the recent political violence and repression but that incurred as a result of varied forms of structural violence that operate locally and the social conditions that perpetuate disadvantage. In doing so, some of the contradictions of suffering emerge, for example, community opportunism may win out over cooperation, leading to further internal violence. The structural violence to which I allude here goes beyond what is usually understood as exploitation to include a multidimensional conceptualization of social injustice, what Iris Young (1990) has referred to as the "five faces of oppression": exploitation, marginalization, powerlessness, cultural imperialism, and random acts of violence. In addition, humiliation and fear, as well as denial of dignity and integrity—that is, the psychological and spiritual effects of violence—are crucial components of structural violence. Structural violence is embedded in national as well as local social institutions and cultural perceptions. Individuals not only experience the direct effects of violence and power in their lives but also the more subtle cultural effects of violence and power that may permeate local social relations and social structures within communities (Poole 1994). The suffering produced by extreme poverty in rural Guatemala, for example, resulted not only in excessive and often preventable morbidity and mortality, hunger, and disease but also in the destruction of cultural institutions. We know that Mayas are poor as a result of five hundred years of exploitation and oppression; the microsocial processes of both violence and suffering have been less fully explored.

In chapter 2 I explore three overlapping social processes—the relationship between commodified and noncommodified forms of production, community formation, and labor exploitation—to explicate how power has been historically reconfigured. In particular, I discuss how structural violence operated within communities, opening spaces for the possibilities of political violence. Not only did these processes of structural violence effectively drive the majority of Mayas to the margins of society; they may have also rendered communities and families vulnerable to preconditions for internal political violence. Why this was the case in some communities and not in others needs to be empirically explored. John Watanabe (1992), for example, has argued in his ethnography on Santiago Chimaltenango that a moral economy of community reinforced the social fabric of community frayed by structural transformations and that this sense of belonging had been sufficient to ward off the ravages of internal violence, something that was not the case in Xe'caj or many other highland communities. Anthropological concerns with the local economic and power structures and social relations that form the connective networks among people may help us puzzle out some answers as to why internal violence happened in some communities and not in others.

Meanings of Survival

One day when I was walking through the town square I noticed that someone had spilled a small amount of rice in front of the health center. A young boy, six or seven years old, who was passing by, stopped, took off his hat, and painstakingly placed the grains into it.

—Fieldnote, August 1989

When I began this study in 1988, my central focus was on the economic activities—survival strategies—of rural Mayan widows and their children as they struggled to rework their lives in the aftermath of war. What were the effects of violence on poor households' livelihoods? In the villages of Xe'caj I found that 15 to 25 percent of the households were headed by women, the majority of whom were widows from la violencia. How were these newly formed female-headed households coping? How did they mobilize labor? How did they procure an income? What were the mechanisms the women deployed to survive? Who was responsible for household decision making?

Initially my theoretical orientation drew extensively from the rich literature on peasant studies and feminist concerns with issues of household reproduction, as well as from Mesoamerican ethnography that situated the locus of Mayan cultural identity in the community, language, dress, and

FIGURE 1.2
Woman with young child preparing corn to cook. (*Jonathan Moller*)

religion.[7] Yet, Western notions of rational economic strategizing, which treat people's behaviors mechanistically overlooked what Eric Wolf has termed "connective networks among people in communities" (1986:327). Likewise, cultural theories that located the essence of Mayan identity in community traits and traditions were unable to account fully for the complex riddles of people's lives as they are subjected to the continual play of culture, power, and history. Perhaps quite fittingly, my first lessons about the complex nature of survival came, in part, from one of the most important symbols and practices at the heart of Mayan cultural identity: the production and consumption of corn.

For centuries, rural Mayan people have eked out a subsistence livelihood from their milpas, the small, rain-fed parcels of land on which they grow a mixture of corn, beans, and squash. Yet, particularly for the last hundred years, each subsequent generation's struggle for survival has become an ever more precarious enterprise. Guatemala has one of the most unequal systems of land distribution in all of Latin America 2 percent of the population owns between 65 and 70 percent of the arable land—and this, coupled with a population growth rate of about 3 percent per year and a population doubling time of twenty-six years, has left most rural *campesinos* (peasants) today with land holdings that Uruguayan writer, Eduardo Galeano (1967:5), has characterized as "plots of land the size of graves."

The rural Mayan economy has long been based on a gendered division of labor. Men work the milpas, as well as procuring cash from wage labor. April and May are months of intense activity in Xe'caj. After the first rains in early May, the agricultural cycle begins anew with the planting of the milpas. A month or so beforehand, men begin to prepare the fields—backbreaking, arduous work in the hot sun—turning the soil with simple hand-held hoes, pulling or burning old corn stocks and weeds that have sprung up since the last harvest. During the planting and harvesting phases of milpa production, Mayan men often work together: fathers, sons, uncles, brothers. The workforce moves from milpa to milpa completing the tasks efficiently and quickly.

Although there is no explicit cultural prohibition against women working in the milpas, they have done so most often only out of necessity. Women are preoccupied with the multiple daily domestic tasks necessary to the rural subsistence household: hauling water, searching for firewood, making tortillas, childrearing, weaving cloth, raising small animals such as chickens and pigs, and looking for wild plants and fruits to supplement the food supply. For the widows in many of the communities in Xe'caj, there was a scarcity of male labor to draw from even when they turned to their extended families. Many of those families had lost not only husbands but fathers, brothers, sons, uncles, and cousins. "We are both mama and papa now" was how many of the widows described their precarious situations. Some widows hired local men as day laborers, or *mozos*, to prepare and plant their milpas, but this required a substantial outlay of cash.[8]

In early June, during the first year I lived in Xe'caj, doña Margarita asked if I would help her to buy fertilizer for her milpa.[9] She had just planted her four *cuerdas* (a cuerda is a twenty-by-twenty-foot parcel of land), and she needed two to three hundred pounds of fertilizer. Without the fertilizer, the harvest would be meager, and she was counting on a crop yielding enough corn for three to four months for herself and her three young children (a family of four needs a minimum of four to five pounds of corn every day). She would be forced to buy the remainder on the open market, where prices rose exorbitantly by mid-July, when most families had little left of their own corn reserves.

Requests soon came from other widows whom I had begun to visit regularly. Over the next several weeks, I hauled hundred-pound bags of fertilizer in my pickup truck to Xe'caj from Guatemala City, where I could get a better price. Already strapped for cash, women repaid me with items they valued: an exquisite piece of handwoven cloth, a small carving, some fruit.

As I watched the widows struggle that year to find the money to hire mozos or to buy fertilizer for their milpas, I wondered why they bothered when they could buy corn more easily at the local market. I had begun to calculate methodically the costs of the production enterprise versus that of market corn, and it seemed as if buying corn would be the most practical solution. Juana and Margarita's indirect answers to my prodding questions, however, disturbed my unitary notions of what survival might mean and what being Mayan might signify.

When we shared food together, doña Juana would frequently repeat to me a commonly held belief that if you have not eaten corn at a meal you had not really eaten. She stressed the centrality of corn to survival, as the necessary staple of the Mayan diet. As for discerning connoisseurs everywhere, quality, appearance, fragrance, and taste are of utmost importance. For Mayas, quality, in part, depends on the altitude at which the corn is grown, how the kernels are ground, and the method of cooking the flat, thick, round pancakes, *la tortilla*. The preference is for highland corn, milled by hand on a grinding stone, and cooked over an open wood fire. Women devote three to four hours to this activity every day.

While we ate, Juana would often tease me, asking me again and again if it were true that gringos don't eat corn. "No, we don't eat *masa* [corn dough]," I would say predictably. Nodding and laughing she invariably replied "Ah, so that is why you gringos are so sickly, you don't eat tortillas. Is it true you grow corn only to feed to your cows? And now to send to us?" Juana would add, referring disparagingly to the corn grown in Iowa or Kansas and sent to Guatemala under the auspices of the U.S. Department of Agriculture PL480 food aid program, which substantially undercuts domestic prices.

"The milpa," doña Margarita explained, "is more than just corn; the milpa is an entire world, a way of life." While initially this may sound like a National Geographic perspective on native life, in fact Margarita described in detail all the practical advantages that the milpa provided. The wild plants, *yerbas*, that grow among the corn plants add important vitamins to the diet, the corn stalks are used as both building materials and sweetener for food, the cobs are boiled to feed pigs, chickens, and cows, and the all-purpose husks have multiple culinary and medicinal uses, for example, as the outer wrappings for steaming corn-based foods, as a component in medicine for coughs, and as bandages.

And, Margarita went on, the milpa too is where her ancestors reside. Many Mayas believe that the dead return to where their surviving relatives live to watch over them. As one elder explained, he not only knew that the *antepasados* (literally, "those who passed before us") were nearby, but working in the milpa actually evoked the presence of his parents and grandparents. For many Mayan campesinos, working the soil reconnects them with the dead, Mother Earth, and the spirits of the mountains, volcanoes, rivers, and trees.

Mayas receive their education in part through growing, preparing, and eating corn. Mayan children learn about the importance of corn through their experiences of everyday life. Young girls copy their mothers as they use their hands to shape the corn dough into tortillas, producing the unmistakable rat-tat-tat that one hears coming from Mayan kitchens at mealtime. Young boys acquire the fundamentals of subsistence agricultural production in the milpa. It is there that grandfathers, fathers, uncles, cousins, and older brothers teach young boys the prayers to the ancestors and spirits that are made at the time of planting. Well before a boy is big enough to wield a hoe on his own, he is allowed to drop the corn seeds into the soil alongside his father, who invokes the help of the antepasados and Mother Earth for a successful harvest. In the milpa too a young boy learns about the catastrophes of life, the vagaries of weather that can leave the family with too little food to survive in the coming year. And without corn, his family tells him, he is without food, even though he may have fruits and yerbas to curb his hunger. Corn is identity, a site of not only material but also cultural production and Mayan agency. Through the social relations of production, corn weaves a thread that connects Mayan people with their ancestors and sacred spirits and with their future through their children.

The widows of Xe'caj are now compelled by the exigencies of survival and violence to struggle to plant and harvest their milpas alone, on the margins of their own communities. In the milpas where the spirits of those who died violently are unable to rest, these women reconnect with their past through a reworking of history and memory that has both material and symbolic effects, while simultaneously producing new cultural identities out of the ruptures and discontinuities of their own experiences. This agency, however, is complexly structured. On the surface it seems passive and backward-looking, and in some ways it is. Yet these are the same people who have resisted the vastly stronger Guatemalan state year after year after year.

To understand the consequences of sociopolitical violence and the meanings of survival in the Mayan case requires rethinking intellectual notions of cultural continuity and transformation as dialectical rather than dichotomous processes. Cultural continuity is often thought of as a linear replication of traits and traditions. The Mayas' experience might encourage us to see cultural survival as analogous to the woven cloth for which the Mayas are renowned. The shared history passed on to and reworked with each subsequent generation through memory and myth can be viewed as the warp (or vertical) threads that constitute the basis of the fabric, while the meaning constructed out of the present *and* the possible can be seen as the weft (or horizontal) threads from which the weaver creates her designs. As Stuart Hall has noted, "Difference, therefore, persists in and alongside continuity" (1994:396).

Dilemmas of Fieldwork/Issues of Power[10]

Xe'caj is a pseudonym, a Maya-Kaqchikel word meaning "under the sky."[11] I use a fictitious name following a long anthropological tradition of protecting informants' privacy. The case of Guatemala dictates more extreme caution, however. People's lives are at risk on a daily basis. Thus I have also changed the names of my informants to disguise their identities and the villages where they reside. Although anyone with more than a passing familiarity with the area will probably recognize Xe'caj,[12] this subterfuge will, I hope, provide a modicum of protection to the women, men, and children who so generously and patiently shared their time with me under politically volatile circumstances.

I lived among the people of Xe'caj in a liminal social space that existed between total power and safety, where fear was a way of life for all of us. And my own experiences of fear allowed me to understand, to a small

FIGURE I.3
Young girl holding exploded mortar shell. (*Jonathan Moller*)

degree, the situation of the people who lived there permanently. Yet when I felt most vulnerable I comforted myself with the knowledge that I was free to leave; after all, I had an airline ticket and a U.S. passport. But with that realization also came an overwhelming sense of discomfort: I could leave at anytime, but the people around me had no such escape. Fear joined me to the people and yet separated me from them as well.

I worked with a very capable field assistant, a local woman, Sophia, who was my translator as most of the women with whom I worked spoke only Kaqchikel and my own knowledge of Kaqchikel was rudimentary. Sophia was also my cultural guide, initially helping me to understand a Mayan world-view. Over time Sophia also became my trusted friend. I rented a small house in one of the towns of Xe'caj, after some difficult months of searching, as few people were interested in renting to a *gringa*. At last, a widow agreed to rent me a small adobe house, next to the one she lived in with her three daughters and son and alongside her half-sister and nephew.

Sophia and I traveled daily in my pickup truck to the surrounding communities to visit women and their families. Because of the difficulties arising from this precarious field situation, interviewing and note taking were problematic. No one wanted to be tape-recorded, and most people were uncomfortable with my taking notes. So after each interview Sophia and I would return to the pickup to discuss in detail what had taken place. In fact, the pickup became a refuge for Sophia and me, serving as one of the few places where we felt safe enough to express our thoughts openly to one another. The pickup was our enclave, a place where we could talk freely and record what we were experiencing in ways that we could not have done even at home.

Many women were willing to speak with us at first, as a rumor had spread that the gringa was working with a development project and might have economic aid to give. Some, however, were reluctant to get involved. When it became evident that I was working independently with Sophia, a number of women who had initially expressed interest in participating no longer cared to do so. Others asked me directly how their association with this academic project might benefit them. Given the dangerous situation in which they were living and the fact that they had no say in its inception, I could only respond that it would not.

Yet some women did share their lives with me over the next two years, and when I asked them intermittently why they continued to do so, for the most part their answers were predictable: that the visits were *alegre*, a pleasant diversion from their daily routine. One often-repeated answer, however, both surprised me initially and has remained with me since: "If people knew what was happening to us, they would do something about it."

The responsibility of researching and writing ethnography weighs heavily, particularly under such conditions of repression and social control that exist in Guatemala. I do not claim to be giving "voice to the voiceless" but rather, as suggested by Gerald Sider, "to give voice to sight," to say what I have actually seen (1989:14), to convey my own experiences while living among the Mayas. As anthropologists, we are in a unique position to address the darker side of the human condition—violence, poverty, war, sexism, racism— based on the lived experiences of the people with whom we work.

The practice of anthropology through fieldwork is by its very nature an involved, engaged human exchange. The challenge for anthropologists, as researchers, teachers, and activists is to use the power of our privilege to speak out about what is at stake for us and for our subjects as human beings and to do so without causing more harm.

Another challenge in a study such as this is to link theoretical, political, and ethnographic issues. In this work, I intend to connect subjective emotional experiences to systemic material, political, and economic conditions. As anthropologists, we have too often tended to abstract people from their

humanity, leaving them devoid of their complexities, contradictions, and the very real suffering of their daily lives, reducing the relations between people to relations between concepts.[13] Often missing from much of our work are insights into suffering and historical processes and how poverty and domination turn on a dialectic of both national and local power. In an attempt to understand the mechanisms of violence and humanity at work locally in the most recent brutal period in Guatemala history, David Harvey's admonition in paraphrasing Raymond Williams is apt: "Never forget the brute ugliness of the realities of lived experience for the oppressed. We should not estheticize or theorize those lived realities out of existence as felt pains and passions. To do so is to diminish or even to lose the raw anger against injustice and exploitation that powers much of the striving for social change" (1996:37).

Simultaneously, acknowledging the multifaceted ways in which anthropological knowledge is created out of shared experiences and personal engagement with others can chip away at one of the lingering residues of the Cartesian legacy: the fieldworker not as a living person but only as a mind (Hastrup 1994). The experiences shared between fieldworker and ordinary people are never egalitarian. In fact, they are inevitably charged by the political and economic inequalities that structure the world in which we live; in Cindi Katz's words, "It oozes with power" (1992:496). As anthropologists we go into the field in an attempt to render intelligible the contradictions and complexities of people's lives. In doing so we become, at least for a time, both witnesses to and participants in those very lives. And we return from the field with two languages at our disposal: the language of the intellectual, with our sophisticated theoretical apparatus of representation, and the language we have learned in the field, not simply the spoken language but the language of people's cultural practices and perceptions. What is called for is not a simple translation from one perspective to the other but instead an effort to address the complex linkages between the perspectives that recognizes the "situatedness and thus partiality of all knowledge [so that] we can develop a politics that is empowering because it is not just about identity—a descriptive term—but about position" (Katz 1992:504). As such, anthropology can contribute significantly toward creating a more just and humane world.

Some practitioners of postmodern anthropology, following the "linguistic turn," have limited their mode of inquiry to discourse and representation in the writing of texts.[14] They contend, quite rightly, that writing can be a source of domination. Yet reducing the terms of struggle to concerns with discourse and textual strategies with an exclusive focus on interpretation lends a myopia to their work that neglects the existence of the material world, the "macro-logics of power," of global capitalism, imperialism, repression, and patriarchy (Katz 1992). And while postmodern writers celebrate difference, it has also led to an "aestheticism of indifference" (Ghosh 1995:41) that often ignores the harsh realities of people's lives and shuns questions of the lived realities of violence and suffering, of domination and exploitation, as well as of truth and engagement. Anthropological writing, despite being embedded within what Edward Said (1978) has called "universalizing discourses" about the Other, can also be used as a tool for struggle (Binford 1996), providing critical and transforming accounts of lived reality so that history and memory are not forgotten even after particular instances recede in time. As the poet Carolyn Forche has noted, memory can act as a "reliquary in a wall of silence—it is important to have scenes that will continue to speak" (1994:5).

FIGURE 2.1

Mayan priest holding a cross inscribed with the ages of those killed in his family. Behind him are crosses bearing the names of murdered neighbors and community members. (*Jonathan Moller*)

2. the altiplano: a history of violence and survival

> Claims to ethnicity are not the same everywhere and the same at all times. They have a history and that history—differently stressed in different situations and at different points of conjunction—feeds back in various ways upon the ways in which people understand who they are and where they might be at any given historical point in time.
>
> —Eric Wolf, "Perilous Ideas: Race, Culture, People" (1994)

Land of Eternal Spring

Guatemala is often characterized in tourist literature as the "land of eternal spring," and perhaps no region deserves this epithet more than the broad expanse of territory known as the altiplano.[1] Tourists hurtling along the Pan-American highway en route to the emerald waters of Lake Atitlan or the famous indigenous market town of Chichicastenango travel through a stunning landscape. Bounded to the north by 10,000-foot mountain ranges and to the south by more than two dozen volcanic peaks, the altiplano, with its isolated verdant valleys, high plateaus, and upper piedmont, is indeed breathtaking. Travelers may glimpse men bent low with heavy loads suspended on trumplines or women and their children in brightly colored clothing—for which the Mayas are renowned—laboring over the plots of broccoli and snow peas for export that have sprung up amid the traditional milpa. To many tourists, the Mayas represent a simpler way of life, free from the demands of the modern world.

The altiplano is Indian Guatemala, home to over five million rural Mayas, who together with their urban counterparts, constitute 65 percent of the Guatemalan population.[2] The majority of Mayas, who inhabit the towns, villages, and scattered settlements that together make up over 150 local municipalities in the eight departments of the altiplano, live on the darker side of modernity.[3] These families experience the degrading underside of capitalist economic relations shored up by a repressive state apparatus. Most Mayas live in grinding poverty, without the most basic social services, potable water, sanitation facilities, health services, adequate housing, or education. Four out of five Mayan children under age five are malnourished, and many of them die of easily preventable illnesses such as cholera, influenza, and measles.[4] Over 50 percent of the active labor force is either unemployed or underemployed; 87 percent of the population lives in poverty, and 67 percent of those live in extreme poverty, that is, the monthly family income is not adequate to meet the costs of procuring basic foods (PAHO 1994). Illiteracy rates are especially high among indigenous people, with 73 percent of the men and 91 percent of the women illiterate (Clay 1996).

Modern Mayas

Although the ancient Mayas are glorified for the great achievements of their pre-Conquest civilization in art, architecture, and astronomy, Mayas of today are often characterized in pejorative terms by white elites and ladinos (i.e., non-Indians) as *tontos* (stupid), *brutos* (animals), and *sucios* (dirty). Modern Mayas are presumed by some to be a derivative culture of peasant farmers who are products of the colonial experience,[5] and many have identified their continuity as a distinct culture as a primary obstacle to Western economic development in Guatemala. Yet the Mayas have been absolutely crucial to the economic development of Guatemala, particularly through their labor. The contradiction, of course, lies in the disjuncture, the simultaneous ideological rejection of the Mayas and their crucial inclusion in the political economy of Guatemala.

Mayas have steadfastly resisted cultural incorporation, however incomplete, into the hegemonic society. Over the past century, varying attempts have been made to assimilate them, first by the nineteenth-century Liberal State, later by the democratic governments of Arévalo and Arbenz (1944–1954), and today as part of the neoliberal economic agenda promoted by Western development policies and sanctioned under the terms of the peace accords. One USAID official commented in a 1989 interview with me, "You can't maintain a traditional society and have better education for kids, roads so they can get to the hospital if they have to. Maintaining [Mayan] peasant culture and progress are incompatible." This blame-the-victim ideology defines the problems of poverty and underdevelopment as intrinsic to Mayan culture, equating and conflating being Indian with being poor and hence primitive. Such sentiments would not be expressed publicly today in Guatemala, where cultural diversity is now embraced in the national public discourse. Yet Diane Nelson found in private interviews with ladino state bureaucrats that some of them continue to imagine the Mayas as existing in a world apart, timeless and premodern. One official suggested "that the Maya are obsolete—that the Maya express themselves through handwoven cloth in the age of the microchip and satellite transmission" (1996:298). Revenues from international tourism, however, are second only to coffee in importance to the Guatemalan economy, and these same obsolete Maya are packaged as the main tourist attraction.[6]

While Mayas constitute the majority of the population, non-Indians have maintained control of economic and political power since the Conquest. Yet the bases of racism and ethnic divisions between Mayas and non-Indians are more cultural than biological. What characterizes an individual as Mayan and predisposes him to social racism are the obvious cultural markers so well described by anthropologists: dress, community allegiance, language, and *costumbre* (Mayan spiritual practices that connect the living, the dead, and the natural world).

During the early colonial period, the distinction between the Spanish and the Mayas rested on consanguinity, and the term "ladino" referred simply to Spanish-speaking Mayas or acculturated Mayas (Sherman 1979). Later, "ladino" came to mean the offspring of miscegenation, usually between a Mayan mother and a Spanish father.[7] Throughout the years of colonization, ladinos too existed mostly on the economic and social periphery of society. Yet, while their liminal social status denied them entry into the domain of the privileged white Spanish, it also spared them from the vicissitudes and the violence of domination that the Mayas routinely confronted (Watanabe 1992). And for the Mayas during that period, the colonists and the Catholic clergy, not the ladinos per se, were the agents of their subjugation, although the ladinos were often willing accomplices.

Independence from Spain in the early nineteenth century did nothing to redress the inequities imposed on the Mayas by the colonists. Throughout the century, as elite ladinos assumed national, regional, and local positions of power,[8] the social divisions between the Mayas and the ladinos became more pronounced even though racial distinctions were often undiscernible. The construction of ladino identity depended on its Other, namely, the marginalization of the Mayas. By the late nineteenth century, many more ladinos had taken up residence in indigenous communities in the altiplano as representatives of state power and authority. Working as labor contractors and overseers on coffee plantations, members of army militias, tradesmen, and appointed officials, ladinos became the local executors of Mayan oppression (Smith 1990a). Then, as today, in the rigid social hierarchy that defines Guatemalan society, ladinos, whatever their class status, characterized themselves as superior to Mayas.

One of the most damaging effects of the violence of racism is the doubleness of its effects. Many Mayas are proud to identify themselves as indigenous and see themselves as superior to the lazy, untrustworthy ladinos, while at the same time they have incorporated a sense of themselves as the inferior Other. This doubleness is crucial to understanding how some villagers could denounce their unwitting neighbors to the army or (less often) to the guerrillas. The Mayan people as object of racism simultaneously become its subject (Hall 1994).

While some Mayas have shed their indigenous identities altogether and become "ladinoized" as a survival tactic in urban areas as well as rural communities, Mayan women continue to wear their *traje* (traditional clothing fashioned from handwoven cloth) as a symbol of pride even as it marks them for denigration as Indians. To many, cultural recognition—what the widows in Xe'caj referred to as an expression of "la dignidad de ser humanos" (the dignity of human beings)—is as integral to and inseparable from their struggles for economic and social justice in Guatemala as it is to the participants in the Zapatista rebellion in Chiapas, Mexico (Nash 1995; Gossen 1996; Sider 1996).

Land of Eternal Tyranny

Senorita, imagine Indians with education, with arms, with money. If they are learning to better themselves it is a great danger, you see, to whites. The Indians educated, armed, could take the country away from us.

—Edna Fergusson, *Guatemala* (1930)

By the early 1980s, the altiplano had become infamous in international human rights circles as the "land of eternal tyranny," because of the carnage wrought by the Guatemalan military.[9] By then, Guatemala was notorious not only for the political murders, kidnappings, and disappearances that had become almost daily occurrences since the mid-1970s in both urban and rural areas but also for the wholesale massacres, mutilations, and burnings—even of the elderly, children, and pregnant women—in indigenous villages in the highlands (Amnesty International 1982). The sheer barbarity of the atrocities committed in Guatemala during the civil war is perhaps in the end inexplicable; the threat to the Guatemalan state, however, was more than the sum of armed revolutionary forces and their supporters. Another very real, looming danger was posed by unarmed civilians—peasants, the poor, and workers—who dared to challenge long-standing structures of domination and exploitation at the local and regional levels.[10] And as the historical record demonstrates, violence has been the modus operandi of the state to control any threat to the status quo by poor Mayas and ladenos alike.

Side Effects of Repression

Rigoberta Menchu, a Maya-K'iche and the 1992 winner of the Nobel Peace Prize, has claimed, as have others (Handy 1992; Manz 1988), that one of the unacknowledged goals of counterinsurgency was to weaken and eventually eradicate Mayan culture through the destruction of their communities. By the Guatemalan Army's own admission, over 440 rural villages in the altiplano were completely destroyed, and countless others were partially razed. It was the most extensive attack on highland indigenous communities since the Conquest. The physical destruction of communities, of both peoples and places, was massive. In Xe'caj many women and children were forced to watch as family members and neighbors were brutally murdered. Some were able to hide in the nearby mountains, where they foraged for food and shelter while being pursued by the military. Those who remained behind were forcibly relocated by the army to towns or makeshift camps where they could be more easily controlled. Between 1983 and 1985 some one million people—out of a total population of about eight million—were internally displaced in rural Guatemala.

Little has been reported, however, about the subtle ways in which counterinsurgency war also reshaped social relations in Mayan families and

FIGURE 2.2
Civil patroller near Todos Santos. (*Dede Faller*)

communities. Doña Tomasa's story exemplifies some of these unacknowledged consequences. One day Tomasa, a woman I had known for well over a year, invited me to visit her at home for the first time. As I sat crouched on a low wooden stool in one of the small anterior rooms of her adobe house, doña Tomasa, kneeling on a woven grass mat, began with quiet dignity to relate to me the particularly gruesome death of her husband at the hands of the army.

As my eyes became accustomed to the semidarkness of the windowless room, I focused on the wall behind her, where, prominently displayed, was a framed photograph of a young man in Kaibil uniform. The Kaibiles are the elite special forces of the Guatemalan army, trained in counterinsurgency tactics.[11] Somewhat confused by that image's seeming incompatibility with her story, I asked doña Tomasa about the photograph. She replied that it was of her oldest son and acknowledged his occasional presence in the household but said nothing more. On a purely objective level, of course, in Guatemala it is dangerous to talk about such things with outsiders. Perhaps too she felt that her son's photograph might provide her with some protection in the future. At the same time, how might a mother feel imagining that her soldier son likely performed the same brutish acts as those used against her husband and her neighbors?

The Guatemalan military's strategy of using Mayan boys as foot soldiers in the counterinsurgency war and using local men as civil patrollers and military commissioners to carry out surveillance on their neighbors and at times to commit murder has led to severe ruptures in family and community social relations. Not only has it undermined the sense of trust and cooperation among family members and neighbors, but the dividing of such loyalties has been instrumental in perpetuating fear and terror, as family members themselves are implicated in the acts of violence. This complicity, not surprisingly, has a devastating impact on the special potency of kinship and community relations.

The violence against women took many forms during the counterinsurgency war. Not only were they witness/survivors of the brutal repression; at times they were its victims. Stories from *aldeas* (villages) relate unimaginable brutalities: pregnant women eviscerated, their unborn babies used as balls to play with; women forced to cook for the soldiers after having watched their husbands tortured and killed. And, of course, rape. Rape was often used as a counterinsurgency tactic, with double effects: as Cynthia Enloe has noted, it was "a technique for socializing [unwilling recruits] into a kind of brutality, thereby severing their ties with their civilian counterparts" (1993:121), and it also served as a way of humiliating both the women who were the victims and the remaining men in their families, some of whom were forced to watch. Rape also was a mechanism for inscribing the societal violence on individual women's bodies and memories. The psychological effects of sexual assault are long-lasting and include shame, fear, and self-degradation. Widespread use of rape during counterinsurgency war was a gendered way in which the military attacked the social fabric of family and community life. Widows in particular are forced to confront multidimensional problems as they struggle to survive: not only the loss of family members but in some cases the rupture of family ties and outright hostilities within families, in some cases leading to domestic violence; not only the crisis of taking on the dual economic and social role of head of household but the prolonged psychological impact of their own intimate suffering.[12]

Splits and animosities among Mayas have existed in and between communities in the altiplano for centuries (McCreery 1994). Yet the particularly brutal and insidious nature of the recent state-sponsored violence in the altiplano and the perpetrators' continuing immunity from any punishment have been unprecedented, and the consequences have been profound. Today, even though the civil militias have been demilitarized, locally the internal power divisions created and perpetuated by their presence are not so easily resolved. The fragile, intricate bonds that held communities together have been severed by the effects of the violence that resonate throughout daily life. Demilitarization is not easily accomplished. Although demobilizing troops and decommissioning civil militias, as decreed by the 1996 peace accords, are important first steps, without the establishment of rule of law and state legitimacy a legacy of violence and repression remains embedded within daily life. Moreover, the majority of human rights violations committed by civil patrollers and military commissioners remain unpunished.

Commenting on local violence in San Pedro de la Laguna during the 1980s, Benjamin Paul and William Demarest reveal how local factionalism was manipulated and exploited in highland communities, contributing to a breakdown in social structure. It should be noted that San Pedro, the area on which they focused, was less affected by direct army repression and guerrilla activity in the 1980s than were many other communities, among them Xe'caj, yet local death squads terrorized the population for over four years. Paul and Demarest noted:

> It may be tempting to land the outbreak of violence in San Pedro on social divisiveness and settling old scores, but the temptation should be resisted. Religious competition and vigorous political infighting were features of San Pedro life for decades before 1980 without producing violence. The same can be said for interpersonal antagonisms. They arose in the past and were settled by means short of murder. What disrupted the peace in San Pedro was not the presence of difference and divisions, but the army's recruitment of agents and spies that had the effect of exploiting these cleavages. (1988:153–54)

Yet as early as the 1960s, June Nash (1967) noted an increase in homicides in a Mexican village in Chiapas, as the result of the breakdown of belief in the ancestors and competition from new economic arrangements.

In this chapter I explore the dynamic relationship between structural inequalities and political violence locally by examining the linkages among subsistence, social relations, and suffering historically. I trace three overlapping processes—labor extraction, community formations, and the social relations of commodified and noncommodified forms of production—to explicate how economic and cultural practices were reworked locally. The structural violence in effect laid the groundwork for political violence.

Cycles of Exploitation

Ever since the Spanish Conquest in the sixteenth century and up to the present, Mayas have been the major source of non-Indian wealth and privilege as a cheap, exploitable labor force. Yet over the centuries Mayas have been reluctant participants, and their labor has been extracted most often by coercive means. Throughout the colonial period, until Guatemala gained independence from Spain in the 1820s, the Spanish Crown, Catholic missionaries, and the settlers of the region all depended on indigenous labor as the principal source of their enrichment.[13] In the case of the clergy and the colonists, an autochthonous workforce was integral to survival. Several strategies were utilized to harness Mayan labor, including tithes, taxes, *ecomiendas*, and *repartimento* (Hill 1992; Lovell 1992; Farriss 1984).[14]

While Mayas were ostensibly freed from these multiple economic obligations after independence,[15] by the end of the nineteenth century, Mayan labor was again crucial to the Guatemalan state for the creation of coffee plantations for large-scale export production. The labor demands of coffee were considerable, and coercion—through debt contracts, labor drafts, and, later, vagrancy laws—again became the principal means by which a seasonal, migratory workforce was secured from the towns and villages of the altiplano (McCreery 1990; Cambranes 1985).[16] A repressive state apparatus was expanded to include an increasing military presence in the altiplano to quell resistance to the expropriation or privatization of community-held lands and increased labor demands (McCreery 1994; Handy 1994; Cambranes 1985).

In 1944 a democratically elected government took national power for the first time in Guatemalan history, and soon thereafter the last vestiges of forced labor were removed. By then, however, the exigencies of survival had compelled most land-poor Mayan peasants to make their way south to the large coffee plantations in order to earn much-needed cash. Wages, although minimal, had become essential to rural subsistence livelihood. Although by 1952 the government of Jacobo Arbenz (1950–1954) had begun to redress the inequitable land tenure system with the passage of the Agrarian Reform Law, a CIA–backed coup d'état in 1954 returned most expropriated lands to their previous owners.[17] By the mid-1970s over a half-million peasants were making the annual trek from the altiplano to the coastal coffee, cotton, and sugar *fincas* (plantations), where the working conditions were increasingly deplorable.[18]

By the 1980s declines in world market commodity prices for Guatemala's leading export crops—coffee, cotton, and sugar—led some finca owners to shift production to less labor-intensive crops such as soy, sorghum, and beef, reducing the demand for a migratory workforce. Thus in the last decade of the twentieth century, many fewer residents of the altiplano journey to the plantations. Those that do continue to live in crowded open-air dormitories housing four to five hundred people without adequate sanitation or health services and work ten or more hours each day in the hot sun to earn less than US$2 per day.[19]

In many communities in the altiplano today the economic situation is far worse than it was twenty years ago. The economic destruction and impoverishment resulting from the political violence have been massive, leading to extensive changes in local patterns of cultivation, trade, and the labor movement in the altiplano (Smith 1990b). Many rural people became increasingly impoverished as some were forced to leave their villages because of the violence, while others were constrained by the demands of the community civil militias, even as the need for a large plantation labor force was declining. Men were not able to migrate to the coastal plantations to earn cash. (To be absent from his turn at patrol, a man needed to find a replacement, more often than not paying someone to take his place. If he just did not show up to take his turn, he would be suspected of being a guerrilla supporter. Moreover, during the war finca administrators were reluctant to hire laborers from regions of the altiplano where there was extensive political violence.) In the department of Chimaltenango, where Xe'caj is located, there were no corn harvests in some communities between 1981 and 1983 as a result of population displacements (Krueger and Enge 1985). In some communities in Xe'caj where people did not return to their villages until 1984 or 1985, many found their homes and household possessions in ruins. Relief aid in the form of aluminum roofing, hoes, pots, and blankets offered people the basics as they began in earnest to rebuild their homes and their lives in the wake of the scorched-earth campaign.

By the mid-1980s, USAID was actively promoting nontraditional export production in the altiplano as a means to alleviate rural poverty and promote economic development, in lieu of substantive land reform.[20] The oligarchy's intransigent stance on land reform was one of the major contributing factors to the civil war. For many Mayan families in Chimaltenango Department, rural factory work and cultivation of winter vegetables grown on converted milpa lands have become a necessity for economic survival in the aftermath of war. Several recent studies, however, have shown that both the production of vegetables for export—such as snow peas and broccoli—and *maquilas*—export apparel assembly plants—while providing economic opportunities, rely heavily for their profits on access to a cheap labor force (Rosset 1991; AVANCSO 1994; Peterson 1992; Conroy, Murray, and Rosset 1996). To mention one example, Mayan adolescents—both boys and girls—who work in the maquilas that have recently sprung up along the Pan-American highway earn about US$4 per day for twelve- to fourteen-hour days. Laboring in factories the size of football fields under adverse conditions, the workers readily acknowledge the exploitative nature of their situation, yet with few available options to procure much-need cash, their choices are limited. As several youths noted, it is better to earn four dollars a day than nothing.

Most disturbing to the workers, however, are the ways in which factory work affects their relationships with their families. Rising before dawn and often not returning home until after nine o'clock in the evening six days a week, the young workers feel as though they have abandoned responsibilities to their families. Unlike in earlier migratory strategies that kept young people away from home for months at a time, these youths continue to live in their communities and families but are for the most part absent. As a result, they are frequently put in the difficult situation of having to choose between their individual needs and their sense of mutual aid and obligations to their family and community groups. Likewise, these adolescents no longer have the time, and in some cases the desire, to weave or work the milpa (Green 1997b).

Contract farming too leaves peasant farmers in precarious circumstances. On land previously used for the milpa, peasant producers cultivate snow peas and broccoli for sale to intermediaries for export, mostly to the United States. Land that had been utilized previously to produce basic grains for subsistence or for sale on the domestic market now is being devoted to export crops (Garst and Barry 1990). With the influx of imported basic grains, the local market value of corn and black beans has been undercut, eroding the already precarious independence of the peasant farmer. While some small farmers have profited, recent studies have shown that overall this is risky business, as many farmers suffer crop failures because of the vagaries of weather or cannot sell what crops they produce because of gluts in the market (Rosset 1991; Conroy, Murray, and Rosset 1996; AVANCSO 1994). As a result, many farmers have had to default on their loans and have lost their land. Production relations are organized so that peasants bear the brunt of the failures, and when they fail, speculators take over the land and the production contracts, thus increasing the pressure on the remaining campesino producers. Intermediaries provide high-interest loans, seeds, and fertilizers, which are then deducted from the price of the harvest. Prices themselves are notoriously unstable, and it is not uncommon to see vegetables that have been rejected for poor quality or high pesticide residues dumped on the side of the roadways. Only a few farmers with significant landholdings are able to sustain a profit (Carter, Barham, and Mesbah 1996).

Not only are new kinds of crops being grown—and this in itself has significant, albeit subtle cultural consequences—new kinds of commodity relations between Mayan farmers and international markets are being formed that often override commodity relations with local markets, which are different in both kind and degree. These changes in turn open up new kinds of power relations both inside and outside communities (Green 1997a). Contract farming reworks social relations of production. While the peasant farmer continues to own the means of production and to control his own labor, it is the contractor who dictates the conditions of labor and the "pace and rhythm of work" (Watts 1992:82). Growing snow peas, in particular, unlike working the milpa, is extremely labor intensive and therefore involves the use of extensive family labor for even moderate success in cultivation.[21] Contract farming disguises the exploitation of the peasant farmer, who on the face of it remains an independent rural entrepreneur. These new labor practices—in maquila employment and contract farming—have the greatest potential for reshaping Mayan cultural practices by reworking notions of time, place, and social relations.

A Genealogy of Community

An awareness of particular historical processes of community formation is crucial to understanding the tensions embedded in Mayan survival and violence in the altiplano. Awareness of the historical context is vital because it underscores how processes of accommodation and collusion, as well as resistance, are integral to how power operates. And community as an expression of culture has been for the Mayas, over the past five centuries, their central locus of struggle and contestation, as well as the space and place of their domination.

In the past sixty years North American, European, and Latin American anthropologists have attempted to unravel the complexities of Mayan material and symbolic life through a combination of field investigations and theoretical models. In general, these studies have sought to account for the peculiarities of autochthonous cultural persistence in a modernizing world that inevitably dooms them to extinction. The conceptualization of community and its relationship to culture has been fundamental to these pursuits. Two studies, in particular, were pivotal in shaping subsequent anthropological understandings of social organization in rural Guatemala.

In 1937, when Sol Tax identified the Guatemalan *municipio* (township) as the site of local ethnic allegiances, he stressed the enduring qualities of Mayan culture. Specific traje, local language dialects, and particular customs, especially pertaining to religious feasts honoring saints of the cofradia denoted community loyalties. Tax argued further that the origins of community could be traced to the pre-Conquest period (1941). As Inga Clendinnen notes in *Ambivalent Conquests* (1987), Mayan elites had rights to material and social resources and political power that commoners did not enjoy. In return, they were obliged to guide and protect the ordinary people under their care. Yet what this emphasis on the quid pro quo over the inequalities obscures is the complexities of both domination and resistance in pre-Conquest Mayan politics (Ortner 1995).

Some twenty years later, Eric Wolf's seminal 1955 article on closed corporate communities delineated the ways in which the internal social and cultural characteristics of peasant communities of "shared poverty" were molded by the vicissitudes of conquest and later capitalism. In contrast to Tax, Wolf stressed the dynamic nature of community formation in relation to external forces. Taken together, these studies shed light on the abiding yet contingent nature of Mayan culture and community. Neither of these two perspectives, however, revealed much about the organizing principles of Mayan society beyond shared territory as a site of shared loyalty.

Less frequently addressed has been the "nexus of social relations" that form the fabric of family and community structures and organization (Watanabe 1992) and the importance of land as the material basis of those relations. Indigenous communities reshaped by differing structures of inequalities since the Conquest have continued to be rooted in kin-based social relations, and many of these social bonds have endured. Mayan principles of reciprocal aid and obligations to both the living and the dead, based on a relationship with land, continued to be expressed routinely through practical activities of survival and cultural symbols such as corn production and consumption. And it is the extended family, as historian Nancy Farriss maintains, that tells us something about the principles, purposes, and structure of Mayan communities, where "individual survival is a collective enterprise" (1984:48). The ways in which land was distributed and utilized were important to how the Mayas have understood and practiced mutual aid and obligations as well as to how these relations have been reshaped over time. Moreover, for the Mayas, corporate bonds were not necessarily egalitarian (Farriss 1984). The hierarchical nature of community and familial social organization simultaneously enhanced the Mayas' ability to withstand the brutalities of colonialization and reinforced gender and generational inequalities.

Extended families have been the basic unit of Mayan social life since the Conquest and most likely since long before. Although theoretically nuclear families could have subsisted with a man planting the milpa and his wife tending the household, without the larger social network a core household would have been too vulnerable to cope with the indeterminacy of survival, such as disease, death, or disaster (Farriss 1984). For most of Mayan history, since the Conquest, extended families were embedded in larger community social structures, initially in scattered residential settlements, called *chinamits*, and later in the cofradias.

Just prior to colonization, Mayas in the highlands were living in chinamits made up of clusters of peasant families with an elite family at the helm.[22] Chinamits, like extended families, were hierarchical and corporate with divisions established along gendered and generational lines of authority. The elite leaders and later the council of elders were responsible for the sociopolitical and spiritual well-being of their settlements. Patrilocal residence seems to have been the norm, with extended families sharing residential dwellings, labor, and food production governed by a system of group support (Hill 1992).

The chinamit structure survived the Conquest and in some cases most of the colonial period because of the peculiarities of Spanish domination. In the decades following the Conquest, Mayas were forcibly relocated into Indian Towns to facilitate the collection of taxes and tribute as well as Christian evangelization. Yet when the Spanish resettled the Mayas they did so, for the most part, as chinamits, rather than as discrete families. Mayas were thus able to utilize the administrative structures of the Indian Towns to retain, albeit partially, the contours of their pre-Hispanic social organization.

In the altiplano, colonial rule was exercised in absentia as non-Indians were forbidden by law to live within the boundaries of Indian Towns. Thus resident indigenous men filling local political offices were primarily responsible for overseeing compliance with tax and labor obligations. Also important was the allocation and use of common lands. Not only did the leaders of the *parcialidades* (as chinamits came to be known in Spanish) adjudicate land and marriage disputes internally, they also represented the group members in negotiations with colonial authorities and were able to influence their clan groups' access to communally held resources. Although the colonists had instituted a townwide governmental structure and appointed officeholders for the administration of duties, parcialidad leaders were often the de facto, albeit circumscribed, power.

In many communities, chinamits cum parcialidades endured as discrete entities within Indian Towns for most of the three hundred years of colonial rule. As a consequence, while Indian Towns remained functionally divided in terms of power, the social bonds of the chinamits allowed for some degree of smaller group cohesion to continue (Hill 1992). A significant land base was crucial to chinamit survival, however, and as this resource became increasingly scarce, intracommunity conflicts became more commonplace

(Monaghan and Hill 1987). The influence of parcialidades extended beyond the boundaries of the town proper. When some group members dispersed to resettle previously cultivated land outside the town center, they maintained alliances with their parcialidad, through both the cofradia and civic responsibilities (Hill and Monaghan 1987).

The cofradia, as religious brotherhoods honoring Christian saints, quickly took on an important role in mobilizing public resources for the clan groups' spiritual and material welfare. Cofradia groups were, for the most part, organized along parcialidad lines and *ejidos* (village common lands) were allocated by clan leaders to raise cattle and crops to finance elaborate religious festivals. Nevertheless, to the distress of the clergy, cofradia celebrations, although ostensibly in compliance with Catholic Church impositions, continued to honor Mayan obligations and responsibilities between the living and the dead, through ceremonies and rituals that venerated their ancestors, local spirits, and deities.

Even as Mayas struggled under the weight of extensive fiscal and labor responsibilities to the Spanish Crown, the colonialists, the local clergy, and the cofradias, they continued to plant their milpas and trade in the extensive highland market system. Because of the peculiarities of colonization in Guatemala, where labor, not land, was crucial to Spanish survival, many Maya were able to avoid the full impact of domination.

At the time of the coffee boom in the late nineteenth century, Mayan towns in the altiplano exhibited a seemingly cohesive character—as in the closed corporate peasant communities theorized by Wolf—more so than in the previous centuries of colonization, when parcialidades had maintained themselves as semi-independent units within the pueblos. In most pueblos, the parcialidades as well a Mayan elite had disappeared altogether as a result of an increase in land scarcity attributable, in part, to population recovery (Hill 1992).[23] With these shifts, communities of the altiplano had taken on a more homogeneous, corporate appearance of shared poverty, where communal allegiances were expressed in the distinctive dress that readily identified a person's natal village and in elaborate cofradia celebrations of each town's patron saint that ostensibly redistributed wealth within the community. Although the cofradias functioned as mediators with the larger society and regulators of internal divisions, recent scholarly work has pointed to the shortcomings of earlier studies that failed to address, in Eric Wolf's words, "the fact and nature of conflicts internal to the corporate communities" (1986:327).

The demands of plantation work led to increasing impoverishment among highland Mayas. Because of the long absences required by plantation labor, Mayas were unable to attend adequately to the diverse economic activities—not only as farmers but as traders and artisans—necessary to their survival. Increasingly drawn into debt, a vicious cycle was created whereby their absences led to further neglect of their milpas in the highlands.[24] In addition, the transformation of alcohol from a social and spiritual adjunct to a colonial and postcolonial tool of labor control further intensified the subjugation of many. The Spanish did not introduce alcohol to the Mayas; Mayas had long used it as an enhancer in their social relations and an offering in their spiritual practices. Mayan use of alcohol as an inebriant and anesthetic, however, both on plantations and in communities, rather than confined to ritual, social, and religious usage, created debts that further necessitated their laboring on the fincas (La Farge 1947; Eber 1995).

Although land expropriated for the creation of coffee fincas did not directly affect communities in the altiplano, where the climate was unsuitable for coffee cultivation, with increasing population pressures and curtailed access to other land, highland communities drew their boundaries ever more sharply. In a strategy probably designed to ward off the formation of alliances between communities, President Justo Rufino Barrios (1873–1885) exploited the growing antagonisms between communities by selectively granting land to communities. In doing so, Barrios gained the allegiance of some communities while fostering animosity between neighboring communities, effectively undercutting the development of pan-indigenous consciousness.

Land titling, an uneven process that had begun after independence and became state-mandated in 1871, effectively transferred ejidal property to individual titles, creating further differentiation, internal divisions, and rancor within some communities and leading in some cases to groups splitting off to form new municipios altogether (McCreery 1994). As land became privatized and commodified throughout the twentieth century, community social relations were critically reshaped under the slow, steady intensification of market relations. While increasing commodification of the rural Mayan economy did lead to new financial opportunities for some, it also contributed to an escalation of economic differentiation among individuals in communities. Moreover, it upset the delicate balance of local power that had mediated between noncommodified and commodified forms of production. These transformations, in which subsistence was subordinated to the market, had a devastating impact on both community and household social relations.

As early as the 1920s, many Mayan families could no longer survive on subsistence agriculture alone—having lost much of their land base—and the annual migratory trek to the coastal plantations to earn cash, however minimal, had become a necessary way of life. And the change produced increasing stratification among Mayas themselves: between those who did have sufficient land resources to meet the minimum requirement for exemption from obligatory work and those who did not (McCreery 1994; Brintnall 1979).

The delicate balance of semi-subsistence production in highland Mayan communities must have been, as Gerald Sider put it when describing similar processes in the context of Newfoundland fisheries, "highly volatile and riven with internal tensions; simultaneously in collusion with and opposed to commodification; simultaneously supporting and undermining non-commodified form of social relations" (1989:27). The subsequent undoing of local indigenous social structures—namely, the cofradias and extended family and kinship networks—that had mediated between individual and community cooperation and opportunism created spaces in which internal political violence could operate.

The Interstitial Tissue of Communities

By the end of the nineteenth century many cofradias in highland towns had melded together into civil and religious responsibilities known as *cargos*, or burdens, that were the primary public institution of local power. Indigenous men, whose wives took on roles crucial to the smooth functioning of their public responsibilities, moved through community service positions alternating between civil and religious duties as they climbed the ladder of community power and prestige. The ideological underpinnings of both community service obligations and extended family responsibilities were based on ideas of internal justice and the ability of older males in the community and the family to negotiate with the larger society and state officials for the benefit of their members (Mallon 1995).

Theoretically, all men had an equal chance of reaching the highest posts; in practice, many did not have the resources to meet the innumerable expenses incurred while serving in all the required posts (Chance and Taylor 1985). The cofradias, like the extended family, were structured along generational and gendered lines of authority: young men submitted to the authority of their elders in return for land inheritance (in the case of the family) and rights to ejidal land (where the cofradia had jurisdiction).

In spite of the multiple pressures placed on communities in the late nineteenth and early twentieth centuries, Mayas were able, to some extent, to reshape the imposed hierarchical political and religious structures in ways that continued to respect corporate land usage and a sense of mutual aid and group identity to both the living and the dead. In the twenty-year period between 1934 and 1954, however, communities in the altiplano underwent significant changes as a result of both external and internal factors. The abolition of debt peonage and the institution of vagrancy laws in 1934,[25] the appointment of outside ladinos to key positions in the local power structures, and the introduction of an orthodox Catholic ideology (Catholic Action), all contributed to intensify divisions within communities (Adams 1970), as did the ten-year democratic opening between 1944 and 1954 (Handy 1994).

The hegemony of the cofradias also was undermined on several fronts. With the appointment of outside intendentes (literally, governors), the civil-religious hierarchies lost much of their official municipal power. With the last vestiges of their public role gone, cargo posts often entailed Mayas simply working in menial tasks for ladino authorities, which reinforced notions of their subordinate position within the community. And with increasing population pressures, communal lands were being privatized, removing, in David McCreery's words, "the vestigial restrictions that custom attached to its use and transfer" (1994:327), thus calling into question the age/grade system of land inheritance itself. As a result communal social bonds were substantially weakened. Land inheritance and the age-gender prestige on which the power of the cofradia rested was breaking down under the impact of commodity production. The cofradia institution, whatever its shortcomings (of which there were many, as Brintnall 1979, Warren 1978, and Falla 1980 have importantly documented), had also served as the interstitial tissue of communities, creating, in part, the social networks and power relations that kept in partial check the potential for internal violence between community members and between men and women.

The hegemony of the cofradia received another blow when foreign priests who opposed the traditional folk Catholicism introduced Catholic Action into rural villages in the 1940s. This conservative orthodox wing of the Catholic Church undermined the ideological basis of the cofradia: the fundamental Mayan belief in the power of the dead. Young local men were trained as lay workers, or catechists, to fill the void created by the severe shortage of priests in rural communities. Many of these young men viewed the cofradia as a force that contributed to the subordinate plight of Mayas locally (Adams 1970; Warren 1978; Falla 1980) and so were often intolerant of cofradia practices that necessitated families selling parcels of land to finance their ritual obligations, a practice that often led to further immiserization for the household.

In the Name of God

Catholic Action had originally been introduced into Guatemala by Archbishop Mariano Rossell Arellano in 1946 in an attempt to ward off the growing influence of Protestantism and the policies of the reformist administrations of Arévalo and Arbenz (1944–1954), which were perceived as making Marxist inroads into rural communities.[26] Catholic Action was also a means for the church to consolidate itself into rural communities long neglected through the lack of priests to minister to campesino spiritual needs.

In addition to contributing to the destabilization of cofradia hegemony in many communities, Catholic Action had other unforeseen consequences. The number of foreign priests and nuns increased substantially after the 1954 coup, and these missionaries were not under the immediate control of the Guatemalan church. A number of these priests—the majority of whom initially were from the American Maryknoll Order or were Spanish Jesuits—were deeply affected by the poverty and misery in which the rural indigenous people were living. With access to independent funding sources, some began not only to tend to the spiritual needs of the poor but also to promote autonomous local-level development, such as potable water and sanitation projects, literacy classes, agricultural cooperatives, and credit schemes.[27] A particularly important aspect of this new ministry flowed from the church's increasing involvement in political action based on fundamental concerns with the plight of the poor worldwide that emerged from the Second Vatican Council of the 1960s. During this period, some progressive church workers began to interpret the Bible in ways that opposed both the traditional cofradias in communities as well as the underpinning of ladino domination locally. By the 1970s the Catholic Church had developed an extensive social network in rural communities in the highlands through bible study groups, Catholic Action groups, catechists, and delegates of the Word of God, which provided spaces for political consciousness-raising.

A progressive offshoot of the Catholic Action and catechist movement was the Cakchiquel Missionary Program (PROMICA) founded in 1976 in the department of Chimaltenango. A group of young Kaqchikel men and women who had been catechists or teachers worked in conjunction with American and Guatemalan priests and nuns in many of the municipios and villages, including Xe'caj, in Chimaltenango Department from the mid-1970s until the early 1980s. The itinerant missionaries promoted local leadership and community organizing skills among the villagers through the formation of base communities. These base communities served as vehicles for local men and women to put their faith into action by redressing the social, economic, and political inequities that defined their lives. Subcommittees—for women, youth, social justice, catechists, married couples—provided a forum for people to analyze their particular situations. The project also promoted the formation of indigenous intellectuals among the young people through literacy in Kaqchikel.

When people began to make demands that challenged local ladino power, particularly over land ownership, these confrontations ended in violence. In one community of Xe'caj the members of the base communities questioned a nonresident ladino's ownership of prime farm land, claiming it was procured by illegal means. This dispute led to the disappearance and killing of several community members. As a result, some community members turned to more active opposition to the Guatemalan state.[28] By 1983 several missionaries and catechists of PROMICA had been killed, and several priests, nuns, and missionaries had received death threats. The project was terminated, and a number of participants went into hiding or exile.

"The Earthquake Not Only Shook the Earth"

Nineteen seventy-six was a watershed year in Chimaltenango Department. A devastating earthquake rocked the region in the early morning hours of February 4, leaving 27,000 dead and thousands more homeless and injured. But as destructive as the earthquake was, it also had many widespread constructive effects in the altiplano. The damage it caused became a catalyst for economic opportunities, political organizing, and the rebuilding of a sense of cooperation and mutual support among many community members in the towns and villages of Chimaltenango. Local leaders were among the first to take an active role in coordinating the relief efforts when the Guatemalan government was unable to mobilize itself quickly and efficiently in response to the disaster.

Doña Marcelina, when recalling the first weeks after the catastrophe, commented that "the earthquake not only shook the earth, but shook us to organize to better our lives." The cleavages and fissures that existed in the communities were nullified briefly after the earthquake. Don Martin, Elena's brother, explained the extraordinary time as one in which "Mother Earth spoke through the earthquake; she called us to unify again as a community, to remember who we are." The structures for community participation and leadership that had been constructed over the past decade were mobilized in the services of those most in need. The successes from these efforts provided further evidence to many of the concrete benefits of mutual cooperation.

By the mid-1970s the altiplano was awash with community organizing activities. A USAID study in 1976 noted that there were over 500 rural cooperatives in Guatemala, approximately 60 percent of which were in the central and western highlands where the majority of the Mayas live (USAID 1982). A vast array of groups representing the spectrum of community organizing and popular mobilization had penetrated Guatemalan society. Peasant organizations, political parties, trade unions, state-sponsored cooperative and colonization schemes, development projects by NGOs (nongovernmental organizations), and literacy campaigns, as well as Christian base communities, were flourishing throughout highland communities, as in Guatemala City.[29]

In the altiplano most of these groups promoted local participation and leadership, presenting new possibilities for a modicum of economic relief and political empowerment to beleaguered Mayas. Ironically, some of the initial funding for community development projects came from USAID (United States Agency for International Development). Some of these civic action projects, such as the construction of roads, schools, and health clinics in rural villages, were part of a larger U.S.-promoted counterinsurgency strategy program for Latin America known as the "Alliance for Progress," initiated under the Kennedy administration. Many of these projects were located in areas where social inequalities were most acute and where the potential support for rebel support was thought to be strongest. The contradiction was that although these USAID-supported projects were intended to shore up consensus to the status quo, in many cases they instead contributed to spaces where many gained an increasing political consciousness of how to redress at the local level their subordinate position within Guatemalan society (Green 1989).

Challenges to Local Power

Introduction of low-cost chemical fertilizers into highland milpa agriculture in the 1960s—part of the Green Revolution—fundamentally altered the relationship of Mayan campesinos to their land, as well as their position in the local economic structure. A decade after the introduction of synthetic fertilizers, for example, the number of men from Chimaltenango Department who were migrating to the fincas had declined significantly (Smith 1990b). During the 1970s, for example, less than 10 percent of the agricultural workforce from many municipios in the department were going to the coastal fincas, and 10 to 15 percent of adult men were engaged in investing profits into land and in small-scale commerce (Smith 1990b). George Lovell has argued that this decline in the available Mayan labor pool "set the stage for a major confrontation between community and state interests" (Lovell 1988:45). While this is certainly an important fact, what I suggest here is that closer inspection of local-level processes is crucial to understanding the ways in which repression happened at the community level.

For the first time, cash became a necessary component of subsistence production, whereas before it had been necessary to sustaining subsistence consumption. With significant land concentration, most Mayan families in the altiplano had to buy at least some of their year's supply of food with the cash they earned through wage labor. Now, rural farmers needed cash to buy fertilizer for the milpa, rather than the customary organic fertilizer that was commonplace.

Initially, it mattered little. The high yields from the chemical fertilizers significantly eased land pressure in areas where tenancy was severely strained. Many older men in Xe'caj recalled those years when their harvest doubled and tripled and fertilizer cost only US$2–$4 per 100 pounds and a 100-pound bag was sufficient for a cuerda. After a few years, however, the miracle harvests began to dwindle in the face of soil depletion, diminishing yields, and increasing problems with pests and disease. In 1990 fertilizer prices had more than quadrupled, with a 100-pound bag selling for US$16–$20.[30] And farmers now needed two to three bags per cuerda as the effectiveness had decreased significantly with extended use. Milpa yields have been declining steadily over the past few decades, as the crops are plagued with grubworms and nitrogen deficiency. Doña Alejandra explains the predicament of landholdings so small that farmers cannot afford to let land lie fallow, as had been widely practiced in milpa agriculture: "La tierra es debil; no puede descansar" (the land it weak now that it cannot rest). Like the failures of the Green Revolution elsewhere, Guatemalan milpa farmers are now dependent on chemical fertilizers that are highly expensive and mostly ineffectual. This situation is particularly burdensome for the rural widows of Xe'caj, who are woefully dependent on the milpa harvest to feed their families and whose options for earning cash are severely limited.

At first, however, the benefits of chemical fertilizers seemed nothing short of miraculous. Some campesinos had surplus crops to sell for the first time in years. Don Miguel and doña Alejandra were fortunate in that regard, and they reinvested their profits in land. After a few years they were able to plant not only subsistence crops of corn and beans but also wheat. Later Don Miguel bought his own truck to transport his crops to sell in Guatemala City. Soon thereafter he was carrying the produce of his neighbors, who preferred to do business with a *conocido* (another Mayan) rather than a ladino. This proved to be a fatal mistake, however: Miguel was not only sidestepping the transport businesses of local ladino middlemen but actually undermining their monopoly. Miguel's personal good fortune, like that of many of his counterparts throughout the altiplano, had begun to challenge long-term local economic and political structures that supported ladino domination and exploitation of Mayas. Several months after the 1976 earthquake that devastated Chimaltenango Department, Don Miguel was disappeared one night from his home by armed masked men. It was the beginning of the era of selective repression in the Xe'caj area. His body was found several days later in a ravine not far from the pueblo, marked with the soon-to-be commonplace signs of torture.

Two overlapping explanations are offered locally for Miguel's disappearance. Like others who dared to challenge the status quo, Miguel was denounced by local ladinos to the military authorities as a guerrilla. The other explanation was that Miguel was denounced by a Mayan family: he was seeing another woman, and that woman's family, with ties to the military, denounced him as a guerrilla sympathizer. Either explanation points to a convergence of issues taking place in the altiplano in the 1970s. And while neither challenges to local power structures nor the breakdown of local-level social relations is unique to the period, what these explanations do reveal is how the forces of structural inequalities and political violence intersected, in some cases with lethal consequences.

The Peace Accords

On December 29, 1996, Alvero Arzu, the president of Guatemala; the high command of the Guatemalan military; and commandantes of the leftist guerrilla group known as the Guatemalan National Revolutionary Unity (URNG, the Spanish acronym) signed peace accords brokered by the United Nations, officially ending a thirty-six-year civil war. On that day, the central plaza located in front of the national palace in Guatemala City was crowded not with the usual protesters but with celebrants. Many of them wore t-shirts or baseball caps or carried signs openly declaring their allegiance to the URNG, an act unthinkable even in the months preceding the official signing. Somewhat disconcerting, however, was the eerie, distinctive hum of helicopters circling overhead. In another context, they would have passed by unnoticed—simply signaling the presence of the press corps capturing the historic event on film—yet insofar as helicopters were the preferred means for transporting military troops into rural villages during the counterinsurgency war, the constant whirling of their blades was an evocative reminder of a not-too-distant past.

Individual accords between the Guatemalan state and the URNG were negotiated under the auspices of the United Nations over a period of several years before their final ratification. In reality, the war ended on the battlefield in 1984, yet a political settlement took another twelve years to reach, in part because of the intransigence of the ultraconservative faction within the military and the oligarchy that saw no need to negotiate as they had effectively won the war. But increasing international pressure was brought to bear on the Guatemalan state to achieve a political resolution to one of the longest-running insurgent wars in Latin America.

Although analysts of the peace process in Guatemala are fully aware that the accords in themselves do not "add up to a restructuring of the state" (Holiday 1997:72), some have argued that they have provided political spaces for public debate where civil society can make demands for development and democratization. Several of the accords, however, if fully implemented, may actually undermine rather than contribute to the possibility of peace and justice in Guatemala. The peace accords negotiated a settlement to a stalemated armed conflict. Because they did not address the indissoluble link between structural and political violence, they in fact reinforced exploitation, marginalization, and powerlessness. At the root of the accords are two key contradictions: the fundamental paradox between democracy and capitalism—the idealogy of equality alonside persistent and deepening social inequalities under a free-market model. Secondly, the accords ignore the extent and strength of the military project—reinforced by ongoing impunity (see Schirmer 1998).

The Accord on the Establishment of a Commission for Historical Clarification of Human Rights Violations created a commission to investigate and report on the human rights violations that had taken place since the beginning of the thirty-six-year armed conflict. While the mandate of the commission is to document the historical truth about the period and provide the basis for some measure of compensation to victims' families, it does not include naming individuals responsible for human rights violations or using such evidence in subsequent judicial trials. Moreover, in December 1996 the Guatemalan Congress, concomitant with the Accords, approved a National Reconciliation Law (NRL) that "established provisions for 'extinguishing criminal responsibility' for crimes committed by, for example, members of the military, civil patrollers, and politicians between the start of the armed conflict and the date of the law's passage" (Popkin 1997:174).

While the NRL does not provide a blanket amnesty for human rights violators and excludes disappearances, torture, and genocide (although not extrajudicial killings) from amnesty cases, it does hold out the possibility for continued impunity through several key features. First, interpretations of critical phrases such as "in the armed conflict" and "genocide" are left open-ended. For example, the wholesale slaughter of unarmed Mayan campesinos thought to be guerrilla sympathizers may or may not be deemed genocidal. Second, the law places the responsibility for deciding who and which crimes are eligible for amnesty in the hands of the Guatemalan judiciary, infamous for its poor record of administering justice in human rights cases (Popkin 1997).

The Accord on the Identity and Rights of Indigenous Peoples was signed in March 1995. That accord, for the first time in Guatemalan history, officially recognized the multicultural, multiethnic, and multilinguistic character of the nation. The document acknowledged the centuries-long discrimination against Mayas and acceded a Mayan identity grounded in a worldview based on land, corn, and culture (Saqb'ichil 1995:5). While the accord goes a long way toward redressing the more flagrant exclusions of Mayas from Guatemalan society, it is not likely to have any more positive material effects on Mayan well-being than independence from Spain did. For one thing, it does not address the extreme conditions of socioeconomic inequality, in particular the vastly inequitable land tenure system that profoundly affects the majority of Mayan lives, whether in rural or urban areas. While the accord recognizes the importance of land and the growing of corn as fundamental elements in Mayan cultural production, it fails to demand land redistribution, a factor vital to rural Mayan economic and cultural survival. Moreover, the neoliberal economic policies the accords promote have intensified the push to pave over some of the prime farm lands in Chimaltenango Department for the construction of more maquila factories or second homes for wealthy Guatemalans and to grow nontraditional crops for export. The majority of rural Mayan people thus are left to bear not only the high costs of war but the high costs of peace as well. As such, the accords have the potential to do more harm than good, separating widespread Mayan beliefs even further from a material reality.

Similarly, the Accord on the Socioeconomic Aspects and the Agrarian Situation does not articulate precise terms that would guarantee a fundamental restructuring of the national economy through agrarian reform or other means that would provide possibilities for economic justice. In some aspects this accord—with provisions that extend only until 1999—mirrors the goals of Western development put forth by the major international financial lending institutions, such as the World Bank and the International Monetary Fund, which include fiscal austerity measures that have led to increasing disparities of wealth in the society as a whole and elsewhere have had a devastating impact on power relations between men and women. Moreover, the accord conceptualizes modernization as an expansion of free trade zones and contract farming whose profits rely on cheap and docile labor force.

While these accords address the issue of basic rights for Mayas in Guatemalan society—rights systematically denied them—most Mayas, as well as their poor ladino counterparts, have not had a central voice in these negotiations and have been denied the power to define their own realities or their own vision of the future. In addition, the 1996 Guatemalan Peace Accords that resulted from the negotiations defined peace and security in its narrowest terms, equating peace with the absence of war and security with the absence of military threat. These restricted definitions both overlook the multifaceted problems that circumscribe Guatemalan society—economic, ecological, demographic, narcotic, and gender issues—and discount their importance in constructing lasting peace and justice in Guatemala. The accords serve to limit and in fact make illegitimate other visions of possibilities for substantive change in Guatemala.

Despite the relentless exploitation, violence, and trauma that have marked their lives since the Spanish Conquest over five centuries earlier, Mayas have endured as a distinct culture. Quite clearly, contemporary Mayas are not the same as their ancestors. Peoples lives, and therefore their culture, have changed over the centuries, as has the world around them. War, trauma, Christianity, loss of land, loss of control over their labor, poverty, and the introduction of farming crops and modern institutions have influenced who the Mayas are today. And each generation has had to respond anew to the challenges of survival under different historical and structural circumstances. Yet Mayas have reworked their economic organization and ideological apparatus within kinship and community structures as best they could to reinvigorate what they deemed important and desirable under conditions not of their own making.

What is unique about the present situation for rural Mayas in the altiplano is that there has been a substantial weakening of the spaces that they have long utilized to survive. The land surrounding their communities, where for centuries they have established their milpas, is being penetrated by new forms of global capitalism. Their communities are militarized in unprecedented ways, and daily life is under surveillance. Today Mayan communities as refuges from the outside world—whatever their shortcomings, factions, and cleavages—have been reshaped under the weight of violence and repression.

FIGURE 3.1
Kaibil counterinsurgency troops (1989). (*Kathleen Foster*)

3. living in a state of fear

The tradition of the oppressed teaches us that "the state of emergency" in which we live is not the exception but the rule.
—Walter Benjamin

No power so effectively robs the mind of all its powers of acting and reasoning as fear—
To make anything terrible, obscurity seems to be necessary.
—William Burke

People want the right to survive, to live without fear.
—Doña Petrona

Fear is a response to danger, but in Guatemala rather than being solely a subjective personal experience fear has also penetrated the social memory.[1] And rather than an acute reaction it is a chronic condition. The effects of fear are pervasive and insidious in Guatemala. Fear destabilizes social relations by driving a wedge of distrust between family members, neighbors, friends. Fear divides communities by creating suspicion and apprehension not only of strangers but of each other.[2] Fear thrives on ambiguities. Denunciations, gossip, innuendoes, and rumors of death lists create a climate of suspicion. No one can be sure who is who. The spectacle of torture and death and of massacres and disappearances in the recent past have become more deeply inscribed into individual bodies and the collective imagination through a constant sense of threat. In the altiplano, fear has become a way of life. Fear is the arbiter of power: invisible, indeterminant, and silent.

What is the nature of the terror that pervades Guatemala society? How do people understand it and experience it? And what is at stake for people who live in a chronic state of fear? In this context survival itself depends on a panoply of responses to a seemingly intractable situation.

In this chapter, I look at the invisible violence of fear and intimidation through the quotidian experiences of the people of Xe'caj. In doing so, I examine the insecurity that permeates the lives of individual women wracked by worries of physical and emotional survival, grotesque memories, ongoing militarization, and chronic fear. The stories I relate below are the individual experiences of the women with whom I worked, yet they are also social and collective accounts by virtue of their omnipresence (cf. Lira and Castillo 1991; Martin-Baro 1990). Although initially the focus of my work with Mayan women was not explicitly on the topic of violence, I came to understand that its usages, manifestations, and effects were essential for comprehending the context in which the women of Xe'caj were struggling to survive. Fear became the metanarrative of my research and experiences among the people of Xe'caj. Fear is inseparable from the reality in which the people live. It is the hidden "state of emergency"—individual and social—that is factored into the choices women and men make. And although this "state of emergency" has been the norm in Guatemala for over a decade, it is an abnormal state of affairs indeed. Albert Camus (1955) wrote that from an examination of the shifts between the normal and the emergency, between the tragic and the everyday, emerges the paradoxes and contradictions that bring into sharp relief how the absurd (in this case, terror) works.

Violence and Anthropology

Given anthropology's empirical tradition and the fact that anthropologists are well positioned to speak out on behalf of ordinary people, it seems curious that until recently so few have chosen to do so. Jeffrey Sluka has suggested that the practice of sociocultural anthropology with its emphasis on a "cross-cultural and comparative perspective, holistic approach, reliance on participant observation, concentration on local-level analysis and 'emic' point of view" is particularly well suited to understanding "the subjective, experiential, meaningful dimension of social conflict" (1992:20). Anthropologists, however, have traditionally approached the study of conflict, war, and human aggression from a distance, ignoring the harsh realities of people's lives.

Although the dominant theoretical paradigms utilized in anthropological inquiry over the last century—evolutionism, structural functionalism, acculturation, and Marxism—have examined societal manifestations of violence, the lived experiences of research subjects have often been muted. Social conflict and warfare were often problematized in abstract terms, divorced from the historical realities of the colonial or capitalist encounter. Throughout the twentieth century, most studies by political anthropologists emphasized taxonomy over process, for example, the classification of simple or indigenous political systems, political leadership, law, domination, and intertribal relations. After World War I, funding from private sources, such as the Rockefeller Foundation, influenced the research agenda of North American and British anthropologists, which was characterized by studies of order and disorder within a functionalist paradigm (Vincent 1990).

In Mesoamerica, Robert Redfield's 1927 investigation of Tepoztlan is exemplary of the ahistorical nature of acculturation studies (1930). Redfield stressed the harmony and consensus existing among the Tepoztecos, describing in detail their cultural traits and "life ways" without mention of recent historical events (the Mexican Revolution) or political realities (ongoing local turmoil in Tepoztlan during his own fieldwork). There were exceptions, of course. Alexander Lesser (1933), Monica Hunter (1936), and Hilda Kuper (1947), for example, were producing politically and socially relevant ethnography during the same period. These studies concerned with the impact of colonialization on marginalized people were marginalized, however (Vincent 1990).

With the upsurge of internecine warfare since World War II, the number of anthropological studies focusing on conflict and change increased exponentially. With the advent of the cold war in the 1950s, counterinsurgency warfare became a common response to the dramatic rise in revolutionary movements in many third world countries. While repression itself was not new, distinct patterns of repression and new organizational forms for its implementation emerged in close association with U.S. security programs.[3] Some anthropologists became involved in studies of the effects of U.S. military presence (for example the controversial Cornell University Studies in Culture and Applied Science), while other anthropologists participated in intelligence activities during the Vietnam War. The emergence of two distinct analytical frameworks within anthropology—neoevolutionary theory (Service 1962; Sahlins and Service 1960; Fried 1967) and Marxism (see Gough 1968; Hymes 1969)—mirrored the increasing polarization taking place in United States in the 1960s. Yet systematic inquiry into human rights violations remained elusive. Despite an alarming rise in the most blatant forms of transgressions, repression, and state terrorism, the topic has not captured the anthropological imagination until recently (Downing and Kushner 1988; Binford 1996; Wilson 1997). Overwhelming empirical evidence demonstrates that state-sponsored violence has been standard operating procedure in numerous contemporary societies where anthropologists have conducted fieldwork for the past three decades.[4]

Paul Doughty (1988:43), in a stinging commentary of anthropology's claim to authority on the subject of Native Americans, has questioned why most monographs have not addressed systematically "the most vital issues that deeply affected all Native Americans since European conquest": death, discrimination, displacement, dispossession, racism, rampant disease, hunger, impoverishment, and physical and psychological abuse. Nancy Scheper-Hughes (1992) is insightful in this regard. In her ethnography of everyday violence in northeast Brazil, she argues that "a critical practice of social science research implies not so much a practical as an epistemological struggle" (172). Perhaps this is what lies at the heart of anthropology's diverted gaze. What is at stake are the struggles between the powerful and the powerless, and what is at issue for anthropologists is to decide with whom to cast their lot.

Today a number of practitioners who work in dangerous field situations are beginning to deconstruct the insidious and pervasive effects and mechanisms of violence and terror, underscoring how it operates on the level of lived experience (Nordstrom and Martin 1992; Feldman 1991; Scheper-Hughes 1992, 1996; Lancaster 1992; Suarez-Orozco 1990, 1992; Peteet 1991; Nordstrom and Robben 1995; Daniel 1996; Nordstrom 1997). Andrew Turton (1986:39–40) has remarked that an examination of power must "include the techniques and modalities of both more physically coercive forms of domination and more ideological and discursive forms and relations between the two, in which fear may be a crucial factor."

In Guatemala recent works by Carmack (1988), Manz (1988), AVANCSO (1992), Falla (1983, 1992), Wilson (1991, 1995), Stoll (1993), and Warren (1993) have begun to document the testimonies of individual and collective experiences during the most recent reign of terror. Ricardo Falla (1992) in his haunting account of the massacres of the Ixcan in Guatemala between 1975 and 1982 asks the chilling question, why should one write about massacres (and terror)? And the question is not rhetorical but expresses the profoundly moral commitment of his inquiry. The narratives of the people who survived the war speak most forcefully to the unresolved issues of impunity and accountability that continue to plague this beautiful yet deeply divided country.

FIGURE 3.2
Soldiers doing a routine search of a bus. (*David Maung*)

The Nature of Fear

Writing this chapter has been a challenge, not only because of the nature of the topic itself but also because of the difficulty of putting fear and terror into words. I have chosen to include some of my own experiences of fear during my field research rather than stand apart purely as an outsider and observer. It soon became apparent to me that any understanding of the women's lives would include a journey into a state of fear where terror reigned and shaped the very nature of my interactions and relationships in Xe'caj. These shared experiences established common grounds of understanding and respect.

Fear is an elusive concept, yet you know it when it has you in its grip. Fear like pain can be overwhelmingly present to the person experiencing it, but it may be barely perceptible to anyone else and almost defies objectification.[5] Subjectively, the mundane experience of chronic fear wears down one's sensibility to it. The routinization of fear undermines one's confidence in interpreting the world. My own experiences of fear, and those of the women I know, are best described as swinging wildly between controlled hysteria and tacit acquiescence.

While thinking and writing about fear and terror I tried to discuss what I was doing with colleagues knowledgeable about la situacion in Central America. I described to them the eerie calm I felt most days, an unease that lay below the surface of everyday life. Most of the time the experience was more visceral than visual, and I tried laboriously to suppress it.

One day I was relating to a friend—a fellow researcher with extensive experience in Central America—how it felt pretending not to be disturbed by the intermittent threats that were commonplace throughout 1989 and 1990 in Xe'caj. Some weeks the market plaza would be surrounded by five or six tanks while soldiers with painted faces and M-16s in hand perched above us, watching. His response only made me more nervous. He said that initially he had been upset by the ubiquitous military presence in Central America and he had assumed that the local people felt the same. But lately he had been rethinking his position after having witnessed a number of young women flirting with soldiers or small groups of local men leaning casually on tanks. Perhaps we North Americans, he continued, were misrepresenting what was going on, projecting our own fears onto the experiences of the Central Americans. I went home wondering if perhaps I was being hysterical. Had I become too preoccupied by the violence while doing fieldwork? Was I misconstruing the terror I had felt? Gradually I came to realize that terror's power, its matter-of-factness, is exactly about doubting one's own perception of reality. The routinization of terror is what fuels its power. Such routinization allows people to live in a chronic state of fear behind a facade of normalcy, even while that terror permeates and shreds the social fabric. A sensitive and experienced Guatemalan economist noted that a major problem for social scientists working in Guatemala is that to survive they have to become inured to the violence, training themselves at first not to react and then later not to feel or see it. They misinterpret the contexts in which people live, including their own. Self-censorship becomes second nature, Bentham's panopticon internalized.

How does one become socialized to terror? Does it imply conformity or acquiescence to the status quo, as my friend suggested? While it is true that with repetitiveness and familiarity people learn to accommodate themselves to terror and fear, low-intensity panic remains in the shadow of waking consciousness. One cannot live in a constant state of alertness, and so the chaos one feels becomes diffused throughout the body. It surfaces frequently in dreams and chronic illnesses. In the morning, my neighbors and friends would sometimes speak of their fears during the night, of being unable to sleep or being awakened by footsteps or voices, of nightmares of recurring death and violence. After six months of living in Xe'caj, I too started having my own dreams of death, disappearances, and torture. Whisperings, innuendoes, rumors of death lists circulating would put everyone on edge. One day a friend, Tomas, from Xe'caj, came to my house feeling very anxious. He explained, holding back his tears, that he had heard his name was on the newest death list at the military encampment. As Scheper-Hughes (1992:223) has noted in the Brazilian context, "the intolerableness of the[se] situation[s] is increased by its ambiguity." A month later, two soldiers were killed one Sunday afternoon in a surprise guerrilla attack a kilometer from my house. That evening, several women from the village came to visit, emotionally distraught; they worried that la violencia, which had been stalking them, had at last returned. As doña Alejandra said, violence is like fire: it can flare up suddenly and burn you.

The people in Xe'caj live under constant surveillance. The local *destacamento* (military encampment) looms large in the pueblo, situated on a nearby hillside above town. From there everyone's movements come under close scrutiny. The town is laid out in the colonial quadrangle pattern common throughout the altiplano. The town square, as well as all the roads leading to the surrounding countryside, is visible from above. To an untrained eye, the encampment is not obvious from below. The camouflaged buildings fade into the hillside, but once one has looked down from there it is impossible to forget that those who live below do so in a fishbowl. Military commissioners, civil patrollers, and *orejas* (spies) are responsible for most of this scrutiny. These local men are often former soldiers and willingly report to the army any suspicious activities of their neighbors.[6]

The impact of the civil patrols (PACs) at the local level has been profound. One of the structural effects of the PACs in Xe'caj has been the subordination of village political authority to the local army commander. When I arrived in Xe'caj, I went to the *alcalde* (mayor) first to introduce myself and ask for his permission to work in the township and surrounding villages. But midway through my explanation he cut me off abruptly, explaining impatiently that if I hoped to work there I really needed the explicit permission of the commandante at the army garrison. The civil patrols guard the entrances and exits to the villages in Xe'caj, he said. Without permission from the army, the civil patrols would not allow me to enter. My presence as a stranger and foreigner produced suspicions. "Why do you want to live and work here with us? Why do you want to talk to the widows? For whom do you work?" the alcalde asked. The local army officers told me it was a free country and that I could do as I pleased, provided I had *their* permission.

One of the ways terror becomes defused is through subtle messages, much as Carol Cohn (1987) describes in her unsettling account of the use of language by nuclear scientists to sanitize their involvement in the production of nuclear weaponry. In Guatemala language and symbols are utilized to normalize a continual army presence. From time to time, army troops would arrive in an aldea obliging the villagers to assemble for a community meeting. The message was more or less the same each time I witnessed these gatherings. The commandante would begin by telling the people that the army was their friend, that the soldiers were there to protect them against subversion, against the communists hiding out in the mountains. At the same time, he would admonish them that if they did not cooperate, Guatemala could become like Nicaragua, El Salvador, or Cuba. Subtienente Rodriguez explained to me during one such meeting that the army was preserving peace and democracy in Guatemala through military control of the entire country. Ignacio Martin-Baro (1989) has characterized social perceptions reduced to rigid and simplistic schemes as "official lies," where social knowledge is cast in dichotomous terms, black or white, good or bad, friend or enemy, without the nuances and complexities of lived experience.

Guatemalan soldiers at times arrived in villages accompanied by U.S. National Guard doctors or dentists who would hold clinics for a few days. This was part of a larger strategy developed under the Kennedy doctrine of Alliance for Progress in which civic actions are part of counterinsurgency strategies.[7] Yet mixing so-called benevolent help with military actions does not negate the essential fact that violence is intrinsic to the military's nature and logic. Coercion is the mechanism that the military uses to control citizens even in the absence of war (Scheper-Hughes 1992:224)

I was with a group of widows and young orphaned girls one afternoon watching a soap opera on television. It was in mid-June, a week or so before Army Day. During one of the commercial breaks, a series of images of Kaibiles appeared on the screen; they were dressed for combat with painted faces, clenching their rifles while running through the mountains. Each time a new frame appeared there was an audible gasp in the room. The last image was of soldiers emerging from behind corn stalks while the narrator said, "The army is ready to do whatever is necessary to defend the country." One young girl turned to me and said, "Si pues, siempre estan lista que se matan la gente" (well, yes, they are always ready to kill the people).

The use of camouflage cloth for clothing and small items sold at the market is a subtle and insidious militarization of daily life. Wallets, key chains, belts, caps, and toy helicopters made in Taiwan are disconcerting in this context. As these seemingly mundane objects circulate, they normalize the extent to which civilian and the military life have commingled in the altiplano. Young men who have returned to villages from military service often wear army boots, t-shirts denoting in which military zone they had been stationed, and their dog tags. The boots themselves are significant. The women would say they knew who it was that kidnapped or killed their family members, even if dressed in civilian clothes, because the men were wearing army boots.

When my neighbor's cousin on leave from the army came for a visit, the young boys brought him over to my house so they could show off his photo album. As the young soldier stood in the background shyly, Eduardo and Luisito pointed enthusiastically to a photograph of their cousin leaning on a tank with his automatic rifle in hand and a bandolier of bullets slung over his shoulder; in another he was throwing a hand grenade. Yet these same boys told me, many months after I had moved into my house and we had become friends, that when I first arrived they were afraid I might kill them. And doña Sofia, Eduardo's mother, was shocked to learn that I didn't carry a gun.

In El Salvador, Martin-Baro (1989) analyzed the subjective internalization of war and militarization among a group of 203 children in an effort to understand to what extent they have assimilated the efficacy of violence in solving personal and social problems. While generalizations cannot easily be drawn from the study, Martin-Baro found that the majority of the children interviewed stated that the best way to end the war and attain peace was to eliminate the enemy through violent means (whether this was understood as the Salvadoran army or the FMLN [Farbundo Martí National Liberation Front]). Martin-Baro has referred to this tendency to internalize violence as the "militarization of the mind" (1990).[8]

The presence of soldiers and ex-soldiers in these communities is illustrative of lived contradictions in the altiplano and provides another example of how the routinization of terror functions. The foot soldiers of the army are almost exclusively young rural Mayas, many still boys, only fourteen or fifteen years old, rounded up on army sweeps through rural towns. The recruiters arrive in two-ton trucks grabbing all young men in sight, usually on festival or market days when large numbers of people have gathered together in the center of the pueblo. One morning at dawn I witnessed four such loaded trucks driving from one of the towns of Xe'caj, soldiers standing in each corner of the truck with rifles pointed outward. The soon-to-be foot soldiers were packed in like cattle. Little is known about the training these young soldiers receive, but anecdotal data from some who were willing to talk suggests that the training is designed to break down their sense of personal dignity and respect for other human beings. As one young man described it to me, "Soldiers are trained to kill and nothing more" (see Forester 1992; Sanford 1993). Another said he learned to hate everyone, including himself.

The soldiers who pass through the villages on recognizance and take up sentry duty in the pueblos are Mayas, while the officers, who cannot speak the local language, are ladinos from other regions of the country. A second lieutenant explained to me that army policy dictates that the foot soldiers and the commanders of the local garrisons change assignments every three months to prevent soldiers from getting to know the people and the commandantes from getting bored. A small but significant number of men in Xe'caj have served in the army. Many young men return to their natal villages after they are released from military duty. Yet their reintegration into the community is often difficult. As one villager noted, "They leave as Indians, but they don't come back Indian." During their service in the army, some of these soldiers have been forced to kill and maim. Set adrift, these young men often go on to become the local military commissioners, heads of the civil patrol, or paid informers for the army. Many are demoralized, frequently drinking and turning violent. Others marry and settle in their villages to resume their lives as best they can. Padre Juan, a local Catholic priest at the time of my fieldwork, said that many ex-soldiers in Xe'caj would get drunk before going to confession, where they intermittently sobbed as they related to him in brutal detail what they had done and seen while in the army.

The Structure of Fear

The culture of fear that pervades Guatemalan society has roots in the trauma of the Spanish invasion five centuries earlier. Fear and oppression have been the dual and constant features of Guatemalan history since the arrival of Pedro Alvarado and his conquistadores in the early sixteenth century. The words written in the Anuals of the Cakchiquels almost five hundred years ago are as meaningful today as then:

Little by little, heavy shadows
and black night enveloped
Our fathers and grandfathers
And us also, oh, my sons . . .
All of us were thus.
We were born to die.

Terror is the taproot of Guatemala's past and stalks its present. When speaking of la violencia of the 1980s, I was struck by how frequently people used the metaphor of conquest to describe it. "Lo mismo cuando se mato a Tecum Uman" (it is the same when they killed Tecum Uman), doña Marta said when describing the recent whirlwind of death, alluding to the Maya-K'iche hero who died valiantly in battle against the Spanish. Although references to the Spanish conquest became more commonplace on the cusp of the quincentenary in 1992, in 1988 and early 1989 rural constructions of local experiences in terms of the invasion were striking, haunting, as if a collective memory had been passed generation to generation. In this way, history engaged through memory becomes a social force comprising "both group membership and individual identity out of a dynamically chosen selection of memories and the constant reshaping, reinvention, and reinforcement of those memories as members contest and create the boundaries and links among themselves" (Boyarin 1994:26).

George Lovell (1992: epilogue 34) has compared some of the occupation strategies of the Spanish Crown with those of the modern Guatemalan state and concludes that "the policy remains the same: to dismantle existing forms of community organization, to drive a wedge between people and place; to force families to live not where they wish but where they are told, in nucleated centers where movements are scrutinized, routines disrupted, attitudes and behavior modified." Franciscan documents from the sixteenth century describe the disorder resulting from a local judge's order to burn down towns when Indians refused to comply with official degrees. Lovell writes (1992:35): "Chaos ensued. Roads and trails were strewn with poor Indian women, tied as prisoners, carrying children on their backs, left to fend for themselves." Five hundred years later, publications by anthropologists (Carmack 1988; Manz 1988; Falla 1983, 1992) and numerous international human rights groups (America's Watch, Amnesty International reports throughout the 1980s) recount violations of a similar magnitude.

Fear has been the motor of oppression in Guatemala. As Brecht

(1976:296–97) noted, "Fear rules not only those who are ruled, but the rulers too." The elite, dominant classes are driven by racist fears of *indios* (a pejorative term for Indians) and in more recent decades by the red menace of communism to perform the most brutish acts to protect the status quo. There are upper-class ladinos in Guatemala City who deny that the massacres in rural areas ever really happened. A ladina journalist noted that "one of the reasons why repression did not cause too big a commotion among Guatemalans in the capital was because it was mainly Indians that were affected. All the suffering that took place was not really suffering because it happened to Indians. The Guatemalan upper class believes that Indians cannot really feel, that an Indian woman will not truly suffer if her husband or children are killed because she is not the same as us" (Hooks 1991:48). Suarez-Orozco (1992) has described the process of denial in Argentina during the years of the "dirty war" as a psychological mechanism for coping with the terror, yet what stands apart in Guatemala is not the denial of the unthinkable but a dismissal of suffering that is rooted in racism. For the women and men of Xe'caj, fear is a way of life, and injustice is the rule. The unimaginable (to us) has already happened (to them).

Like most fledgling anthropologists, I had been nervous about getting my first major research project under way, particularly in view of the special circumstances in which I had chosen to work. By the time I began fieldwork in Guatemala in 1988 it was permissible to discuss openly and publicly la situacion and la violencia of the past eight or so years, and the plight of widows and orphans was becoming a matter of public record.[9] Yet the fragile democratic opening that had been welcomed by the majority of the population in 1985 and buoyed by a sense of hope when Vinicio Cerezo took office—the first elected civilian president in sixteen years—was in grave danger by 1988. An attempted coup d'état in the spring of 1988 (followed by another in May 1989) dashed any hopes for significant social reform. The military remained firmly in charge, although backstage. Still, even the military recognized the need for international and national legitimacy through a return to civilian rule in order to address the nation's severe economic and political crises.

In retrospect, political analysts now define the May 1988 and May 1989 coup attempts as "successful" short of toppling the presidency. What little power the military had relinquished during the electoral process in 1985 had reverted back to the generals. Although, as these coups demonstrated, the army was far from a monolithic institution (Jonas 1991; Anderson and Simon

1987; Mersky 1989),[10] it was becoming clearer that Cerezo's role was to be directed toward an international audience. He had in effect yielded power to the military without vacating the presidential palace. Human rights violations in the capital and in rural areas continued unabated.[11]

International human rights organizations documented the continuation of systematic human rights violations (America's Watch 1990 and Amnesty International 1987). The U.S.-based Council on Hemispheric Affairs named Guatemala as the worst human rights violator in Latin America for 1989, 1990, 1991, and 1992. The massacre of twenty-one campesinos in El Aguacate, San Andreas Itzapa, Chimaltenango in 1988; the political assassinations of Hector Oqueli from El Salvador, Gilda Flores, a prominent Guatemalan attorney, and the political leader, Danilo Barillas; the killings and disappearances of university students and human rights workers; the 1990 murder of the anthropologist Myrna Mack, who was stabbed to death in the street in front of her office; the murder of the North American Michael Devine; the systematic torture of Sister Diana Ortiz; and threats and intimidation against countless others throughout the period, all these point to the persistent violence and repression used by the state against its citizenry. While the state denounced the atrocities, it also tried to explain them away as crimes by delinquents. While it vowed to investigate and prosecute fully those responsible, no one in the high command of the military has ever been convicted or served a prison term for human rights violations, despite the fact that frequently there has been substantial evidence indicating the complicity of the state security forces. Thus, with a wink and a nod to its citizens, a policy of impunity makes it clear to everyone who retains power and under what conditions. As Ignacio Martin-Baro noted: "The usefulness of violence is its effectiveness and the crucial point concerning the proliferation of violence in Central America is its impunity under the law" (1990:344).[12]

Despite this hideous record of documented human rights abuses, the United Nations Commission on Human Rights decided in 1992 to downplay Guatemala's record for the fifth consecutive year, placing it in the "advisory" rather than "violations" category. Yet inside the country, repression continued unchecked.[13] Repression is used selectively: to threaten, intimidate, disappear, or kill one or two labor leaders, students, or campesinos is to paralyze everyone else with fear. If one crosses the arbitrary line, the consequences are well known; the problem is that one cannot be sure where the line is, nor when one has crossed it, until it is too late.

After several months of searching for a field site, I settled on Xe'caj because although it had seen much bloodshed and repression during the early 1980s, la situacion was reportedly *tranquila* (calm) in 1988. The terror and fear that pervaded daily life were not immediately perceptible to me. Military checkpoints, the army garrison, and civil patrols were clearly visible, yet daily life appeared normal. The guerrilla war, which reached a climax in the early 1980s, had ended at least in theory if not in practice. Although guerrilla troops moved throughout the area, clashes between them and the army were limited. The war had reached a stalemate. While the army claimed victory, the guerrillas refused to admit defeat. The battlefield was quiescent, yet political repression continued. Scorched-earth tactics, massacres, and large population displacements had halted, but they were replaced by selective repression, militarization of daily life, and relentless economic insecurity. Army General Alejandro Gramajo's now infamous inversion of Clausewitz—"politics as a continuation of war"—was clearly accurate. The counterinsurgency war had transformed everyday life in the altiplano into a permanent state of repression, fortified by economic arrangements that led to increasing poverty, hunger, and misery (Smith 1990b).

Silence and Secrecy

The dual lessons of silence and secrecy were for me the most enlightening and disturbing. Silence about the present situation when talking with strangers is a survival strategy that Mayas have long utilized. Their overstated politeness toward ladino society and seeming obliviousness to the jeers and insults hurled at them, their servility in the face of overt racism, make it seem as though Mayas have accepted their subservient role in Guatemalan society. Apparent Mayan obsequiousness has served as a shield to provide distance and has also been a powerful shaper of Mayan practice. When Sophia disclosed to a journalist friend of mine from El Salvador her thoughts about guerrilla incursions today, her family castigated her roundly for speaking, warning her that what she said could be twisted and used against her and the family. Alan Feldman (1991:11), writing about Northern Ireland, notes that secrecy is "an assertion of identity and symbolic capital pushed to the margins. Subaltern groups construct their own margins as fragile insulators from the center."

When asked about the present situation, the usual response from almost everyone was "pues, tranquila"(calm, peaceful), but it was a fragile calm. Later, as I got to know people, when something visible broke through the facade of order and forced propaganda speeches—for example, when a soldier was killed and another seriously injured in an ambush in Xe'caj—people would whisper of their fears of a return to la violencia. In fact, the unspoken but implied conclusion to the statement "pues, tranquila" is "ahorita, pero manana saber?" (for now, but who knows about tomorrow?). When I asked the head of a small (self-sufficient) development project that was organizing locally if he was bothered by the army, he said he was not. The army came by every couple of months and searched houses or looked at his records, but he considered this "tranquila."

Silence can operate as a survival strategy, yet silencing is a powerful mechanism of control enforced through fear. While I talked with the women, at times our attention would be distracted momentarily by a military plane or helicopter flying close and low. We would all lift our heads, watching until it passed out of sight yet withholding comment. Sometimes, if we were inside a house we might all step out to the patio to look skyward. Silence. Only once was the silence broken. On that day, doña Tomasa asked rhetorically, after the helicopters had passed overhead, why my government sent bombs to kill people. On another occasion, at Christmas Eve mass in 1989, twenty-five soldiers entered the church suddenly, soon after the service had begun. They occupied three middle pews on the men's side, never taking their hands off their rifles, only to leave abruptly after the sermon. Silence. The silences in these cases do not erase individual memories of terror but create more fear and uncertainty by driving a wedge of paranoia between people. Terror's effects are not only psychological and individual but social and collective as well. Silence imposed through terror has become the idiom of social consensus in the altiplano, as Suarez-Orozco (1990) has noted in the Argentine context.

A number of development projects in Xe'caj work with women and children who have been severely affected by the violence. Most do not address the reality in which people live. These projects provide a modicum of economic aid but without acknowledging the context of fear and terror that pervade Xe'caj. When a Vision Mundial (World Vision) administrator explained the project's multitiered approach to development, he spoke proudly of the group's emphasis on assisting the whole person, materially, emotionally, and spiritually. When I asked him how the project was confronting the emotional trauma of war and repression in which the widows live, he admitted obliquely that it did not. To do so, of course, would put the project workers and the women at jeopardy. Yet not to address the situation perpetuates the official lies. Development aid, by constituting itself as apolitical, serves to legitimate the status quo (Uvin 1998), which in the case of Guatemala has deadly consequences.

On Breaking the Silence

Despite the fear and terror engendered by relentless human rights violations and deeply entrenched impunity, hope existed during this period. With the appointment in 1983 of Archbishop Prospero Penados del Barrio, the Guatemalan Catholic Church had become more outspoken in its advocacy of peace and social justice. The Guatemalan Bishops' Conference, in particular, issued a number of pastoral letters that have become important sources of social criticism in the country; the 1988 "Cry for Land," for example, was an extraordinarily articulate commentary on one of the country's fundamental structures of inequality. In 1990 the Archdiocese of Guatemala opened a human rights office to provide legal assistance to victims of human rights abuses and to report violations to national and international institutions. And more recently, in 1994, the archdiocesan office began the Interdiocesan Recuperation of the Historic Memory Project (REHMI). The goal of the project was to collect individual stories of repression to document as precisely as possible under the present circumstances the extent of the violence that had taken place. The project began collecting testimony in 1995 from thousands of mostly indigenous people in rural communities whose stories would have likely not been heard by the formal Truth Commission created under the tenets of the peace accords. The official report was published in April 1998. Perhaps what is most remarkable about the project is the use of Mayan promoters to gather the testimonies, often in Mayan languages, throughout the regions most affected by the violence. As such, the project had the potential of rebuilding people's ties to one another through "recuperating memory" and breaking the silence, a necessary component of ongoing repression and impunity. In effect, the project laid the groundwork for ongoing political struggles between the state and the victims and survivors over the interpretations of the history of the war. Its findings may effectively serve as a counterpoint to the Amnesty Law and Truth Commission created by the peace accords.

Collective responses to the silence imposed through terror began in 1984 when two dozen people, mostly women, formed the human rights organization called the GAM (Grupo de Apoyo Mutuo). Its members are relatives of some of the estimated 42,000 people who have disappeared in Guatemala over the past three decades. Modeled after the Mothers of Plaza de Mayo in Argentina (Agoson 1987), this small group of courageous women and men decided to break the silence. They went to government offices to demand that the authorities investigate the crimes against their families. As they marched in silence every Friday in front of the national palace with placards bearing the photos of those who had disappeared, they ruptured the official silence, bearing testimony with their own bodies to those who have vanished.

In 1990 Roberto Lemus, a Guatemalan judge in the district court of Santa Cruz del Quiche, began accepting petitions from local people to exhume sites in the villages where people claimed clandestine graves were located. Family members said they knew where their loved ones had been buried after having been killed by security forces. While other judges in the area had previously allowed the exhumations, this was the first time they were performed with the intention of gathering physical evidence for verbal testimonies of survivors in order to corroborate reports against those responsible. (Judge Lemus was eventually forced to seek political exile.) During the same period, the eminent forensic anthropologist Dr. Clyde Snow assembled and trained a Guatemalan Forensic Anthropology Team with assistance from the Argentine Forensic Anthropology Team.[14] There are estimated to be hundreds, perhaps thousands, of clandestine cemeteries throughout the altiplano. These cemeteries and mass graves are the *secreto a voces*: something everyone knows about but does not dare to discuss publicly.

In Xe'caj, people would point out such sites to me. On several occasions, when I was walking with them in the mountains, women took me to the places where they knew their husbands were buried and said, "Mira, el esta alli" (Look, he is over there). Others claimed that there are at least three mass graves in Xe'caj itself. The act of unearthing the bones of family members allows individuals to reconcile themselves to the past openly, to acknowledge at last the culpability for the death of their loved ones, and to lay them to rest. Such unearthing is, at the same time, a most powerful statement against impunity because it reveals the magnitude of the political repression that has taken place. These are not solely the work of individuals with individual consequences; they are public crimes that have deeply penetrated the social body and contest the legitimacy of the body politic.

Thus, as has been the case in Uruguay, Chile, Argentina, Brazil, and El

Salvador (Weschler 1990), the dual issues of impunity and accountability are obstacles in the way of peace and social justice in Guatemala. As such, amnesty becomes both a political and an ethical problem, with not only individual but social dimensions. Ramiro de Leon Carpio, the Guatemalan human rights ombudsman (who later served as Guatemalan president between 1993 and 1995) suggested that to forgive and forget is the only way democracy will be achieved in Guatemala. In a newspaper interview in 1991, he said: "The ideal would be that we uncover the truth, to make it public and to punish those responsible, but I believe that is impossible. . . . We have to be realistic" (*La Hora* 1991).

Certainly, the idea of political expediency has a measure of validity to it. The problem, however, turns on "whether pardon and renunciation are going to be established on a foundation of truth and justice or on lies and continued injustice" (Martin-Baro 1990:7). Hannah Arendt has argued against forgiveness without accountability, because it undermines the formation of democracy by obviating any hope of justice and makes its pursuit pointless (1973). Further, while recognizing that forgiveness is an essential element for freedom, Arendt contends that "the alternative to forgiveness, but by no means its opposite, is punishment, and both have in common that they attempt to put an end to something that without interference could go on endlessly" (Arendt 1958:241). The military's self-imposed amnesty, which has become the vogue throughout Latin America in recent years, forecloses the very possibility of forgiveness. Without a settling of accounts, democratic rule will remain elusive in Guatemala as has been the case elsewhere in Latin America. Social reparation is a necessary requisite to healing the body politic.

Living in a State of Fear

During the first weeks we lived in Xe'caj, Sophia and I drove to several villages in the region talking with women—widows—in small groups, asking them if they might be willing to meet with us weekly over the next year or so. At first many people thought we might be representing a development project and therefore distributing material aid. When this proved not to be the case, some women lost interest, but others agreed to participate. During the second week, we drove out to Ri Bay, a small village that sits in a wide U-shaped valley several thousand meters lower in altitude than Xe'caj and most of the surrounding hamlets. The only access is a one-lane dirt road that cuts across several ridges in a series of switchbacks before beginning the long, slow descent into the valley.

Fortunately for me, there was little traffic on these back roads. Bus service was suspended during the height of the violence in the early 1980s, and by the early 1990s it was virtually nonexistent, although a few buses did provide transport to villagers on market day. The biggest obstacle to driving is the possibility of meeting head on logging trucks carrying rounds of oak and cedar for export. With their heavy loads, it is impossible for them to maneuver, and so I would invariably have to back up- or downhill until I found a turnout wide enough to allow the truck to pass. Yet the most frightening experience was rounding a curve and suddenly encountering a military patrol.

On this day in February 1989 it was foggy and misty, and a cold wind was blowing. Although the air temperature was in the fifties (degrees Fahrenheit), the chill penetrated to the bone. "El expreso de Alaska," Sophia laughed, wrapping her shawl more tightly around her. Heading north, we caught glimpses of the dark ridges of the Sierra de Cuchumatanes brooding in the distance. The scenery was breathtaking. Every conceivable hue of green was present—pine, cedar, ash, oak, bromeliades, and the wide lush leaves of banana trees—and mingled with brilliant purple bougainvillea and ivory calla lilies that lined the roadway. The hills, the softness of the sky, and the outline of trees created an unforgettable image. This was the Guatemala of eternal spring.

On each side of the road, houses were perched on the slopes, surrounded by the milpas, which lay fallow after the harvest in late January, only the dried stalks left half-standing, leaning this way and that. In the altiplano several houses made from a mix of cane or corn stalks, adobe, and wood are usually clustered together. The red tile roofs seen further west have all but disappeared from Xe'caj. Most people now use tin roofs (*lamina*), even though they make houses more oppressively warm in the hot dry season and colder when it is damp and rainy. The department of Chimaltenango was one of the hardest hit by the 1976 earthquake in which nationwide more than 75,000 people died and one million were left homeless. Many people were crushed under the weight of the tiles as roofs caved in on them. Today, half-burned houses stand as testimony to the scorched-earth campaign, while civil patrollers take up their posts nearby with rifles in hand.

Although we frequently saw people on foot, most women and children ran to hide when they saw us coming in the truck. Months passed before women and children walking along the road would accept a ride with me. And even then, many did so reluctantly. Most would ask Sophia in Kaqchikel if it were true that I wanted to steal their children and that gringos ate children.[15]

On this particular day, Sophia and I drove as far as we could and then left my pickup at the top of the hill when the road became impassable. Walking the last four miles down to the village, we met local men repairing large ruts in the road where the heavy September rains had washed away the soil. Soil in this area is sandy and unstable. Most of the trees on the ridge above the road had been clear-cut, and the erosion was quite pronounced. The men were putting in culverts and filling in the deep crevasses that dissected the road; their only tools were shovels and pickaxes. Although the pay was only US$1.50 per day, it was desirable work, one of the few opportunities to earn cash close to home rather than away on the coastal plantations.

As we descended to the lower elevations, Sophia and I mused over the fact that there were only seven widows in Ri Bay, a village of 300 people. In the several other villages where we had visited women, there were thirty to forty widows, or about 15 to 20 percent of the current population. Perhaps there had not been much violence in Ri Bay, I suggested. It was one of the notable features of the military campaign known as scorched earth that neighboring villages fared quite differently. One might be destroyed and another left untouched, depending on the army's perceived understanding of guerrilla support. The military's campaign of terror had happened in two phases. Army strategy began with selective repression against community leaders not only to garner information but also to spread fear. The second phase of the counterinsurgency plan included cutting off rural areas from the city. This began with sweeping operations' that fanned out from the city first westward to the department of Chimaltenango and then south to Quiche and later further north and westward (see Falla 1992). The massacres and brutality seemed to occur according to some deliberate plan, despite the disorder and panic they provoked: while some villages were left unscathed, others were completely razed. For example, according to an eyewitness of the massacre in the village of Los Angelas, Ixcan, on March 23, 1982, the soldiers had a list of pueblos and villages that were to be targeted (Falla 1992). And in numerous testimonies of survivors, the army more often than not launched its so-called reprisals against the guerrillas by brutally killing the population at large.

Sophia and I found Marcelina, Eufemia, and a third younger woman sitting in front of the school where we had agreed to meet. We greeted the women and sat down in the sun that was just breaking through the clouds. The women had brought several bottles of Pepsi for us to share. I asked doña Marcelina, a small thin woman with an intelligent face, why there were so few widows in Ri Bay and held my breath waiting for the hoped-for answer: that the violence there had been much less. She replied that it was because so many people had been killed, not just men but whole families, old people, children, and women. The village was deserted for several years, its inhabitants had fled to the mountains, the pueblo, or the city. Many people never returned, whether because they were dead or merely displaced, no one knew for sure.

This was the third village we had visited, and each time it was the same. The women, without prompting, took turns recounting their stories of horror. Using vivid detail, they would tell of the events surrounding the deaths or disappearances of their husbands, fathers, sons, brothers as if they had happened the previous week or month rather than six or eight years before. And the women—Marcelina, Eufemia, Juana, Martina, Alejandra, Elena—continued to tell me their stories over and over during the time I lived among them. Why? At first as strangers, and then later as friends, why were these women repeatedly recounting their Kafkaesque tales to me? What did they gain by the telling? What was the relationship between silence and testimony? As Suarez-Orozco has noted, "Testimony [is] a ritual of both healing and a condemnation of injustice. . . . The concept of testimony contains both connotations of something subjective and private and something objective, juridical and political" (1992:367). The public areas used to thwart surveillance were transformed into a liminal space that was both private and public during the recounting.

In each of the villages where I met with women, the routine was always the same in the beginning. We would meet in groups of three or four in front of the village health post, the school, or the church, always in a public space. It would be three months or more before anyone invited me into her home or spoke with me privately and individually. Above all else, they did not want the gringa to be seen coming to their houses. Under the scrutiny of surveillance, the women were afraid of what others in the village might say about them and me. And when I did start going to people's homes, rumors did spread. The reports themselves seemed innocuous to me—that I was helping the widows or that I was writing a book about women—yet the repercussions were potentially dangerous.

During one particularly tense period, my visits caused an uproar. One day when I arrived to visit with Juana and Martina, I found them both very anxious and agitated. When I asked what was going on, they said that the military commissioner was looking for me, that people were saying I was helping the widows and talking against others in the community. "There are deep divisions within the community. People don't trust one another," explained Juana. "Families are divided, and not everyone thinks alike," Martina added.

When I said that I would go look for don Martin, the military commissioner, they became very upset. "He said that he would take you to the garrison; please don't go, Linda. We know people who went into the garrison and were never seen again." "But I have done nothing wrong," I said. "I must talk with them, find out what is wrong." I worried that my presence might reflect negatively on the women. So I went. Sophia insisted on accompanying me, dismissing my concerns for her well-being by saying, "Si nos matan es el problema de ellos" (if they kill us, it will be their problem). Fortunately for us, the commissioner wasn't home, so I left a message with his wife.

The next day I decided to go to the destacamento alone. The trek uphill to the garrison was a grueling walk, or so it seemed to me. The last one hundred yards were the most demanding emotionally. Rounding the bend, I saw several soldiers sitting in a small guardhouse, a machine gun perched on a three-foot stanchion pointed downward and directly at me. Franz Kafka's *The Trial* flashed through my mind, with its protagonist Joseph K., accused of a crime against which he had to defend himself but about which he could get no information. "I didn't do anything wrong. I must not look guilty," I repeated this mantra to myself over and over. I had to calm myself. Finally, stomach churning and nerves frayed, I arrived, breathless and terrified. Ultimately, I knew, I could be found guilty merely because I was against the system of violence, terror, and oppression that surrounded me. I asked to speak to the commandante, and he received me outside the gates. This struck me as unusual and increased my agitation, as on every other occasion when I had been to the garrison—to greet each new commandante and to renew my permission papers to continue my work—I had been invited into the compound. The commandante said he knew nothing about why I was being harassed by the military commissioner and the civil patrol in Be'cal, and he assured me that I could continue with my work and that he personally would look into the situation. A few days later, the commandante and several soldiers arrived in the village, called a communitywide meeting, and instructed everyone to cooperate with the gringa who was doing a study.[16]

When the matter had been settled, some of the women explained their concerns to me. They told stories of how widows from outlying villages who had fled to the relative safety of Xe'caj after their husbands had been killed or kidnapped had been forced to bring food and firewood to the soldiers at the garrison and then were raped and humiliated at gunpoint. As one story goes, a brave woman with a baby on her back went to the garrison demanding to see her husband. The soldiers claimed he was not there, but she knew they were lying because his dog was standing outside the gates and the dog never left his side. Either they still had him, or they had already killed him. She demanded to know which and told them to go ahead and kill her and the baby because she had nothing more to lose. Today she is a widow.

The stories continued. In the hour before dawn on a March day in 1981, doña Marcelina recounted, she had arisen early to warm tortillas for her husband's breakfast before he left to work in the milpa. He was going to burn and clean it in preparation for planting soon after the first rains in early May. He had been gone only an hour when neighbors came running to tell her that her husband was lying in the road, shot. When Marcelina reached him, he was already dead. With the help of neighbors, she took the body home to prepare it for burial. Marcelina considers herself lucky because at least she was able to bury him herself, unlike so many women whose husbands were disappeared. The disappeared are among what Robert Hertz (1960) has called the "unquiet dead," referring to those who have died violent or unnatural deaths. Hertz has argued that funeral rituals are a way of strengthening the social bond. The Mayas believe that without proper burial souls linger in the liminal space between earth and the afterlife, condemned in time between death and the final obsequies. And yet these wandering souls may act as intermediaries between nature and the living, buffering as well as enhancing memories through the imagery of their violent history.

Sitting next to Marcelina was her daughter, Elena, also a widow. Elena took Marcelina's nod as a sign to begin. In a quiet voice, she said that she was seventeen when her husband was killed on the patio of her house while her two children, Marcelina, and her sister stood by helpless and in horror. It was August 1981, five months after her father had been killed. Soldiers arrived before dawn, pulled Elena's husband out of bed, and dragged him outside, where they punched and kicked him until he was unconscious and then hacked him to death with machetes.

Just as Eufemia was beginning to recall the night her husband was kidnapped, a man carrying a load of wood stopped on the path about fifty feet away to ask who I was and why I was in the village. Don Pedro was the military commissioner in the community. I introduced myself and showed him my permission papers from the commandante of the local garrison. After looking at my papers, Pedro told me I was free to visit the community but advised me to introduce myself to the head of the civil patrol as well.

Eufemia anxiously resumed her story. Her husband had been disappeared by soldiers one night in early 1982. Several days later she had gone to the municipio to register his death, and the authorities told her that if he was missing he was not considered dead. Some weeks later, she did find his mutilated body, but she did not return to register his death until several years later. She was then told that she now owed a fine of Q100 because of the lateness of her report. Eufemia planned to leave in a few weeks to pick coffee on a piedmont plantation to earn the money. She also wanted to secure legal title to her small parcel of land and the house, which her husband had bought in 1981 but for which he never received official papers. This village had been a finca de mozos. The owner of the coffee plantation also held land in the highlands that he rented to the campesinos in return for the labor during the harvest.

Las Guardiaespaldas (The Bodyguards)

After the disconcerting visit to the commandante at the destacamento, I had walked away somewhat wobbly legged to sit on the bench outside the alcalde's office to wait for a bus to return to one of the other pueblos in Xe'caj. As I sat there reading, occasionally glancing up to watch the children playing at recess, I suddenly noticed Commandante Lopez walking across the square toward me, dressed in his Kaibil uniform; next to him was a slightly taller man also dressed in a special forces uniform but, instead of the maroon beret of the Kaibiles, wearing the black beret of the parachute forces. Closely surrounding the two were their bodyguards, their M-16s at the ready. Neither of the two officers had guns, but each had a long sheathed knife hanging off his belt. They walked slowly and deliberately toward me. I took a deep breath and waited. Commandante Lopez introduced the other to me as an officer from the *Zona Militar* 320 (military base 320) in Chimaltenango who also wanted to meet me. This fellow sat down on the bench next to me and began to speak in English. When I asked where he had learned to speak English so well, he told me he had spent some time in North Carolina and Georgia. After asking very detailed questions about what I was doing in the region and for whom I was working, they left as abruptly as they had arrived.

Later, on the ride home, a very old man who had lost both eyes boarded the bus. Wearing a tattered but clean traje, he was being led by a young boy in patched clothing, his grandson, I presumed. They were obviously poorer than most. As I sat there wondering about their story, in my mind's eye I contrasted the two images: the commandantes with their bodyguards walking toward me in the square, self-assured in their perfectly pressed combat uniforms, their bodies straight and tall, and this old man with his empty sockets, hunched over and smiling, being led tenderly by his grandson. As one pair of bodies echoed stories of privilege and discipline, the other spoke of suffering and dignity. Each in its own way embodied a representation of Guatemala's reality.

a legacy of survival

part two

FIGURE 4.1
Women's garden project. (*Jonathan Moller*)

4. from wives to widows: subsistence and social relations

"What is most difficult for you, being a widow?" I asked several women in Ri Bay, an aldea of Xe'caj.

"Being both mother and father now," replied Marcelina.

"And," Petrona added, "being alone."

"So, do you want to marry again one day?" The women met my question with a burst of laughter.

"Yes, if he were a good man," giggled Rosa. "But," she added, "it's hard to find a good man."

"What makes a good man?" I prodded.

"Ah, a good man is one who walks alongside his woman," Eufemia offered. "A man who works hard, has land, and has respect for himself and his family."

"Some had good husbands, men who worked hard and did not drink. Some widows who had good husbands married again quickly, thinking they would have a good man again. Some of us do not want to marry again, because it is better to be alone than be with a man who drinks and who hits his wife and children," explained Eufemia.

This conversation reveals some of the dilemmas rural widows in Xe'caj face. As they assume the role of sole caretakers of their children in a local economic and cultural system that has long been based on a gendered division of labor, the women must cope alone with the psychological and social effects of the deaths of their husbands and other family members as a result of political violence. The widows say that options for reshaping their lives are limited. Even the most obvious possibility—finding another mate—is unlikely as repression and fear, poverty, alcohol abuse, and domestic violence have taken their toll on family and community life.

What does it mean to be a woman alone in the villages of Xe'caj? When I arrived in Xe'caj, I was especially interested in understanding the survival tactics of women who were heading households alone: their coping mechanisms, how they mobilized labor, and how they fulfilled their dual economic roles after they became de facto heads of households. In particular I wanted to know how widowhood reshaped women's behavior, what Diane Wolf has called "household practices," "the entire bundle of . . . activities, decisions, and interactions" (1992: 263). Over the next two years of fieldwork, I not only learned about the economic plight of widows but also began to understand something about how the multiple dimensions of survival—social, psychological, cultural, and political—operate within a dynamic of both structural and political violence.

In the first part of this chapter I explore how structural violence operated internally within families prior to the political violence. By focusing on the linkages between subsistence and social relations I situate the present circumstances of the widows historically and ethnographically. The connection between kin relations and social and gender relations of power, among subsistence, the household economy, and marriage practices are central to this analysis. The structural violence I am referring to here reflects a particular historical set of economic, political, and cultural arrangements under twentieth-century capitalism in Guatemala that is embedded in social institutions and social relations through a nexus of class-race-gender inequalities. The daily experiences of ordinary people reveal the ways in which their lives are objectified by structural violence. Moreover, these arrangements render invisible the subtle, though intensely destructive, influences of structural violence not because its effects are hidden but because they are taken for granted (Scheper-Hughes 1996). Structural violence also permeates people's subjectivities.

As Mayan communities underwent profound economic transformations throughout much of the twentieth century, the semiautonomous subsistence mediated by traditional forms of community social relations was increasingly undermined by an intensifying agrarian crisis. Concurrently, the position of women in relation to men in households and families was also weakened. These changes are critical to understanding how the misery engendered prior to decades of political violence affects the choices the widows now make in order to survive and the meanings they give to their lives today. These changes are also crucial to understanding how the macro effects of Western capitalist development altered gender, kinship, and household relations locally, adding to women's powerlessness and exploitation.

In the second half of the chapter I explore the dynamic between structural and political violence through an analysis of three projects that came to Xe'caj in the 1980s to assist widows created by the political violence. These projects shaped, to some extent, the daily economic and cultural practices of those widows who chose to participate, as well as the community as a whole. Additionally, through each group's particular construction of the category "widow," they also influenced some women's gendered and political understandings and identities in their communities and beyond.

Marriage, Kinship, and Households

Not marriage, nor kinship, nor the lives of women has been a central focus of the numerous anthropological monographs on the indigenous peoples of Mesoamerica in the last half century. Michael Salovesh attributes this lack of interest in kinship and marriage in part to "accidental history," or the "founders' effect" (1983:181). He notes that the early and influential works of Robert Redfield, Eric Wolf, and George Foster, which emphasized, albeit quite differently, the community as the basic unit of indigenous social organization and anthropological investigation, became the model for most subsequent ethnographic studies. Mesoamerican kinship patterns fit uneasily into the "formal structures and jural forms" (Salovesh 1983:181) that were the hallmark of anthropological theory on tribal peoples at the time. Moreover, as Laurel Bossen (1983) noted, anthropologists did not think that women and their activities were consequential for understanding processes of acculturation among indigenous peoples of Mesoamerica.

These community studies, however, did not totally overlook marriage and kinship as important aspects of social life, and many did make some general observations regarding marriage and kin relations among the Maya.[1] Traditional marriage practices, for example, show considerable variation across the region; the bride-price, postmarital residence, and inheritance are remarkably diverse. The composition of kin groups is not limited solely to consanguinity and affinity but also includes *compadrazgo* (ritual kinship) as a "valid form of kinship in its own right" (Bossen 1983:177). Yet to be fully explored, however, is how marriage and kinship relations functioned as the social fabric that allowed for both a dynamism and an underlying unity in Mayan economic and cultural production practices. Simultaneously, they provided the spaces where the blows of violence—both structural and political—were most keenly felt and reproduced in people's lives.

As in most monographs from the period, women were conspicuously absent from the Mesoamerican anthropological record. When women were mentioned, they were described as being culturally conservative, the bearers of tradition, and their lives were thought to reveal little about processes of modernization (Bossen 1983). Community studies produced ethnographies of men. Yet one of the very real effects of modernization was an assault on subsistence activities that undermined the social and cultural life attached to that form of production, with very palpable effects on women's well-being in their communities and households.

With few exceptions marriage is nearly universal among Mayas of Mesoamerica, even today. Marriage in Mayan communities has usually given women, in particular, social protection, security, and a degree of autonomy. In the rural areas there are usually only a handful of young men and women who do not marry. Doña Juana, for example, at age forty, has never married. She lives with her elderly widowed mother in a separate household that is part of a larger compound belonging to her extended family, including her two brothers, their wives, and their children. Juana participates in two projects for widows in her aldea because she is, as she says, "representing her elderly mother." Juana did not marry when she was young because she never found a good man, and now she feels she is too old. Juana and I would often joke, to the delight of everyone present, that if one or the other of us were to happen on a good man, we would share him, because at the time of my fieldwork I too was an unmarried woman of almost forty. And in the eyes of the women I, unlike Juana, was lacking both a family and the everyday skills so necessary to survive.

Not only is there variation within traditional marriage practices across the Mayan landscape, there is also a mix of different types of conjugal bonds within communities—elopement and cohabitation, civil ceremonies and Catholic and Protestant church weddings—through which young men and women form households and families. Most widows I spoke with agreed, however, that the ideal marriage union is one created through traditional practices that "respect the ways of our ancestors." The ceremony involves a complex series of exchanges and rituals between not only the couple but their extended families and respected community elders as well.

Although several women said they had been married the first time through *pedida* (as the traditional betrothal ritual is called), their subsequent marriages were made through the less formal bonds of cohabitation. A few women said that the first time around they had eloped with their mates, circumventing the elaborate and expensive ritual practices. Yet none of these aldea women reported being married in either a civil or church ceremony, a practice more common in the pueblos of the altiplano. Again, ethnographers from the period neglected to interpret this variation, attributing it simply as a result of acculturation, without taking into account the relationship between economic and cultural production practices.[2]

The marriage stories of Marcelina and Eufemia, widows now in their late forties, not only illustrate their very different individual experiences but also highlight how crucial marital relationships and kinship networks have been to the delicate balance between economic and cultural survival. In addition, the two marriages reveal how in small, seemingly homogeneous communities, even some thirty years ago, social relations of power, of gender, and of cultural production were shifting under the pressures of local economic insecurity perpetuated by larger structures of exploitation.

Marcelina's Story

I recount Marcelina's betrothal in some detail to show not only how the ideal marriage union arranged in the 1950s established proper gendered behavior between men and women but also how power operated locally. These bonds importantly created and reinforced larger kin networks based on beliefs and norms of age-prestige-reciprocity that encompassed both the living and the dead. The material basis of this system rested on filial claims to household land and labor. Marriage functioned at the household and family level in ways similar to how the cofradia system did at the community level. It ordered the distribution of power and land based on age and gender.[3]

FIGURE 4.2
Mayan wedding. (*Jonathan Moller*)

Marcelina was about fourteen years old when she first seriously took note of Pedro. Each afternoon, Marcelina, her sisters, and their cousins would go to the small river nearby to fetch the water needed for preparing the evening meal. Marcelina remembered that in May of that year she noticed that Pedro and several of his friends would frequently be waiting along the path as the girls returned. When Pedro tried to speak with her, Marcelina would run off, as young women were not supposed to speak publicly with men outside their family (see Burgos-Debray 1984). Marcelina said that even though she never answered Pedro's queries directly, neither did she rebuff him. This scenario repeated itself over the course of several months as Marcelina gradually lost her shyness and began to speak with Pedro, albeit briefly.

Taking that as a sign of encouragement, according to Marcelina, Pedro told his family of his interest in her. After some discussion within the family regarding Pedro's choice, his grandmother, a respected elderly woman in the aldea, went to Marcelina's house to make the first formal, public petition on Pedro's behalf. This first step initiated a long process of pedida, which would require the involvement of both extended families, neighbors, community elders, and trusted friends, as well as multiple exchanges of gifts. After several days of knocking on the entryway to Marcelina's house without success, Pedro's grandmother's persistence paid off. Marcelina's mother at last opened the door and received her into the house, where the grandmother expressed Pedro's wish to become engaged to Marcelina. Even though Marcelina had told her parents at the outset of her interest in Pedro, the ritual of initial refusal was a test of Pedro's sincerity, according to Marcelina. Some three months after this initial visit, Pedro's mother and grandmother visited Marcelina's parents, this time bringing with them bread and chocolate for the family and *guaro* (locally made alcohol) for the adults to drink as Pedro's kin made the formal petition for marriage betrothal.

Subsequent visits over the next year, which included Pedro and his father, had what June Nash described among the Mayas of Chiapas as "cyclical and progressive tendencies," referring to the increasing length of the visits, the greater number of people, the growing size of the gifts involved (1970:126). Traditional gifts vary from place to place according to the local sequence of pedida as well as the wealth of the young men and their families.[4] Although money changes hands in these transactions, gifts of food and drink are valued, according to the women, for they are what cements the bonds between family members. Since all were agreeable to the union in this case, Marcelina and Pedro became officially engaged. Yet anytime during the pedida ritual, Marcelina retained the right to refuse Pedro's petition. Likewise, if Marcelina's or Pedro's family objected to the marriage, they too had the right to dissuade the young couple from taking the final step.

In her monograph on Chichicastenango, Ruth Bunzel (1952) noted that parents of both young men and young women tried to guide their children in selection of mates who would prove to be good workers, increasing the likelihood of both success and love in marriage. For a young woman's family, this meant finding a respectable and reliable man who had some land, a trade, and no debts and who neither drank nor had relations with other women.

Another year passed before the official marriage ceremony took place uniting Marcelina and Pedro. At the time of the ceremony, a Mayan priest (*ajk'ik*) and the couple were surrounded by family and community elders, the parents of the young couple, witnesses, younger family members, and friends who joined together to pray to the Mayan gods, spirits, and antepasados that the marriage would serve as a good example to others. Marcelina described this ceremony as one that creates a concentric circle of respect extending from the ancestors to the youngest members of the family, linking the past and the future.

The ceremonial series of pedida exchanges and the marriage are quite expensive, sometimes prohibitively so for land- and cash-poor households. Thus elopement has provided another way for young couples to form conjugal bonds (Paul and Paul 1963). A couple may even start the pedida process and then decide to run off before its completion and take up residence with the young man's family, if they agree to the union. Usually, after initial resistance, the young woman's family will acknowledge the match.

At the time of the marriage ceremony or, in the case of elopement, when the girl's family recognizes the marriage, the parents of the couple decide if they will become *compadres*, establishing ritual kin bonds between them. Although most scholarly work on compadrazgo has focused on the ritual bonds established through Catholic baptism, marriage unions among the Maya have also been a time when compadre bonds may be agreed on between families (Nash 1970). Sidney Mintz and Eric Wolf (1950:355) noted in their study of compadrazgo that these horizontal bonds in peasant communities "make the immediate social environment more stable, the participants more interdependent and more secure," for they provide what George Foster (1961:264) describes as a "social insurance" between families when sickness, poor harvests, and all manner of emergencies can undermine a family's ability to survive. Labor exchanges and ritual participation based on ideas of reciprocity—the entitlements of compadrazgo—strengthen social bonds beyond the households and may serve in some cases to mitigate disruptive behavior within communities, such as drunken fights and brawls (Zingg 1938).[5]

A few days after the ceremony, Marcelina went to live with Pedro's family. Patrilocal marriage residence is the norm among the Maya of Guatemala, although virilocality may be an alternative.[6] Thus initially the young couple becomes part of the husband's household. Later, the husband receives land from his father, and the couple establishes its own nuclear residence, usually nearby. Marcelina and Pedro lived with his family for almost five years before Pedro's father gave him ten cuerdas to farm and a small parcel of land on which Pedro built his own house.

While living in his father's household, Pedro and his unmarried brothers worked the fields jointly with their father. Pedro and two of his brothers would also go to the coast together to pick coffee and cotton to earn cash, which they would turn over to their father for distribution. As was his prerogative, Pedro's father allocated all male labor and assets. In this system, Pedro was dependent on his father to gain his own eventual economic independence. Land is not only the material basis of survival but also the material symbol of continuity between generations. Although a young man may acquire land through a variety of other means—renting communal or private land or, if he has capital, buying his own—access to ancestral lands has usually only been meted out to sons when filial responsibilities are fulfilled (Gross and Kendall 1983). For Pedro's father, a sufficient and diversified labor force provided by a large family allowed him to take on important cofradia commitments, thereby increasing his own power and prestige in community affairs.

Meanwhile, Marcelina's fate was tied both to Pedro and, in the early years, to that of her mother-in-law. Like most new wives, Marcelina worked under the watchful eye of her *suegra* (mother-in-law), who was responsible for female labor and the doling out of resources within the household. A young daughter-in-law is quite vulnerable as she enters into a household where she has few legitimate claims, and this in itself can often be a source of tension and conflict for a young couple. Yet women are not expected to suffer, and if a young wife is being poorly treated by the husband or his family, she is free to return to her natal household without stigma. This is more likely to happen before there are children, however, as the children's inheritance usually comes through their father. Although a woman may inherit land from her own family, this is based on her ability to fulfill filial obligations to her parents, which is rendered difficult by her patrilocal residence as well as by the diminishing landholdings available to most families.

Marital instability is not uncommon. A third of the women I worked with in Xe'caj, for example, reported having more than one conjugal bond. If a marriage does survive, the cycle will complete itself when the couple in later years assumes authority over their own extended family (Bossen 1984).

Eufemia's Story

In sharp contrast to Marcelina, Eufemia's story poignantly underscores the crucial role that kinship and marriage play in shaping the extent to which women can lose control over their lives because of particular marriage arrangements. Eufemia, unlike Marcelina, was quite reticent about describing in detail the painful circumstances surrounding her own marriage.

Eufemia was thirteen when her father "gave" (actually, sold) her to an itinerant trader who frequently passed through their village. Eufemia's own mother was dead, and her stepmother readily agreed to the transaction.

Eufemia said her family was very poor, her father had little land, and as a child she had spent considerable time working on the coffee fincas. She had no idea how much money her father received in exchange for her nor why he forced her to marry Marcos, the man who was her husband for twenty-five years. When Eufemia's father sent her away, he told her that she would not be welcomed back into his household.

According to Eufemia, there were problems from the start. Marcos was much older than she, and he frightened her as he was often drunk and abusive. They had moved to a hamlet of Xe'caj some distance from Eufemia's natal village and set up an independent household. Marcos was often gone for long periods of time peddling his wares, leaving Eufemia to fend for herself, often without food or money. Much of the time, Marcos was a poor provider. Although he planted a milpa, he refused to buy fertilizer, and his harvests yielded little.

In the early years of their marriage, both Eufemia and Marcos migrated to the coast to pick coffee for several months each year, but he always kept whatever money she earned. After the death of her first child from diarrhea while Eufemia was working on a coffee finca, she stopped going altogether. Some ten years passed before she migrated again to the coast out of desperation and hunger.

Over the years, Eufemia had eight more children, although four of them died young, from diarrhea, cough, and *susto* (fright). Often strapped for food and cash, Eufemia would make *atole* (a corn-based drink) or raise a pig to sell in the local market. Without the help of her neighbors and at times her sisters, Eufemia says she does not know how she would have survived.

While Eufemia's sad story is an extreme case, according to the women it was by no means a singular tragedy. On a personal level, without any significant kin network Eufemia was left without even a modicum of social protection. Feeling she had little recourse because of her children, Eufemia endured the situation as best she could. Now as a widow, life is hard, yet Eufemia readily admits that it has improved for her. What little money she earns, she is able to control herself, and she no longer is the object of abusive behavior. "Without a good man," she says, "it is better to be alone."

Marcelina's story gives us some insight into how marriage ties and kinship are integral to forming the ideological, structural, and social bases for collective family survival—and for power relations within the community—while providing a modicum of personal, social, and economic options for women.

Eufemia's account brings into sharp focus how changes in marriage practices and kin responsibilities leave families less cohesive and women, in particular, more vulnerable. Although Marcelina's narrative demonstrates the epitome of Mayan marriage practices where corporate yet hierarchical relationships based on age and gender are strengthened, other women I spoke with, such as Eufemia, indicated that not all their experiences can be reduced to this cultural model.

While many of these women have experienced degrees of protection, choice, and power within the confines of their families and households, as Laurel Bossen (1984) aptly demonstrated in her four-community study of women and economic change in Guatemala, gendered relations are not solely the result of "cultural traditions and family roles" (42) but also embedded within a social and historical reality and structures of power. As land became increasingly privatized and commodified beginning in the late nineteenth century, a process that intensified after 1944, community and household social relations were critically reshaped.

For rural Mayan campesinos, sufficient communal and familial landholdings were key factors in maintaining their integrated cultural and economic system of subsistence both at the community and household level. The breakdown of this system through the steady intensification of commodified social relations also had important gendered ramifications. As traditional marriage practices based on noncommodified local relations became increasingly obsolete, so too did the linkages among and between families created by the ritual kin bonds of compadrazgo. As a result women were left more socially and economically vulnerable.

Subsistence and the Market

By the 1950s an agrarian crisis was intensifying in Mayan communities as a result of both population growth and a highly skewed pattern of land distribution and concentration, leaving most poor Mayas working plots too small to supply their subsistence needs.[7] As a consequence, rural campesinos needed cash to maintain subsistence whereas formerly it had only been used to augment rural livelihood. In the altiplano, an Indian market economy had thrived since pre-Conquest times, with people from across the highlands buying and selling their wares in a vast regional market system. Noncommodified productive relations (both land and labor) had been at the center of local economic practices for the rural poor. Marcelina, when asked, summed up the changes that had taken place in the following way: "Before no one went hungry. If someone did not have tortillas, neighbors would come to help."

Notwithstanding, subsistence had been for the past century only partially autonomous, and money garnered from surplus domestic production or wage labor bought, among other things, essential items such as salt, chiles, coffee, hoes, and machetes. By the 1950s, however, the entire regional economy had become "highly market dependent" (Smith 1990a:210), as cash was now essential to subsidize subsistence production. The commercialized artisans and traders—the weavers, potters, and leatherworkers of Totonicapan along with the commodity food producers of Solala and Chimaltenango—and the part-time campesinos from all over the altiplano, who make up the bulk of the migratory labor force on the coastal fincas, were locked into an interdependent relationship. Each group depended on the others to generate what it was no longer able to produce for itself domestically (Smith 1990a).

While increasing commodification of the rural Mayan economy did lead to new financial opportunities for some, it also contributed to an escalation of economic differentiation among individuals within communities and upset the delicate balance of local power that had mediated between non-commodified and commodified forms of production. These transformations, in which subsistence was subordinated to the market, had a devastating impact on both community and household social relations. Community social bonds were substantially weakened. Traditional social institutions, such as the cofradia and the pedida, became moribund. The material bases to support these practices were no longer viable. Land inheritance and the age-gender-prestige authority on which they rested were breaking down under the impact of commodity production. Yet these institutions, whatever their shortcomings, had also importantly served as the interstitial tissue of the communities, creating in part the social networks and power relations that kept the potential for internal violence between community members and between men and women partially in check. In addition, the once near-total community and household power of the elders and the hegemony of the ancestors, exercised through land inheritance, was severely undermined (Brintnall 1979). The integral relationship between the growing of corn and a Mayan worldview that premised survival on collective enterprise dissolved, producing widespread social and cultural suffering and conflict among the Maya. The material and symbolic bases for cultural and historical continuity were effectively destroyed.

As feminist scholarship from the 1960s and 1970s in Guatemala has revealed (Bossen 1983, 1984; Chinchilla 1977; Ehlers 1990), the declining importance of subsistence production to rural livelihood was particularly deleterious to social relations between men and women in the household. While the content of the gendered division of labor between Mayan women and men did not ostensibly change, the value attached to that labor changed significantly during the twentieth century.

Marriage and the Market

In rural Mayan households, subsistence activities have long been organized around a complementary division of labor between men and women. Men are responsible for basic work in the milpa, providing the family at minimum with the essential staples of corn and beans. Women's work is carried out in or near the home, where they are primarily concerned with food preparation—in particular, the conversion of corn to tortillas—weaving clothes for the family, and caring for the children.

As long as subsistence activities predominated, the complementarity of gendered practices created a mutual dependency between men and women. Since the work of both was crucial to the enterprise of economic and cultural survival, the relationship between men and women was characterized by a degree of respect and cooperation. As in most peasant agricultural societies, a Mayan campesino would have had difficulty farming his land productively without a woman's contribution (Bossen 1984). As necessary partners, women have had a degree of leverage within the household economy. If a man failed to share at least partially the rewards or decisions of subsistence with his wife, he risked undermining his own productive potential if she resisted fulfilling her obligations to the household or decided to leave him. Moreover, a Mayan man without a wife was limited in his social mobility within the community, as an unmarried man was not allowed to assume the more powerful positions in the cofradia.

In addition to their subsistence activities, men and women alike had found a myriad of ways to earn cash. Wage labor, like subsistence labor, was also gendered. Men most often garnered cash from work on fincas or through commercial trade. While women too went to the fincas, they did so less frequently. Their cash was most often procured through producing household crafts or raising small animals for sale in the local market. The cash earned by both was reinvested in the household, used to procure durable goods—machetes, hoes, and grinding stones—to purchase or rent land, or to acquire small animals to raise.

While these gendered domestic labor divisions are readily observable even today in the rural aldeas of Xe'caj, giving one a sense of continuity and timelessness, the balance between subsistence and wage labor has shifted, leading to women's increasing dependence on men as wage earners. As cash has become integral to the viability of the household economy—essential for shoring up the entire bundle of economic tactics—the opportunities to earn income available to men and women differ vastly. This has created what Laurel Bossen (1984) has called a "redivision of labor" that has negatively affected rural women's well-being.

The economist Esther Boserup (1970) was one of the first scholars to document how modernization and Western economic development strategies had contradictory effects for men and women in the third world. The rural highlands of Guatemala are no exception. As the modern market economy and new technologies increasingly came to dominate the economy locally, the importance of the subsistence sphere was substantially weakened (Bossen 1984). As noted, household economic partnerships between men and women were similarly destabilized as a result, producing what Tracy Ehlers (1996:14) has described as the "individualization of income and concentration of other opportunities in men's hands," with the effect of devaluing and marginalizing women's contributions. Although customary opportunities were still open to women to earn cash, the income was sufficient only to supplement not to subsidize subsistence. To earn cash, women, like men, could migrate to coastal fincas, where their earnings were comparable to men's (Bossen 1984), but women's responsibilities to their children placed restrictions on this practice, as Eufemia's situation poignantly illustrated. Likewise, petty commodity production continued to be a source of cash for women, yet the scale of their activities and its compensation were minimal.

The introduction of new technologies further eroded women's productive worth. By the 1970s most Mayan men in the altiplano had begun to wear Western clothes rather than the traditional traje. Yet in most cases the loss of this productive activity of weaving clothing for household members was not replaced by new opportunities to earn cash independently (Bossen 1984). Although women could weave for the increasing number of tourists passing through the altiplano, these opportunities were limited and only open to women who had access to tourist routes (Maynard 1963). Increasingly, cash was also needed to buy other goods previously manufactured at home, such as soap, candles, and thread.[8]

New opportunities created by mainstream development projects in rural Guatemala were consistently geared toward men. Men's participation in literacy programs, rural cooperatives, agricultural schemes, health projects, and political parties all served to intensify their economic independence from women and widened the discrepancy between men's and women's contribution to the household economy.

As men became more fully integrated into a market economy, women's increasing economic dependency on men resulted in increasing social vulnerability. Although men still require women's domestic service, its contribution to household survival has been devalued and marginalized as cash has taken on increasing importance in the domestic economy. Many of the widows of Xe'caj spoke openly and critically about their husbands' irresponsible behavior toward their families, particularly drinking and abusive practices. Yet the women say they had little choice but to accept the situation. Women's communal social safety nets tore with the destruction of subsistence relations, and with few economic alternatives because of the dominance of wage labor, they were left with little choice but to accept male irresponsibility (Ehlers 1996).

Women's Roles

In the ethnographic literature Mayan women have been portrayed for the most part as passive, submissive, and conservative (see Tax 1952). And their public behavior seems to bear out this analysis. Women have little to say publicly when men are present, and they often appear shy, timid, or embarrassed when talking with strangers. Women, especially older ones, will often avert their eyes in public, covering their mouths with their shawls. It is not unusual to see a woman walking along village roads a few paces behind her husband. Moreover, all women continue to wear traje, the traditional clothing, while only a few old men in Xe'caj continue to do so. Most older rural women speak no Spanish, only Kaqchikel, and few have had any formal education. Women do seem to act submissive to men in the household, where, for example, men receive their food first at mealtimes.

Yet these observations belie the active role that Mayan women have played economically and culturally in their families and communities for centuries.

Many make economic decisions in their households, manage their own labor and their small incomes, and make decisions about household consumption. Of the forty widows I interviewed, the majority said that at least some time in their marriages they and their husbands made all household decisions jointly. Moreover, women have well-honed market skills as traders and customers. In their homes or in private groups, women's lively talk and opinions are noteworthy, and their sense of self is demonstrated in their humor, their aesthetic sensibilities, and their bodily presences. Their once-important public roles either in the community alongside their husbands in the cofradia or as active agents in their own right as Mayan priests, healers, midwives, and mediators in traditional marriage practices reveal their social independence and worth as members of their households, families, and communities.

These apparent contradictions in women's behavior and roles—being submissive to men in one domain yet self-sufficient in others—point to the increasingly unstable economic and social position of Mayan women in their families and community. Perhaps their behavior reflects not so much traditional roles as key tensions in their lives: the loss of social protection and support from their families and communities in marital relations, the lack of power within and beyond their households, the difficulties of poverty, and the dearth of real economic and social opportunities for them as poor Mayan women.[9]

These contradictions were not lost on popular groups working locally in the period immediately preceding the repression. Some communities in Xe'caj were aware of the increasing effects of structural violence on women's lives—the devaluation of women's labor and of women themselves—and the need for local mechanisms to attend to these problems. For example, in the early 1980s, a group of Kaqchikel lay missionaries working with PROMICA set up women's committees at the behest of community leaders. These committees not only taught aldea women literacy and nutritional skills but also intentionally reasserted a public role and public voice for women in their communities, providing a forum for women to analyze their status and roles within their household and communities. Moreover, because PROMICA worked throughout the department of Chimaltenango, it was able to begin linking women into a regional network. As I noted earlier, however, this program, along with other community-based organizations, came to an abrupt halt during the period of intense political repression.

From Wives to Widows

Given the increasingly precarious social and economic standing of many rural women in Xe'caj prior to the political violence, the transformation from wives to widows was particularly devastating, creating enormous suffering in their lives and leaving them bereft of economic, social, and emotional support. The violence and repression uprooted people from their communities as they were forced to flee the onslaught of the army's scorched-earth campaign, abandoning their homes, their crops, and their possessions. Many of the women and their children, after witnessing the brutal deaths or disappearances of their husbands and other family members, were displaced; they fled to the mountains or to nearby towns to hide or sought the anonymity of Guatemala City. The residents of Xe'caj lived far from the borders of Mexico, effectively cut off from that escape route, unlike many people in the western and northern highlands, who crossed into the relative safety of Mexico.[10]

Doña Marcelina and her children, for example, lived in the mountains near her village for two years before seeking refuge in a pueblo of Xe'caj, where she survived working as a domestic servant for another year before returning to her aldea. Doña Eufemia was instructed by soldiers to move with her children to another town in Xe'caj, where there was a military garrison. Eufemia, like Marcelina, worked as a domestic, washing clothes and making tortillas, earning about US$6 per month, before returning to her aldea some three years later. Some widows settled in the towns where they initially sought refuge, crowding into small rented rooms. Many of these women chose not to return to their natal villages at all, fearing reprisals there even when it was relatively safe to go home.

Women Alone

Of the women who did return to their rural communities, many found their houses looted or partially destroyed. They had lost most of their possessions, including their animals, their crops, and their few domestic tools. Relief agencies assisted the returning families by providing them with such necessary items as blankets, cookpots, hoes, and sheets of aluminum for roofs. Other development agencies, such as UNICEF and CARE International, as well as European NGOs, provided small loans or materials for rebuilding homes.

Local groups, such as KATOKI, a Chimaltenango-based cooperative, canceled loans that husbands had incurred prior to the violence.

Yet as women tried to reestablish their lives economically they found themselves betwixt and between. Although most widows in the rural area of Xe'caj did continue to live in some configuration of a kin-based group, in many cases only a few men remained in their entire extended families. Thus the women lacked both the labor of a milpa producer and a wage earner. Most women had land, yet few had more than three to four cuerdas, far less than is adequate to support a family. Moreover, most of the women and their preadolescent children were unable to work the land themselves. In the highlands, men use only a hoe to turn over the often rocky, hard soil before planting the milpa, arduous work at best. It takes two men a full day to prepare a cuerda for planting. Without access to male labor, the widows had to hire local men as day laborers at a cost of US$1 per day per person, plus lunch.[11] Although it seemed little to pay, the women had few resources for procuring cash.

The majority of the women with whom I worked were in their thirties and forties at the time of my fieldwork, and they had on average of three children. Few had received any formal education, and no one had attended school beyond the third grade. With few marketable skills and even fewer opportunities to piece together a livelihood, they had to rely in part on the assistance offered by development projects. Far from becoming accustomed to handouts—an attitude attributed to them by some development workers—the women worked in projects because they were desperate for cash to cultivate their milpas and also to buy necessary household items such as coffee, salt, chiles, and tomatoes. Most of the women expressed ambivalence about participating in the projects, yet they felt that they had little choice but to do so.

Socially and politically, the situation for widows was quite precarious. The divisions that existed in communities prior to the political violence were only exacerbated by the repression. The stories of doña Tomasa and doña Alejandra, which I recounted in chapter 2, poignantly reveal how the intricacies of political violence and repression operate locally. In some cases, widows knew who had denounced their husbands to the military as guerrilla sympathizers or to the insurgents as spies. Some of these informers continue to live nearby as neighbors, while others were military commissioners or leaders in the civil patrols. Not surprisingly, these events have created multiple social and political divisions within communities, between widows and the rest of the population, between family members with different sympathies, and among the widows themselves. These antagonisms, whose history was often unknown to anthropologists and development workers alike, contributed to persistent tensions in communities and frequently undermined the objectives of relief projects. The fact that much of the material aid coming into villages after the violence was directed exclusively to widows was a constant source of friction among many villagers. In fact, in several villages in Xe'caj, aid workers were periodically denied entry. Moreover, as the stories of Marcelina and Eufemia reveal, not all women's lives before the violence were identical, and therefore the resources, both economic and social, that they were able to bring to bear on their present circumstances as widows also differed. This furthered the difficulties and jealousies among the women.

Aid for Widows

During the course of my fieldwork, a number of projects assisted widows in the villages and pueblos of Xe'caj. In this section, I examine three of those groups: a small locally based NGO run by an order of Catholic nuns; PAVYH, a state-financed project to aid those widowed by the political violence; and CONAVIGUA, a national, mostly indigenous group of rural women widowed by the violence. I focus on these projects—one outside NGO, one state-sponsored, one Mayan—to explicate the multifaceted ways in which widows were constituted as widows by each project and thus the effects of that aid, both positive and negative. Additionally, the projects, in most cases unintentionally, created spaces where women without intact kin-based households could refashion a network of support in their quest to survive.

La Ayuda

The NGO project under the auspices of the Catholic sisters that I refer to as La Ayuda began working with widows in Xe'caj in 1986. In addition to a large weaving project, which I discuss in some detail in chapter 6, the sisters also supported small-scale income-generating projects for widows in several aldeas. These included raising small animals and making soap and candles and woven baskets for sale in the local market. Although the projects were ostensibly designed to provide material assistance for widows produced by the violence, women who were heading households alone, whether because they were abandoned or because their husbands had died of natural causes, were also included.

In the aldea of Be'cal, twenty-five women on average worked together raising egg-laying hens and making black soap. For a year I observed the widows as they worked diligently caring for the hens, whose eggs they sold weekly to a local orphanage, and making black soap to sell in a nearby weekly market. Because the widows had a steady buyer for their eggs, the hen project was by far the more lucrative. Over the course of the year they saved Q1000 (US$350 at 1989 exchange rates) jointly in addition to meeting the expenses of caring for the hens, buying special feed and vaccinations as well as replacing hens who died. Working in groups of five, the women took turns caring for the hens, rotating the chores weekly. Usually each woman invested two to three hours per week in the project. Unfortunately, misfortune befell the widows during the first year I observed them. One of the project coordinators responsible for depositing the money from the egg sales into a bank account for the widows quit his employment with the sisters and absconded with the money.

Soap making was more labor intensive and less profitable. It required constant vigilance on the part of one or two women throughout the twenty-four-hour period of preparation, as well as collecting and hauling sufficient firewood for the cooking process and procuring cow fat, a prime ingredient. The women made soap twice a month and tried to sell it at the large weekly market in one of the pueblos of Xe'caj. Sales, however, were often sluggish as there was much competition from women in other communities throughout the area. The women invariably returned home with soap unsold. In this effort, the women rarely turned a profit, mostly just meeting their expenditures.

Despite its good intentions, the project never really succeeded in providing adequate material assistance for widows, nor was it able to spur the entrepreneurship it was supposed to inspire. The project focused on economic activities specific to women, assuming that collectively the widows would generate enough income to sustain themselves. Yet the project's plans, like most mainstream microenterprise development projects, were grounded in an unrealistic assumption that economic advancement is based solely on hard work, a little capital, and education, ignoring the very real structural limits that configure people's lives. In fact, the women earned very little cash, although they invested significant time and resources in the project. Even though the women had a regular customer for their eggs, that project required a regular and rather substantial investment of time to maintain the hens. Moreover, only as long as the project lasted was there a market for the products. The positive impacts only reached a small proportion of the population, which increased resentment among villagers. Additionally, the project concentrated on activities that have long been a part of women's domestic production. While these activities provided women with a source of cash to contribute to the household economy, the project planners overlooked the fact that these tasks were importantly tied to men's income production. Without its complement, the income generated from women's labor was wholly inadequate. And with its focus solely on economic need, it did nothing to address the profound psychosocial problems of the widows and other community members.

One of the more important consequences of the Ayuda project, however, was that it fostered collective work and social sharing on the part of the women, a feature previously limited to the extended family for some women. For others who participated, La Ayuda provided a public space in which they could reconnect with other women in a relatively safe arena, even while under the surveillance of the state security apparatus, particularly the locally based military commissioner and civil patrol. What this did for some women was to encourage them to interact with nonkin women; some thus formed friendships with neighbors that helped to sustain them economically, emotionally, and socially. Marcelina did not really know Eufemia very well even though they lived in the same aldea. Both of them eventually dropped out of the project, yet they continued to work together, often sharing ideas and resources in their struggles to subsist. This was particularly important for Eufemia, whose social network, even before the violence, was limited.

La Ayuda intermittently gave the widows in the project food, such as oil and powdered milk, and secondhand clothes for their children, which set the widows apart and created discord between them and others in the community who were not beneficiaries of the project. Because La Ayuda treated widows as if they were a coherent group, it overlooked both the economic and political context of their lives and what set them apart in their villages and among themselves, both the resources available to particular women and the internal divisions that existed depending on who killed their husbands and why. In the end this limited significantly the positive effects of the project, and in some cases further contributed to divisions among the widows themselves.

PAVYH

[In the highlands after the massacres] we watched the widows: how many were there, how they obtained their food, who gave them food, and where the orphans were located and who took care of them [in order to determine who and where the subversives were].
—Defense Minister Gramajo (quoted in Schirmer 1993:46).

PAVYH, a program of assistance for widowed and orphaned victims of the violence, was a special project mandated by the Guatemalan Congress in 1987 and administered through the Ministry of Special Affairs. Its stated intent, according to then-president Vinicio Cerezo, was to repay a social debt to the widows and orphans of the political violence. A pilot program was started in 1988, and by 1989 the first phase of the project had been completed in all fourteen departments to be covered under the program.[12] The program consisted of three phases. First, a census took place in Xe'caj in 1988, asking for information about each widow: name, residence, age, literacy level, circumstances of the husband's death or disappearance, the kind of work she did, whether she owned her own house, the type of dwelling, whether she was in debt, her husband's name, and the age and names of her children. The widows were also asked to supply evidence to substantiate their claims.

In an interview I conducted with officials at the project headquarters in Guatemala City, I was shown computer printouts reflecting the data gathered from the census, which had been entered into the state computer system, a fact unknown to the widows in Xe'caj. The implications of this were chilling in a country where the state had just participated in massive killing of civilians, many of whom were the very husbands and family members of these widows. Moreover, as the epigraph above indicates, the Guatemalan state had contradictory understandings of widows, viewing them as both victims of the war entitled to relief aid and as enemies of the state suspected of guerrilla sympathies.

The second phase of the PAVYH project consisted of six food distributions. Every fifteen days for three months, ten pounds of corn, a can of powdered milk, and one liter of oil per family were disbursed. As one PAVYH administrator explained, the idea behind the second phase was to encourage the women to participate. Yet to be eligible for the food a widow had to answer the census questions. Many women I spoke with in Xe'caj refused to participate in the census, but many others did so out of desperation. There seemed to be some confusion among the widows as to how long the food distribution would continue. Several women I spoke with had initially thought they would be receiving food every two weeks for an indefinite period of time.

The third phase was the initiation of income-generating projects in each village. The widows from each village had to submit proposals as a group to receive a one-time distribution of aluminum sheets for their roofs, or they could choose a diesel corn mill to operate collectively, a treadle sewing machine (one per village), or initial capital to run a small store. By 1990 women from several aldeas of Xe'caj had petitioned PAVYH for assistance, but nine months later, they had not received replies to their requests.

Intermittently, the women sent a messenger to the provincial office to make inquiries regarding the status of their proposals. For some of the women, it was the first time they had had direct contact with state administrators. On one such trip, I accompanied several of the widows who in halting Spanish tried to describe their desperate situations and their need for assistance. Rebuffed and ill treated by the two officials with whom they spoke, the women returned home dismayed. When discussing the incident at length with other women in the group they concluded that this was the treatment that they as Mayan women should have expected from ladino men and from a state that both consigns them to the margins and had killed their husbands. Later, when speaking to other aldea widows who had also submitted proposals to no avail, they decided that the attitude of the project officials was pervasive, and they abandoned any hope of getting aid from that quarter.

The experience, however, did provide a venue of analysis for the widows, as for many this was the first time they had directly experienced state-level racism and sexism. And now many widows had groups within which to reflect on those very experiences from their positions as poor Mayan widows. Until then, many of the women had been buffered from these encounters by their husbands, who had interacted with state officialdom.

CONAVIGUA

CONAVIGUA (National Coordination of Guatemalan Widows) is a national widows' group founded in 1988 by Mayan widows throughout the rural highlands to make demands on the state for human, women's, and citizen's rights. CONAVIGUA brought public attention to the dire situation of widows and demanded state compensation to those whose husbands were killed during

FIGURE 4.3
National coordinator of Guatemalan widows participating in a protest march in Guatemala City in 1989. (*Tom Mattie*)

the counterinsurgency war. They called for an end to forced recruitment of their sons into the military, and, working in conjunction with the Argentine and Guatemalan Forensic Anthropology Teams, began literally to unearth the long-denied number of clandestine cemeteries scattered throughout the highlands.

Locally, CONAVIGUA began organizing village widows not only around their immediate needs but also around their positions as indigenous women within the nation-state and their communities. Through critical discussions regarding the horrors of rape, torture, disappearances, and death, as well as on the domestic violence that many of the women had experienced firsthand, the widows began to make connections between their individual economic and political situations. Membership in this larger imagined community of indigenous women lessened their senses of isolation and alienation. Moreover, women in CONAVIGUA began to make connections between human rights and women's rights, initiating a political consciousness among the women themselves as wives and widows and also influencing their daughters (Schirmer 1993).

The activities of CONAVIGUA did not go unnoticed by the local power structure or the military. A story repeatedly told by some widows in Be'cal on my return in December 1992 is emblematic of the surveillance and suspicion surrounding CONAVIGUA and the widows in Xe'caj.

In the fall of 1992, CONAVIGUA had organized a public demonstration in Guatemala City to demand that the army stop the forced recruitment of widows' sons into the military. Seven busloads of men, women, and children went from Be'cal to Guatemala City to attend the protest. Several days after the demonstration, a platoon of soldiers arrived in Be'cal from the local garrison, warning people, and the widows in particular, that if they continued their association with CONAVIGUA the village would be leveled. All the women who related the story to me dropped out of public participation in CONAVIGUA, although their analysis of their present circumstances was reinforced. In this sense, some of these local women fashioned a sense of themselves as Mayan women that for the first time extended beyond the borders of their households and communities.

For most of the century, Mayas have been struggling to maintain their traditional economic base (the land) and their traditional support network (their kin) as both steadily eroded under the forces of modernization. Women's roles within their communities and households have undergone major transformations as their contributions to subsistence were undermined by the increasing dependency on cash, which altered the balance of power between men and women in households. Political violence accelerated and exacerbated these trends, breaking apart families and communities. As Peter Uvin (1998) has argued, in some cases structural violence actually sets the stage for political violence. Uvin implicates development aid in shaping processes that lead to violence by providing a large share of financial and moral resources to nation-states, thus playing a crucial role in processes of elite reproduction, social differentiation, political exclusion, and cultural change. In the aftermath of war, development aid for widows again reproduced locally inequality, exclusion, and humiliation by disregarding people's creativity and knowledge in defining and solving their problems.

The category of widows was constructed in a variety of contexts—social, cultural, political, and economic—that existed simultaneously and overlapped. There is no clearcut, easily generalizable construct of widowhood, yet each construction has implications on women's lives and daily practices. Coming together under the auspices of development projects many widows struggled within a radically changing world, complicated by their dislocation from land and community. One social response was to search for a niche within the projects that at least in part served to create a sense of community. The women found ways to rework their identities that included their experiences as widows and as Mayan women. They became aware of the ways in which their suffering had been shaped by gender as well as class and ethnicity. As the women sought solutions to their complex and seemingly intractable problems, some too began to forge new identities from the marginal positions they occupied in Guatemalan society. Yet even as these women have become subjects of their own collective history, their subjectivities, notwithstanding, remain objects of subjugation.

FIGURE 5.1
Woman at home with her children. (*Jonathan Moller*)

5. the embodiment of violence: lived lives and social suffering

The body is the vehicle of being in the world and having a body is, for a living creature, to be involved in a definite environment to identify oneself with certain projects and be continually committed to them. . . . My body is the pivot of the world. . . . I am conscious of the world through the medium of my body.

—Maurice Merleau-Ponty, *The Phenomenology of Perception* (1962)

Political violence of the sort that took place in highland Guatemala in the late 1970s and early 1980s both maimed and killed people literally and figuratively. Many of the widows have suffered doubly, as both victims and survivors. As victims they not only witnessed the unimaginable atrocities of the disappearances or brutal deaths of family members and neighbors, but in some cases they themselves were violated and raped. As survivors they live on the economic and social margins of their impoverished communities; more, they continue to experience the trauma engendered by the violence to both their bodies and memories. In addition, as I noted earlier, the Guatemalan state views widows in contradictory terms. As victims entitled to compensation, they represent what President Vinicio Cerezo described in 1988 as a social debt, a status now consolidated in the peace accords. At the same time, widows are labeled by the military as threats to state security when they demand, among other things, that the state end forced recruitment of their sons into the army or when the women actively assist the Guatemalan Forensic Anthropology Team in exhumations of clandestine cemeteries.

Not surprisingly, given the misery and repression that continues to circumscribe many widows' lives, they cope with hunger and fear as well as multiple and ongoing bodily ailments. Many suffer from chronic headaches, gastritis, stomach ulcers, weakness, diarrhea, irritability, insomnia, and anemia, symptoms often classified as post-traumatic distress syndrome (see Young 1995). Some too experience what medical anthropologists have described as folk illnesses: *nervios* (nerves), *susto* (fright), and *pena* (pain, sorrow, grief).[1] Yet to categorize their sufferings as either manifestations of clinical syndromes or culture-bound constructions of reality is to dehistoricize and dehumanize the lived experiences of the women.[2]

Doñas Marcelina, Eufemia, Alejandra, Elena, Juana, and Martina, along with many other women in Xe'caj, live in a chronic state of emotional, physical, spiritual, and social distress. One of the ways in which the women express their suffering is through illness; their hungry, painful bodies bear witness to their harsh lives. Although the voices of the women have been mostly silenced by the state of fear and repression in which they live, their bodies speak poignantly of trauma and sadness, of loneliness and desolation, of chronic poverty and doubt. Yet these women are not simply passive victims of violence; through their bodies they also chronicle the social, cultural, and political transgressions that have been perpetrated against them. The widows' voices have been silenced by a repressive state, but their illnesses are the language of the body. And for some widows illness has generated sites of dialogue among themselves.

In what follows I explore ways in which one group of widows has made sense of and given meaning to their experiences of simultaneous corporeal and emotional distress. I argue that for many, the body is not experienced as an appendage to the self but as the locus of subjectivity, the very fabric of self, what Merleau-Ponty described as "being-in-the-world" (Diprose 1995). Illness represents a shift not only in one's experiences but also in one's experiences of oneself. For many widows this has meant coming to terms with a new self, a self constructed through experiences of trauma and violence.

Illness brought about by political violence also has a social component. Some women have incorporated the past into the living body of the present. Their communities as places of refuge, as locales in a physical environment, have been drastically altered. Loss of land, the destruction of social institutions within communities, cultural attacks against the ancestors, and the rupture of social relations have reworked both place and spaces where Mayan people and culture previously endured. The body, as a last resort, has become a repository of both history and memories, much as ancestral lands had been before. In this way the body is an oppositional space, a space of resistance. The resistance to which I refer is both passive and active. It is passive in that pain is individually felt, yet illness has also generated agency among the same women when animated in a group. The body bears witness to the violence perpetrated against not only individual women but the Mayan people, as their memories are sedimented into their bodies. As such, sensation and emotion are simultaneously experienced and Western notions of mind-body, subject-object dualisms break down.[3]

Bodies and Embodiment

Until recently much of the theoretical work on the body in the social sciences remained essentially an examination of representations and images of human physicality. While such analyses are useful, they tell us little about the body's implication in human agency, about the productive capacities of the body, or about the history of bodies and peoples experiences, the lived body. Moreover, these studies to a greater or lesser degree treat the body as the focus of analysis while taking embodiment for granted; that is how culture is grounded in the human body (Csordas 1990).

Likewise, medical anthropology has long been concerned with the physical and emotional suffering of the body that results from illness, disease, and death, yet the body itself remained unproblematized until quite recently (Lock 1993). Even recent work discussing the body explicitly has often not addressed the phenomenological aspects of human experience. While this work has looked at issues such as bodily representation, sexuality, and illness, it has tended to produce an incomplete portrait of the body that Terrance Turner (1994) has described as the autonomous "disembodied body." Such theorizing has largely neglected the concrete and specific suffering of people, particularly the complex consequences of that suffering.[4]

Recently, medical anthropologists have begun to pay closer attention to war, conflict, and human aggression (Das 1997; Farmer 1997; Kleinman 1996; Scheper-Hughes 1992, 1996) that structure people's everyday realities and social relations. Not only do violence and warfare produce suffering and alienation, but they may also give rise to human and humane possibilities (Nordstrom 1997; Green 1998).

The Mayan widows' experiences help us rethink notions of illness that highlight the relationship among individual, social, and political bodies (Scheper-Hughes and Lock 1987), between lived experienced and culture (Csordas 1990), and structures of inequality and acts of human agency (Turner 1994). While these concerns are far from new to sociocultural anthropology and medical anthropology, by examining the relationship among violence, culture, and social relations, I bring these bodily concerns into sharp focus.

By problematizing the notion of embodiment as lived experience, or "being in the world" (Merleau-Ponty 1962; Csordas 1990), I want to challenge conventional understanding of mind/body dualism and call into question distinctions between structure and agency, object and subject, materiality and meaning, society and the individual. An examination of the relationship between violence and embodiment reveals vividly the inseparability of sensate experience and cultural representation in lived reality and show how power, history, and gender operate through embodied subjectivity and concrete bodily activity. The body is both a sociological and historical phenomenon, and knowledge is gained through the senses and sensory immersion in the natural and supernatural world. Embodiment, in this sense,

FIGURE 5.2
Quiche women meeting. (*Harvey Finkle*)

is neither a metaphor for social relations nor a text to be read but the actual contested terrain where human beings struggle.

El Grupo

During the course of my fieldwork I met regularly with a group of widows in one of the pueblos of Xe'caj who participated in what is best described as a Protestant base community.[5] Knowing of my interest in working with widows, a Kaqchikel friend who was involved with the group asked me if I would like to take part. I met regularly with the women over the course of two years.

There were thirty members in the group, most of them widowed by the political violence, though the husbands of several women had died of illness, and one woman's husband had abandoned her. The women ranged in age from the midtwenties to the late sixties, with the average age being around forty. All the women were heads of their households, struggling to survive with their often young children as best they could. Many of the women were from outlying aldeas who had fled to the pueblo during the violence and chosen to remain there. Some lived with family members, while others rented single rooms.

The group had formed a year before I began working with them. The meetings took place in Kaqchikel, and the format was such that each woman was given the time and opportunity to express her opinions and reflect on her circumstances through an analysis of the Bible. At most meetings fifteen to twenty women were present, and those who could not attend often sent another family member—often an adolescent daughter—to represent them at the meeting as customary courtesy.

The women expected that I would take an active role rather than merely attend the meetings as an interested observer. Because I was also a nurse, trained in Western-based medicine, I suggested that offering my services in that role might be one way that I could help them. I envisioned my job as one of recording and organizing discussions on specific health issues. My plan had been to explain to them, for example, the physiological effects of gastritis on the body and the possible common treatments that might be available to alleviate their suffering. Surprisingly to me, the women rather than simply describing their symptoms, as is often the focus of Western medical practice, emphasized the etiologies of their illnesses, an approach common to indigenous medical practices that in this case had profoundly political and cultural dimensions.

Doña Maria, age fifty-four, had had a constant headache since the day they disappeared her husband several years before. "It never leaves me," she said.

Doña Juana, age sixty, said, "I have pain in my heart." She could not forget witnessing the brutal killings of her husband and son.

Doña Elena was thirty-eight. Her husband was disappeared and killed in another village seven years before. She had constant headaches, gastritis, and heart pain.

The husband of doña Rosa, thirty-three years old, was disappeared nine years before. She had pains in her stomach and head, especially when she thought of him.

Doña Suzanna was forty-four. Her husband had been disappeared eight years before, and she had *nervios*, stomach aches, headaches, and heart pain.

Doña Faustina was sixty. Her father and husband had been killed and two of her sons disappeared nine years before. She did not sleep because of her sorrow.

Doña Margarita was forty. Her husband had been killed eight years before. Since that time, she had had gastritis, ulcers, headaches, and heart pain.

Doña Jacinta, was thirty-eight. Her husband had been killed nine years before. She did not sleep because she was afraid. She had gastritis and pains in her back and shoulders.

Doña Felipa was thirty-eight. Her husband had been killed nine years before. She had gastritis, constant headaches, heart pain, and susto.

Doña Luci was sixty-two. Two of her sons, her father, and her husband had been killed ten years before. She had headaches, heart pain, ulcers, sadness, and susto.

Doña Francisca was sixty-one. Seven years ago her husband had been killed. She could not concentrate or eat much. She suffered from weak blood and nervios.

Doña Petrona was forty-eight. Her husband had been killed five years before. Her body was weak, and she had gastritis, nervios, sadness, and heart pain.

Doña Norma was fifty-five. Her husband had been disappeared eleven years before. She had nervios, susto, sadness, and insomnia.

Doña Martina, age forty-eight, said she cried bitterly the day her young grandson died of respiratory infection while another lay gravely ill, weak and undernourished, his frail body unable to withstand the deadly assault. Martina said that she tried to forget the past, but whenever someone died the pain in her heart (*pena*) returned and her "nerves came on strong." At times, doña Martina become so weak she could barely work. Martina fled from her village in 1981 with her husband and children because of death threats against him. He was hunted down and disappeared in Guatemala City several months later. She returned home to her village to pick up the pieces of her life as best she could. She and her four youngest children shared a compound with an older son and daughter-in-law.

At first, I was at a loss trying to understand the pain and anguish of the women in relation to their explanations of causality. What did it mean to have a headache since the day your husband had been killed over eight years before? Were the widows speaking metaphorically? What was the connection between emotional memory and bodily pain?

Later, I understand that the women had come to (re)present through their bodies the horrors that they had experienced, and as such illness had become a powerful communicative force. Although I am not suggesting this process was wholly conscious—the women had not consciously willed their illnesses—they did know where their pains came from, what had brought them about. They attributed political causality to particular illnesses. And the widespread nature of these complaints forged a commonality and sense of sharing among the women in the group. As the group listened to the narratives of its members, the testimonies acquired a social as well as personal meaning. These individual bodily complaints took on a collective dimension, where possibilities of communities of pain and healing could be realized (see Comaroff 1985; Seremetakis 1991). Rather than separating individual women from each other, pain sustained the bonds among them. The power of naming their suffering as illness, especially its collective implications, created spaces for struggle while giving bodily shape to the image the women have of themselves as widows. Memory and pain served as a source for regenerating community and identity and for political consciousness.

Sickness in these cases is inherently dangerous because illness related to political violence represents a refusal to break ties with the person who was killed or disappeared.[6] It is dangerous because such refusal circumvents the goal of the disappearance or death, which is to wipe out a person's existence. The women embody the acts perpetrated against their husbands. The women's illnesses thus become actual physical representation of the violence against the Mayan population, for which there has yet to a reparation. As such the body stands as political testimony.

The widows' memories of violence were so powerful and essential that they constituted what Carina Perelli (1994:40) called in the Argentine context *"memorias de sangre"*—blood memories—that ran through their veins literally and figuratively. Their memories, like history, were shaped by breaks, discontinuities, and ruptures and now the "perceived continuum of their lives [was] broken down into a before and after" (40). Their painful bodies stood as individual and collective evidence of the violence perpetrated against them, their families, and their neighbors. In this case, pain and trauma, rather than introducing a conscious split between mind and body, self and world, self and other, joined the women in ways that rendered their pain personally and socially meaningful.

Multiple Medical Beliefs and Practices

According to Orellana (1987) two broad categories of illness etiology were recognized in pre-Columbian Mesoamerica. The first involved illness of natural origins, which could be explained by theories of equilibrium (hot and cold theory); the second covered illnesses attributable to wishful harm and supernatural origins. These causal explanations persist today but overlap with biomedical theories of disease causation.[7] Common illnesses not considered to be of supernatural origin—colds, flu, those caused by changes in climate or lack of food, and *aire* (wind)—are usually treated first in the home. If a cure is not achieved, the sick person may turn to traditional healers such as herbalists, bonesetters, midwives, or the local pharmacy. If the illness persists or becomes chronic, *mal de ojo* (evil eye), susto (fright), or other outside forces may be suspected, and a local shaman or *curandero* sought for treatment. With the introduction of Western medicine, many traditional beliefs have been discredited, and a mix of understandings of illness and curing practices is now evident (Cominsky 1977). Most of the women in the group, for example, had been to the pharmacist, an injectionist, and clinics as well as physicians when they could afford the cost.[8] Yet most could not afford repeated visits nor the expensive medicines that are often prescribed.

Doña Alejandra went to a local doctor intermittently for her headaches, which the doctor attributed to high blood pressure. Alejandra knows that there are other causes for her pain, yet she still went to the doctor when she had the money to do so. She knew that he would prescribe medicines that she could ill afford and that often had no effect, but the visit itself provided her with a modicum of relief from her symptoms even if she knew no cure was forthcoming. Alejandra analyzed her situation in the following way: "I have these [health] problems because I am alone. Without my husband [Miguel] I have no one to help me. I must work constantly to survive." She shrugged her shoulders and added, "Such is our life, the life of the campesino."

Many of the other women in the group went back and forth among local healers, the pharmacist, and Western doctors in search of relief for their pains and distress. Yet modern medical practice neglected their noncognitive feelings—fears, anxieties, despair, and grief—bracketing them out. Effective treatment of fear, for example, demands communion with others, affirmations of solidarity, a sense of belonging. As a result of the political violence a new category of chronic problems has emerged among the widows, with symptoms of existential angst, pain, fear, sadness, and grief, whose etiology is political repression. Though these problems are not exclusive to the women, the widows pointedly understood them to be the result of the political violence.[9] These were the problems about which the women in the group were most concerned and for which they sought solutions together.

Trauma and Recovery

In the meetings the women spoke over and over of their fragile health: illness as a consequence of violence, death, and fear. The women expressed a sense of resignation: "es la vida" (such is life), "que vamos a hacer" (what can we do), "la vida es dura" (life is hard), "es que Dios nos manda" (it's what God has sent us). They had little expectation that they would ever be relieved of their suffering. Yet this sense of fatalism did not necessarily translate into a passivity among the group. A spirit of generosity existed among the women, as well as a sense of responsibility for the well-being of their children and a moral sense of struggle for a better future for Mayan people.

Judith Herman (1992) has argued that in trauma the spirit is crippled and sustaining bonds among individuals, their families, and communities are destroyed. The task of healing is to restore a sense of connection to community. For trauma victims, membership in a group provides protection against terror and despair and re-creates a sense of belonging, a sense of solidarity. The women of El Grupo refashioned a sense of community among themselves and found ways in which to nurture their daily lives and cultural practices, reaffirming the possibilities of common values in the midst of violence.

The women decided that they wanted to focus on the use of locally available medicinal plants and herbs. Most said they knew little about the plants.

As Margarita explained, "There are plants in the mountains that our mothers and grandmothers used. I don't know much about them; I only remember a few. Perhaps we might learn to know the plants, and they might help us too." The women felt that the knowledge of their ancestors might provide them with a key to the alleviation of their suffering in the present.

Sophia and I found some books on medicinal plants that had recently been published by a locally based health organization. The author had interviewed a number of elders and indigenous practitioners about what plants to use for different ailments. Initially, I used the book to offer suggestions on how to prepare teas and poultices as well as to identify plants that might be useful in treatments.

Each week one or two women would have a turn discussing health concerns. The meetings often took on a testimonial quality as the women told of their specific worries and problems, their underlying causes, and what they had tried to do to alleviate their suffering. The etiologies of their illnesses were wide-ranging, at times moving from the suffering caused by the violence to the misery produced by poverty and racism as well as afflictions attributable to the intervention of superior forces. Women began to offer suggestions from their own experiences, and soon they were bringing in plants that they found in the mountains to share with the rest of the group.

What was striking to me was that the women connected some of their problems to the past violence and the ongoing misery, indicating a political etiology. "What we need is unity so that we can stand up for what we want as Indians," doña Rosa would often repeat. "We need land and justice to get well." They also felt that the alleviation of their chronic problems lay in a resurgence of traditional practices and was grounded in their own experiences. A war that to a large extent had destroyed the last vestiges of community life, the locus of cultural expression, became the incentive to bring women together in community under new circumstances and to revitalize traditional health practices that had been neglected.

Susto as a Social Manifestation

Susto is a malady with undifferentiated symptomatology common throughout Mesoamerica that appears to have pre-Columbian antecedents. It is understood by its victims to be the loss of the essential life force as a result of to fright. Often reported symptoms include depression; weakness; loss of appetite; restlessness; lack of interest in work, duties, and personal hygiene; disturbing dreams; fatigue; diarrhea; and vomiting. If left untreated, the victim literally (though often slowly) wastes away.

The literature in medical anthropology is replete with interpretations of illness and sickness in terms of cognitive and symbolic models of meaning. Folk illnesses such as susto have commonly been understood as the physiological expression of individual maladaptation to societal expectations. The nature of the etiology of susto in Western terms has left medical anthropologists baffled, although various explanations have been posited, ranging from mental illness (Pages Larraya 1967), to social behavior as a result of stress (O'Nell and Selby 1968; Mason 1973), cultural transgressions, an inability or unwillingness to fulfill role expectations (Rubel 1964), or the assumption of the sick role as a form of protest (Uzzell 1974), to purely biological phenomena such as hypoglycemia (Bolton 1981) and malnutrition (Burleigh 1986).

Logan's findings (1979) among the Kaqchikel Mayas in Guatemala pointed to the variations that existed between two communities as the underlying explanation of why a person might be *asustado* (frightened in a manner that leads to soul loss). He utilized Foster's (1976) distinction between etiological systems—naturalistic and personalistic—to explain variability according to local ecology and subsequent intrasocietal competition and need for social control. What distinguished Logan's argument from earlier functionalist interpretations is that he illustrates the diversity of susto predicated on material bases: the social relations of land ownership and usage. He moves away from a wholly cognitive and symbolic interpretation of susto to one that involves practice.

Michel Tousignant (1979), on the other hand, has linked susto to the cosmological world of Mayan thought, viewing susto as a metaphor for understanding the relationship between the living and the spirit world. He has insightfully pointed out that *espanto* (susto) refers more to a state or mode of existence than to a specific illness (355). It represents a state of weakened resistance, of vulnerability, following the departure of the soul. Recently Rubel, O'Nell, and Collado-Ardon (1991) have suggested a middle ground that understands susto as an interaction between social and biological factors.

While these studies are important steps in discerning the complexities of susto, I suggest that rather than seeking one overarching theory that will encompass all manifestations of susto across Latin America, the affliction, like the *nervos* of Brazilian cane workers, can be thought of as a "polysemic folk illness" (Scheper-Hughes 1992), both across and within cultures. What I propose is an interpretation of susto that is situational, an embodied understanding of complex social and political relations, one that links the lived experiences of the physical body and memory with the social, cultural, and body politic.

José, one of the church leaders who helped start El Grupo gave the following explanation of susto:

> The spirit of the person is nothing more than life itself. All living things have a spirit, although sometimes the spirit of a person will abandon that person physically, socially, psychologically, and morally, when that person is preoccupied, when their energy is low and they are thinking of other things: the violence, how to survive. Something may suddenly frighten them, and their spirit will abandon them and go into the spirit of another living thing, for example, a tree, the earth, water. Then that other living thing has the person's spirit in its possession. One can look at the face of a person and tell when the spirit has left, it is hollow, ashen, vacant. Yet, rather than calling this a "magical" belief of the Mayas, it is better to say that is a social manifestation. When someone is in a weakened state, the spirit of life can go from one to the other, but it is not the result of a fight or a contest between two types of spirits.

In some cases in Xe'caj the susto from which the women and children suffer is directly related to the terror and fear they have experienced as a result of the political violence. Susto in these cases can be seen not solely as social and passive resistance to what has transpired but as social memory embodied. At the same time we might literally take their explanation that they have been asustado: the spirit has indeed left the body. I suggest this is an accurate description of what has happened to them.

Doña Maria's young son Juanito was asustado one evening when he ran head on into a platoon of soldiers as he was returning home on a mountain path. Juanito's father had been killed several years earlier by the army. Juanito eats very little, and his small edematous body is so lethargic that he hardly moves outside the house. Doña Julia was asustada in 1982 when soldiers entered her house and killed her husband in bed as he lay next to her. Don Lucas's daughter, Fermina, was only eight when the army came to her village. Since that event nine years ago, Fermina, who is distant and withdrawn, has grown very little. She is thin and pale, with a distant gaze. She suffers from susto, don Lucas says, and when strangers come to the house, she experiences *ataques* during which she is unable to speak and appears dead. When Fermina does speak, which is rarely, don Lucas describes it as "speaking to everyone and no one." He says that she saw terrible things during the violence, that she was witness to many brutal killings in the village. Don Lucas knows that Fermina's spirit left her body because of fright but he has been unable to help her. To heal the repression that she witnessed, what stole her spirit must be directly confronted.

These frail wasting bodies are themselves testimony to what has happened to Mayan people. Susto, as a result of political violence, is not only an individual tragedy but serves as a powerful social and political record of transgressions against the indigenous population. Like the pena in doña Martina's heart, which is both bodily and emotionally felt, the illnesses the women of Xe'caj are experiencing are more than metaphors of their suffering. They are expressions of both the rupture of the intricate and immediate connections among body, mind, and spirit and of the social relations among the individual, society, and the body politic. The pain and sadness that Martina experiences in her heart is a direct link to the death of her husband. To no longer have pain would be to forget this death, and this Martina says she cannot do because there has not been justice.

The heart is the center of the vital forces of the spirit in Mayan thought and as such it is the center of awareness and consciousness. The alliance between Martina and her husband that helped to sustain her has been broken, as have the social bonds of trust and stability in her community. While I am not arguing that the ongoing chronic pains that the women experience are in themselves a form of social resistance, they do serve to connect the women to each other in their hardships and as such become a mechanism for social commentary and political consciousness. Western medicine can in some instances alleviate their symptoms, but it cannot solve their problems. For the individual body to be cured the body politic must also be treated.

In the meetings of the group the widows discuss their health problems and how they might help one another while at the same time breathing new life into neglected Mayan medical practices. The women speak of their sufferings and illnesses in terms of the violence and oppression they suffer as Mayas. "I have these nervios because I am poor," doña Marta explains to the group. "I have this headache because they killed my husband and now I am alone, and it will not go away because I am afraid," says Tomasa. The medicinal plants they gather in the mountains relieve some of their pains, but the women say that things must change before they can be well. As they share their sufferings, the women's understandings of their predicaments take on a more social dialogue that offers hope for the future.

For some widows the body has become both an individual and social body, an agent as well as an object. The illnesses rather than fully debilitating them actually work to mitigate their powerlessness. The women looking for herbs in the mountains, with their headaches that will not go away until there is justice, are doing something more important than simply revitalizing tradition: they are rebuilding their relations to each other, re-creating their Mayanness in the aftermath of the assault.

FIGURE 6.1
Woman weaving cloth. (*Jonathan Moller*)

6. the dialectics of cloth

Guatemala, with your *huipil* of lazy trees that droop with sleep
of little animals of the air who embroider their flight
celestial blue
of little animals of the earth who leave the tracks of their droppings
on your surface as they flee the mountains.

Guatemala, with your *huipil* of lakes and markets,
of markets sinking into lakes where colored clouds are traded
for fish, fish for turkeys, turkeys for various fruits and seeds.

Guatemala, with your *huipil* of never-ending rains, rains
that never end because they remain sleeping in your sad
suffering eyes

Oh, Guatemala, little dove, mockingbird,
with your *huipil* of tortured machine-gunned blood
beneath the shadow of all the infinities with claws . . .

—Rafael Sosa

The rhythm of doña Marta's life is circumscribed by the demands of survival. Each day, she rises before dawn to grind by hand corn that has been soaking all night in a large clay pot. Although there is now a diesel-powered corn mill in the village thanks to PAVYH, the cost of using it is prohibitive. Marta cannot afford the twenty cents a day she would need to grind enough corn to feed her family. Instead, she mills the cooked corn on a flat stone; later, she makes it into a dough that she pats it into tortillas that she cooks over an open fire for the family breakfast.

At dawn, the day's tasks begin in earnest. Most mornings, with the help of her two children, Marta hauls water from the public spigot, collects firewood, and washes clothes in the nearby stream. In the afternoon she weaves. Marta has been weaving for over thirty years. When she was seven years old, her mother taught her how to make the traditional handwoven blouse, *el huipil*, in the colors and designs of her pueblo in Xe'caj. Marta says proudly that the huipil is the poetry of Mayan women, an art passed down from woman to woman for centuries.

The art of backstrap-loom weaving is an important material expression of Mayan cultural practices that incorporates the great achievements of the Mayan people. It is at once art, architecture, mathematics, and poetry. The cloth, like the sacred Maya-K'iche text, the Popuh Vuh, is a social, political, and historical product. The shapes, colors, and intricate figures formed by combining warp (vertical) and weft (horizontal) threads are infused with Mayan sentiments. Weaving has served to transmit traditions and values from the past to the present, from one generation of women to the next (Nash 1993).

In this chapter, I explore the dialectics of cloth, the contradictions that arise when the meaning and experience of the widows' weaving of cloth are reshaped by the penetration of capitalist formations of production through small-scale development projects. As David Harvey (1989) has pointed out, global capitalism does not always destroy other economic systems. At times, it may simply reorganize the social relations of production in ways that rupture the threads that had previously linked material and cultural production processes together, as in the semisubsistence domestic and agricultural (milpa) arrangements in Guatemala. These new relations transform the ties among the individual, the household, and the community and between the past and the present. In order to explore the changes that are taking place for the widows of Xe'caj and the multiple, often contradictory, ways in which they respond to those changes in the relationship between the function and meaning of handwoven cloth, I examine processes of cultural production, circulation, and consumption (Garcia Canclini 1993) and link these to the ways in which even a small-scale NGO, with the best of intentions to help widows, reinforced a kind of cultural imperialism, negating indirectly Mayan women's experience and interpretation of social life.

Marta's Story

Since her marriage at age seventeen, Marta has sold her huipiles to other pueblo women, especially in the months before the townwide celebration of the patron saint, *la feria*. This extra cash came at a fortuitous point in the agricultural cycle, usually when the household corn supply was critically low and the price of corn at the *tiendas* (local stores) was at its highest. It takes Marta between one to three months (working half days) to weave a huipil, depending on the intricacy of the pattern. A huipil may sell for US$15–20 locally, depending on the quality of the thread used. The material costs to the weaver amount to around US$10.[1] Most women weave with commercial threads—cotton, silk, or acrylics—although several women in the area continue to use the rough, brown handspun fibers called *ixcaco* to make the *sobrehuipil*, a ceremonial blouse. Prices of thread have risen dramatically over the past decade, and many women have begun to incorporate more synthetic fibers into their weavings. When the cloth is intended for a particularly special occasion, such as a wedding or baptism, weavers often use some highly prized, expensive *seda* (silk) or *cedalina* (silklike pearl cotton) even if only in one or two designs.

FIGURE 6.2
Woman carrying water. (*Jonathan Moller*)

Doña Marta has a *sobrehuipil* made entirely of silk thread that belonged to her grandmother. She cherishes this huipil as part of her *herencia* (inheritance) and plans to pass it on to her own daughter. The soft, smooth texture of the garment, fragrant with woodsmoke and copal, an incense used in ritual ceremonies, evokes the special occasions for which it was created. Marta is worried that this year, however, she may have to sell the huipil in order to buy chemical fertilizer for her milpa. On another occasion, doña Marta was visibly upset when she showed me an especially beautiful huipil and asked me to sell it to my gringa friends in Guatemala City. When I admired the workmanship, she told me it was the huipil she had made to be buried in. She was anxious because she did not know if she would be able to make another of the same quality before she died, but she desperately needed the money to buy corn.

Many Mayan widows can now no longer spare the time and money needed to weave only for themselves and their families or the local market. Without ready access or alternatives for earning much needed cash, they are forced by the exigencies of survival to invest their time in weaving cloth to sell to development projects. For many of the widows of Xe'caj, most of the cloth that they now weave is a commodity for sale on the national and global market. The widows need cash, and there are very few ways for them to earn it while remaining in their rural communities. Although women have long been involved in petty commodity production practices and local market trade, it has been men who customarily earned the bulk of the cash needed for household survival. For some women—those who do not speak Spanish, who are older, alone, and have no other marketable skills useful to a free-market economy—there are no options but to weave cloth to sell. Although cloth has long been exploited, traded, bartered, and sold, first to indigenous and ladino consumers and later to the innumerable travelers, collectors, and anthropologists who have passed through Guatemala, these Mayan women are confronting new predicaments.[2]

The women I know are very distressed about this turn of events. They understand only too well the precarious situation they face in trying to meet the new labor demands imposed by the projects. Perhaps Marta summed up their collective worries best when she said, "Tal vez el ano proximo todas de nosotras moriremos de hambre y miedo" (perhaps we will all die next year from hunger and fear). Such is the insecurity that besets daily life.

Although this restructuring of social relations through capitalist economic arrangements is nothing new to Guatemala's Mayas, the degree of penetration into women's cultural practices is qualitatively different. What is new in these modern experiences is their disengaging impact on the cloth production process, where the unity of material and cultural production is disrupted. As I discussed earlier, the direct intrusion of the state into communities, households, and families and the subsequent reorganization of these institutions has been possible in part as a result of the political violence. And this opening has allowed for new types of capitalist penetration in people's daily lives.

Throughout the twentieth century, weavings for sale locally and regionally have long been geared toward consumer preferences and a perception of quality that is influenced by market forces. Weavers nonetheless chose from a range of options. They could choose to sell or not to sell locally at the marketplace or to peddle their wares in other regions. Since the tourist booms of the 1970s and again in the late 1980s at Panajachel, Chichicastenango, and Antigua, this second strategy has been a viable and much-used option.[3] In these cases, however, the weavers retained a degree of control over what and when to weave. Now, as a result of the political violence, there are large numbers of women on their own whose only marketable skill is to weave cloth and whose choices are thus necessarily far more circumscribed.

Weaving as Relief Aid

In the department of Chimaltenango, the first wave of organized relief aid began for survivors of la violencia in 1982. Some of the people who were forced to flee their communities because of the scorched-earth sweeping operations began slowly to return to their villages in early 1983 to reconstruct their lives as best they could. Many of them were sick and hungry. There had not been any harvests in many of the municipios during the violence, and many were afraid to risk traveling to the fincas on the south coast to earn the cash they needed for survival.

A small NGO, PAVA, Programa de Ayuda para los Vecinos del Altiplano (Assistance Program for Highland Neighbors), was one of the first projects that assisted people in the communities of the Chimaltenango region with the basic necessities—seeds, tools, *lamina* (metal sheets) for roofs, clay pots, blankets—in the aftermath of the scorched-earth sweep by the army.[4] At the same time the Berhorst Foundation of Chimaltenango had received special permission[5] from the government of Rios Montt to send an extension team to visit communities in the departments of Solala and Chimaltenango with the aim of assisting destitute women and children, many of whom had been widowed and orphaned as a result of these same military operations. The team consisted of a doctor, a nutritionist, a veterinarian, an agronomist, and a team member sent along to organize widows in weaving projects.[6]

Between the mid- and late 1980s more development groups cautiously began to initiate small-scale projects for widows and their children. Of these, backstrap-loom weaving projects have been some of the most popular low-cost interventions.[7] One of the less perceptible consequences of this strategy, however, has been a shift in the relationship between women and their cloth, although the technology of production has remained unchanged. In one sense, cloth has become a site of subtle control and dependency: women's livelihoods now depend on what is produced, and the content of that product is dictated by outside forces (Etienne 1980).

Every two weeks Marta walks four hours over rugged mountain paths to one of the pueblos of Xe'caj to sell her weavings to a small international development project. This project in many respects is typical of weaving projects for widows that I encountered throughout the altiplano during my fieldwork. My goal in this chapter, however, is not to criticize the work of any particular project nor to question the commitment and good intentions of the project staff, which were clearly evident. Rather, my intent is to unravel more broadly the economic and cultural contradictions embedded in Western development aid through small-scale rural projects and more specifically to explore the ambiguities and complexities the women of Xe'caj face in their struggle to survive under extremely difficult circumstances.

Marta was one of 300 women from the pueblos and aldeas of Xe'caj enrolled in the weaving project, which bought cloth from the widows in seven villages of Xe'caj. This small NGO began the project in Xe'caj in 1987. It was one of several in the region that bought backstrap weavings exclusively from widows. Every two weeks, a project representative came to Xe'caj to buy. The women clustered together in small groups in the shade of the chapel courtyard to wait for their turn to sell their weavings. Marta would wait her turn with the other widows, receive the next batch of thread, and begin the long trek home by midafternoon. Elsewhere, the cloth was sewn into change purses, totes, and place mats for export to North American and European markets.

Making and selling cloth became a survival strategy for many of the Mayan widows of Xe'caj. Yet the women were caught in a double bind: they had to exploit their artistic talents to earn a bare minimum of cash to maintain the household, yet the means by which they earned this money—not even a living wage—transformed and diminished the cultural meaning of their weaving.

The Production of Cloth

The Loom

The elegance of the backstrap loom is in the simplicity of its design. Its barest constituent parts are merely a bundle of assorted sticks made from locally available materials: hard or soft wood, sometimes even bamboo or dried cornstalks. The loom allows the weaver a great deal of flexibility in production. Not only is it mobile, inexpensive, and readily available, but work can be done almost anywhere, inside or outdoors. Today, this once commonplace loom has been replaced by the more complex treadle (or foot loom) in most regions of Mesoamerica (Stephen 1991a), although the backstrap loom is still used by the Mayan women of Guatemala and Chiapas, Mexico (Nash 1993), and by the Huichol women of Jalisco, Mexico (Shaefer 1990).

When assembled the backstrap loom takes its shape when the warp threads are wrapped around two wooden sticks (known as loom bars). One of the loom sticks is then fastened to a tree or the post of a house and the other to a help strap encircling the weaver's hips. The loom literally comes to life when it is embodied by the weaver.

Inserted between the two loom bars are several other sticks around which the warp and weft threads are wrapped and that allow for the passage of weft threads back and forth between the warps. With the backward and forward motion of her hips, the weaver controls the tension of the threads. The warp threads are continuous, not cut as is common on the larger, more complicated treadle loom. Because of this the weaving is complete with four finished sides, or selvages, when it is removed from the loom, ready for immediate use.

Martin Prechtel and Robert Carlsen (1988) in their work with the Tzutujil Mayas of Santiago Atitlan found correlations in beliefs people held about weaving and birth. The Tzutujil believe that the loom sticks are related to the thirteen important female deities and that the sticks are imbued with some of the same powers as the deities. Mayan midwives in Santiago will sometimes use the loom sticks to reposition breech babies before birth. According to Prechtel and Carlsen, Tzutujil Mayan women speak of weavings as being born and infants as being woven.

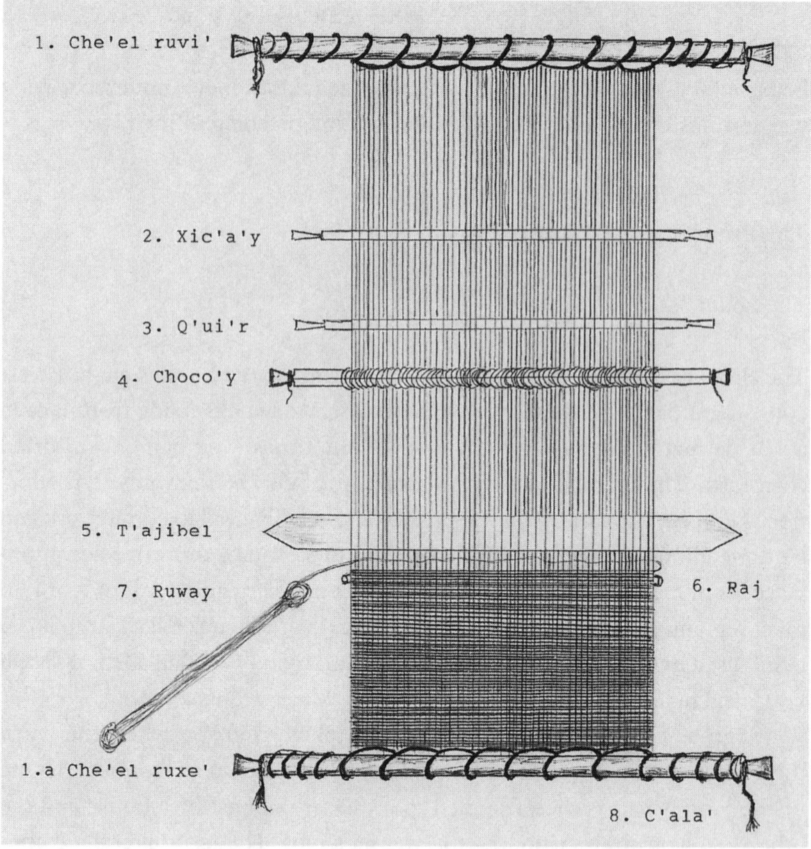

FIGURE 6.3

A Mayan backstrap loom.

1. *Che'el ruvi', che'el ruxe'*: These sticks, about an inch and a half in diameter, support the two ends of the weaving with a thin rope (*pita*) while the weaving is in construction.
2. *Xic'a'y*: A thin, round cane-reed stick that functions to protect the *ruc'u'x* (heart) if the *choco'y* falls or its threads come undone. With this as a safety device, another *choco'y* can be inserted through the ruc'u'x.
3. *Q'ui'r*: A very thin, round cane-reed stick that controls the distance between some threads. It is used to make designs only on the front of the weaving.
4. *Choco'y*: A special thread is attached to a small round wooden stick that is passed between the vertical threads, making a division between them and thus creating the front and the back of the fabric. When the choco'y is pulled up and down, the ruc'u'x (heart, not pictured; the interconnection between the front and back threads) appears. Together, the ruwey and the ruc'u'x create the body of the weaving.
5. *T'ajibel*: A thin and flat wooden stick used with a downward motion on the *ruwey*. The amount of force with which it is applied determines whether the finished cloth will be an open or closed weave.
6. *Raj*: Another very thin cane-reed stick that controls and sustains the width and edges of the weaving. Without the raj, the weaving draws in, and the finished fabric is uneven.
7. *Ruwey*: The threads that feed the weaving. Together with the ruc'u'x they constitute the body of the weaving.
8. *C'ala'*: A thin rope (pita), that ties the ends of the weaving to the che'el ruvi and che'el ruxe.

Most local mythology about what the loom sticks, designs, and patterns of weavings might have meant symbolically to the women in Xe'caj seems to have been lost. Carol Hendrickson (1995), in her extensive study on Mayan cloth and clothing in Tecpan, Guatemala, for example, found only a few people who spoke of such things. And the women I asked said they did not know about such traditional beliefs. Talking with the weavers of Xe'caj about the loom did reveal, however, the significance of the relationship between material and cultural production. Doña Marta explained to me in detail on the day of my first weaving lesson. There is an essential connection among each component of the loom (see figure 6.3), including the rope that ties the loom to the tree or post and the woman kneeling on the earth as she embodies the loom. Through the practice of weaving (the labor process) a meaningful (ideological) association is established between the producer and the natural world. As women weave their cloth, they also reproduce Mayan epistemology that emphasizes the intimate relationship between human beings—both living and the dead—and their universe. And the iconography that appears repeatedly in the cloth—tree of life (*ceiba*), corn plants, flowers, animals, birds, volcanos, people—re-creates visually the world around them. In this way, a weaver produces through her labor and her art a symbolic conduit between the past and the future.

The Art of Creating Cloth

Designs are produced by adding supplementary wefts during the weaving process. Depending on the technique used, the design may or may not be visible on both sides of the fabric. The town of San Antonio Aguas Calientes, for example, is well known for a double-faced weft brocading that creates a mirror image on both sides of the cloth. The process is intricate and time-consuming. It can take the weaver as long as ten minutes to prepare a single round of supplementary threads to pass through the warp, and a complicated weaving can take up to six months to complete (Rowe 1981). The weaver must count and keep track of numerous threads, colors, motifs, all at the same time. The huipiles are often made up of two or three identical pieces. In Xe'caj, for example, after a woman completes the first panel (*lienzo*) of the huipil, she weaves another identical to it so that when the panels are joined together they form a seamless whole. Much of this is done from memory.

Backstrap weaving allows the weaver a great deal of artistic control over the final product. According to Ann Pollard Rowe: "Weaving is one of the world's slowest ways of creating art, a fact not easily appreciated by those who are accustomed to simple machine-made fabrics. Even in our culture, most hand weavers use the treadle loom, which is capable of much greater speed than the backstrap loom, although the artistic potential is significantly reduced" (1981:200). The skill of the weaver is dependent on her knowledge of iconography, her use of color, the quality of the threads, her patience, and her aesthetic sensibility in general. Women create designs from memory, mixing what their mothers and grandmothers taught them with new designs garnered from dreams, local contemporary fashion, or embroidery pattern books. Although the local tradition of the municipio dictates at least some uniformity of overall composition, each cloth produced is unique, infused with the individual preferences of the weaver. The knowledge needed to produce the cloth resides in the imagination of the weaver drawing inspiration from her surroundings.

Reproducing Gender Relations

Weaving on the backstrap loom has traditionally been the work of women. Most young girls are taught to weave when they are around seven to ten years old. Kneeling beside their mothers, their grandmothers, their aunts, or their older sisters, the girls learn about their culture and their place within the world. They learn of the gendered division of responsibilities that they will assume as adult women, whose work is a crucial component of household survival.

Usually, there are no more than a handful of women in rural communities who cannot weave well enough to produce the cloth and clothing necessary for household use. Yet not all women become master weavers, while some, like doña Marta, gain special reputations for the quality of their weavings. Women who cannot weave or do not have the time to do so commission skilled weavers to make huipiles for special occasions. After doña Alejandra's husband was killed in 1976, she began to weave for other women in the pueblo in an effort to support her six small sons. Yet, even weaving full time did not give her sufficient income to maintain the household. And during the violence and its aftermath, fewer and fewer women had the cash to commission doña Alejandra to weave their huipiles.

There are no culturally prescribed rules or sanctions against men weaving on the backstrap loom. Yet it has been uncommon for them to do so. Men who do weave use the treadle loom, which was brought to Mesoamerica in the seventeenth century by the Spaniards. In Guatemala, weaving on a foot loom is referred to as weaving *a machina* (by machine) while backstrap weaving is weaving *a mano* (by hand). Men in the towns of Totonicapan, Quezaltenango, Momostenango, and San Pedro Sacatepequez, for example (Ehlers 1990), have long been involved in the commercial production of textiles on the treadle loom. Most of the women's *cortes* (wraparound skirts), sold in the markets throughout the highlands, are woven by men on foot looms in the department of Quezaltenango, while many of the mass-produced huipiles and *fajas* (woven belts) are made on foot looms in the department of Totonicapan. More recently, cooperatives have formed in the small towns around Lake Atitlan, where both men and women are involved in the production of cloth for commercial sale regionally and international (Hammerschlag 1991; Carlsen 1993; Ehlers 1993). Yet, as Ehlers has pointed out in her study of the lakeside town of San Antonio Polopo (1993), while community women participate in commercial foot-loom production, they do not garner the same profits as men as the women's primary responsibilities are domestic.

Yet although backstrap weaving has remained primarily the domestic occupation and art of women, there are exceptions. In the town of San Antonio Aguas Caliente, a village renowned for its weavings, situated near the popular tourist destination of Antigua, Guatemala, a few men have been weaving on backstrap looms commercially for at least twenty years (Schevill 1990). When the anthropologist Laurel Bossen visited there in the mid-1970s, she encountered a household in which a man who had been ill and could not work his milpa had taken up weaving to make wall hangings for tourists. He did not make huipiles, however. Interestingly, he modified the technique by intermittently skipping sections of weft and tying the warp threads together at regular intervals to make a diamond pattern of weft threads. This innovation was a great shortcut in weaving that was not always perceived by the tourists, uneducated in weaving, who by any local woman's standards paid the same prices for vastly inferior products (Laurel Bossen, pers. comm., 1992).

Doña Alejandra took me to her natal village to meet a man who weaves alongside his wife. When I asked about his decision to take up what has traditionally been women's work, he said he did it in his idle time for economic reasons: it was a way to earn extra money when other means were not available. He is an accomplished artisan, and the women who introduced me to him were proud that he could weave so well. They freely criticized his work, however, giggling as they pointed out how the manner and technique of his weavings differed from theirs. Don Marcos sits in a chair rather than kneeling on a mat on the ground as all women do; he copies the designs his wife has shown him and remains awkward in his maneuvering of the weft sticks, although the cloth he produces is quite beautiful. The cloth woven by his wife and their fifteen-year-old daughter is used for the family's clothing. Don Marcos's cloth is for sale.

Cloth as a Development Strategy

As noted earlier, weaving projects emerged throughout the highlands as a commonplace development intervention to aid Mayan widows after la violencia in the 1980s. The use of weaving as an economic strategy with claims to cultural sustainability appeared to be, at first glance, a pragmatic response to an intractable situation. Yet most of these projects have proven to have little overall impact on the widows' material conditions while contributing to the intensity and reach of capitalism over their daily lives. The changes have created a situation where the women are doubly exploited: economically and culturally. Their art is treated as piecework, from which they cannot earn a living wage, and the social relations under which they labor contribute to the breakdown of their shared values.

Marta worked on her weaving four hours per day for two weeks and received US$6–8 for each finished piece, depending on its size and quality. The widows of Xe'caj were paid by the piece, with the cost of the next batch of thread deducted from their earnings. Marta has never had a weaving rejected as have some of the other women. She wove during the afternoon outside on the patio where the light was good. There is no electricity in her village. Marta said that her back and shoulders ached while she wove and after some time her hands went numb. She wove the same design over and over, day after day, week after week. Marta said she wove to sell because that was what she knew how to do. The money was not enough to meet her household expenses, yet her livelihood depended on this steady income. She added resolutely, "Algo es algo" (something is something); besides, what other choices did she have? Marta's situation was typical of many of the widows that I knew.

The results from a survey of forty widows I conducted in 1990 revealed that women earned between US$12–15 per month from selling their weavings to the project. For the majority, these earnings constituted a significant part of their income. The money did not accumulate, however. In fact, when one added up the number of hours the women spent weaving plus the time it took them to walk to and from the pueblo to sell and then subtracted the expense of thread, the women actually earned nothing for their efforts. The benefit of participation was the regular circulation of cash that moved in and out of the household. This fact was not lost on the women, and some women who stopped participating said "No vale la pena" (it is not worth the trouble). Those who continued in order to receive the cash said, "Por la necessidad" (out of need) or "Luchando por mis ninos" (to struggle for the sake of my children).

The conflicts that arose in the project were not due solely to the failures of economics, although these were certainly relevant. The rupturing of the vital links between economic and cultural production is crucial to understanding what was at stake for the women. Project workers, dismayed when women did not meet the production schedules or dropped out altogether, would say that the widows did not really want to work, that they were simply looking for handouts. This analysis tends to obscure, however, the profound dilemmas that the women faced when social relations were transformed so that the conditions of their material survival were at odds with their values.

In each community of Xe'caj where widows participated in the weaving project, a *presidenta* was selected by the project to represent the other participants. Any announcements or changes in procedures were related to the presidenta, who then passed them along to the others. Often this woman was chosen for her ability to speak Spanish, as many widows spoke only Kaqchikel and the project workers were, for the most part, Spanish-speaking. Many of the women in Xe'caj said that because they did not have a say in the selection of the presidenta, she did not really represent them. Furthermore, this structure did not allow each woman, as a member of the project, the opportunity to voice her ideas, her needs, or her desires publicly to the other members as is customary for many Mayas in making decisions within their families and within some indigenous community organizations. To further complicate matters, in several instances in Xe'caj, there were women who were trying to take advantage of their positions as presidentas for their own material gain, and the other women were well aware of this.

The fact that the projects were established exclusively for widows in the communities also created conflicts and resentments. First, by defining the women as widows, they were categorized and separated from others in the community who had also suffered from the violence and entrenched poverty. Second, this special attention to a single group undermined the ability of the community to organize itself to confront its own problems. This led to divisions and bitterness toward the widows. A number of men and women said that they too were in need of assistance, even though they were sympathetic to the special circumstances of widows and their children.

Time and Aesthetics

Historically, rural women weavers retained control over key elements of the production process. They managed both time and aesthetics and maintained ownership of the tools of their craft, most importantly, the loom. Weavers produced and sold their products free from what E. P. Thompson (1972) has called "the demands of labor discipline," where time itself becomes a commodity. Decisions regarding the aesthetics of cloth were also in the hands of the weaver, rather than determined by the dictates of (global) desire for so-called primitive arts and crafts.

Marta spoke poignantly about the tensions that weaving for the project created for her. She often had trouble adhering to the production schedule, yet she was dependent on the biweekly cash. Because Marta suffered from recurring headaches, vision problems, and nervios, some days she could not weave at all. The fact that some weeks she failed to finish her cloth on time added to her anxieties over keeping the household running.

Marta also said that sometimes she could not meet the weaving schedule because she had to help a family member or neighbor in need, as when an illness or death occurred. The project production schedule was at odds with her sense of mutual aid and obligation to her family and neighbors. Many of the women were put in the difficult position of choosing between their individual needs and their commitment to their family and their neighbors.

Weaving for the project also disrupted the ways in which weaving is connected to time as it flows between the past and the future. Marta worries that she does not have time to teach Rosa, her daughter, the designs her mother taught her. Nor does Rosa have the time to experiment on her own. A generational thread of life and of memory has been frayed between mother and daughter, and at the same time the dialogue with the antepasados has been ruptured, replaced by a new dialogue with the market.

The project discouraged creativity on the part of the weavers, dictating the designs to be woven into the cloth. The women were asked to replicate the same pattern repeatedly without variation, the same motif over and over, week after week. In many cases the colors of thread used in the weavings were at the discretion of the project managers and not the weavers themselves. Pastel blues and light pinks replaced the traditional combinations of vibrant yellows, reds, greens, and black. The knowledge and expertise of the weaver became secondary to the demands of the market.

When weaving for the project, the women no longer created a whole piece of cloth but instead wove fragments intended to be fashioned into something else, somewhere else. Ordinarily if you ask a weaver where she is in her weaving of a huipil, she will invariably answer by describing where the cloth (*lienzo*) will lie on her body: I am at the heart (chest), I am almost up to the shoulder, I have just dropped over to the back. The cloth is imagined in relation to its use on the body as clothing. Divorcing the weaving from its function as clothing eliminates a vital aspect of its significance in the weaver's life.

The Language of Clothing

One of the ways that woven cloth circulates is through traditional clothing known as traje, for which the Mayas are known worldwide. For the most part, it is women who have continued to use the distinctive woven clothes.[8] In the communities of Xe'caj there is little variation in women's attire. Most women and girls dress in the handwoven huipil of their municipio, a corte (a wraparound skirt made from a six-foot-length of cloth), with a faja wrapped around the waist to keep the corte in place, a *delantal* (or apron), often trimmed with elaborate embroidery, and a *perraje* (or shawl).[9] Today, only the huipil and faja are now made by hand on the backstrap loom in Xe'caj. The other elements of the ensemble are mass-produced on the foot loom in indigenous communities such as Totonicapan. This production, however, has allowed Mayan women who do not have the resources to weave all their clothes to maintain an important symbolic expression of their identity.

Many rural women take great pride in their clothing and their appearance. The aesthetics of dressing properly—in the image of the ancestors—is of great importance to them. In Xe'caj most people are poor, and most have only two or three changes of clothing, yet people place a premium on looking their best. When working around the house, a woman may wear her oldest huipil and corte or may turn her huipil inside out to preserve it, but if she has to go out even on a short errand she will groom herself before leaving home. And keeping oneself and one's clothes clean is no easy task, as I was to learn during my time in Xe'caj. Six months out of the year, there is mud everywhere from the heavy rains, and the dry season brings winds and dust and water is scarce.[10]

Traje has been an important marker of Mayan identity historically, but what it has signified has changed over the centuries. Robert Hill (1992) noted that during the colonial period the type and style of traje used distinguished Mayan elites from peasants. It was not until the mid- to late nineteenth century that traje more typically took on a communitywide uniformity that served to reinforce a community hegemony as well as to mark outsiders, whether Mayas or ladinos. Until recently, a huipil could confidently be used to identify which municipio the wearer was from. Traje also serves as a marker of class among Mayas. Women from families with more resources can afford either to use expensive threads in the huipiles that they weave themselves or to buy huipiles made from such fibers from other women.[11]

In the pueblos of Xe'caj, as throughout much of Chimaltenango, there is now the more common practice, especially among younger women, of wearing huipiles with patterns from other municipios, a practice that has been described as "pan-Indianism" (Asturias 1985, 1991; Hendrickson 1995). A women of means may own huipiles from several other municipios besides her own. Women say they wear these other styles "por gusto" (to please themselves), dismissing the significance of wearing a particular pattern of huipil as "no importa, somos indigenas" (it is not important, we are all Indians). Not only do the women buy the huipiles from other weavers in the local market, but some women have learned how to reproduce the designs and colors from other towns. There has also been a resurgence of designs and colors of huipiles *de los ancianas* (from the elders) that doña Marta told me had been all but lost in recent years.

Although the women of Xe'caj have a variety of opinions and preferences about the 150 or so different styles of huipiles that exist in Guatemala today, traje of whatever design remains for them an important signifier of their identities. When I asked women why they used traje for themselves and their girl children, they said that it was a tradition of their ancestors and it was important to them to be identified as indigenas. Robert Carlsen in his recent study in Santiago Atitlan found that people often stated that the reason for using traje was to dress in the eyes of the ancestors and to follow their traditions (Carlsen 1993; Nash 1993).

The use of traje has a double quality to it. While it is both a source of pride and identity for Mayan women and men, at the same time it singles them out as indios, victims of the flagrant racism that prevails in Guatemalan society. Most men in rural Guatemala now wear Western-style clothing, and their only material identifier may be their *morrals* (distinctively woven shoulder bags). Laurel Bossen (1984) has argued that any analysis of this phenomenon needs to be historically and geographically specific. This process of westernization in men's clothing has spanned almost a century and reflects men's greater and differing degrees of subordination to capitalist economy and culture. Many indigenous men, for example, were forced to give up traje when they became the coerced workforce on the newly established coffee plantations in the late nineteenth century, as well as forced conscripts for the expanding military (McCreery 1976, 1990).

Men who continue to wear traje are feeling the economic pressures to wear the cheap Western clothes readily available to them (Carlsen 1993). Men in Xe'caj seemed to stop using traje widely only in the past several generations, although one often sees old men using a modified version of the traditional dress. Some men who continue to wear traje said that they could not afford to buy indigenous clothing for their sons when they were young and so "no tienen el costumbre" (they are not accustomed to wearing traje). One man confided that men who traveled outside the community frequently were more readily ridiculed as "inditos" when they wore their traje (see Ehlers 1993).

The economic and political situation over the last decade has placed increasing pressures on women's ability to maintain their use of traje. In the larger towns and cities of the highlands, it is not uncommon to see poorer Mayan women wearing machine-made *blusas* (blouses) in place of the handwoven or foot-loomed huipiles. In Guatemala City, many women now use a Western-style blouse or even a t-shirt with their corte and dress their daughters entirely in Western-style clothes. As economic conditions have worsened, many Mayan women simply cannot afford to buy or make huipiles for themselves and their daughters. They have no choice but to turn to cheaper, mass-produced cloth and clothing. Used clothing (*ropa americana*) from the United States, for example, sells for twenty cents per item in the secondhand shops of Guatemala City. When asked about this turn of events, the women of Xe'caj said it was sad when someone could not afford to dress like their ancestors, but if a women does give up traje, she remains a Maya if she so chooses, because what makes one Maya, they said, "es aqui en el corozon" (is here in the heart).

On a more disturbing note, during the worst phase of political repression, many indigenous people either stopped wearing traje altogether as a survival strategy or began using traje from other regions so as not to be identified with a particularly contested region and thus marked as subversives.[12] Women in this context were forced to conceal their indigenous identities, a process that begun much earlier for men, as I have said.

Perhaps emblematic of the extent to which the military has intruded into village life was a disturbing scene I witnessed one afternoon at the yearly festival in honor of the patron saint of Xe'caj. As I noted earlier, this is the time of year when women weave and put on their best traje. A little girl, about four or five years old, was dressed in traje, but instead of her huipil being woven in the time-honored pattern of her municipio, it was made from army camouflage cloth trimmed at the neck and sleeves in black velvet.

When Cloth Migrates

The entry of Mayan cloth into the global exchange circuits is not new; in fact, it began five centuries ago when the Spanish first carried cloth back to the Old World. Then, however, artifacts gathered from the New World were not valued primarily as objects of the past but prized as achievements of the present (Clifford 1985). In modern times, Mayan cloth began to migrate across borders when travelers, anthropologists, and missionaries began acquiring cloth for museums, galleries, and private collections. The cloth went in one of two directions: it was housed in anthropology museums as material culture to be scrutinized for scientific data and later showcased, or it became part of private art collections. As cloth has crossed transnational boundaries, it has been transformed into exotic art, an object of desire and curiosity from one of the great civilizations of the past. More recently, with an increased Western consumer demand for material objects from other cultures, cloth has entered into global commodity circulation as tourist souvenirs or folk art (Graburn 1976), or it is sold in specialty shops in Manhattan and Guatemala City as an expensive novelty item. Not unexpectedly, the meaning of the woven Mayan cloth changes, like other material objects of cultural value, in relation to where it is located and its utility (Appadurai 1986). A huipil used daily by a rural Mayan women as a material symbol of her indigenous identity does not have the same decorative and recreational meaning for an upper-class latina woman in Guatemala City who wears a huipil with jeans to a Sunday afternoon cocktail party.

As one strolls along the tree-lined streets of Zona 10, a wealthy residential and commercial section of Guatemala City, one cannot help but notice in the boutique windows designer dresses, jackets, and vests made from exquisitely woven Mayan cloth or bedspreads, tablecloths, or elaborate ceremonial huipiles still intact to be used as household decorations. Hovering mostly unnoticed and unacknowledged in the background are the producers, the rural poor who also have to migrate in search of work as domestic servants, gardeners, and caretakers of the rich. The woven cloth and clothing, which came from some of the same communities as these urban migrants, are reified as emblems of age-old and unchanging traditions valued as part of a national patrimony. While the producers themselves are summarily exploited, killed, or displaced from their natal communities, their cloth and clothing are transformed into objects of desire.

The mystification of these fetishized objects, as Marx aptly pointed out, dehistoricizes the context in which the producers labor, while at the same time it appropriates Mayan history. The object itself comes to represent the culture, but a culture of the past associated with old objects. As Nestor Garcia Canclini has insightfully pointed out, "crafts which might have once been identified by the way in which they were produced today must include in their characterization the social process through which they move, from the time of production to the time of consumption. In part, the term artisanal continues to denote a particular way of using implements, but their meaning is also formed by their reception, through a series of features attributed to objects (age, primitivism etc.)" (1993:107). The ability of the wealthy to purchase, wear, or display the best Mayan cloth becomes a signifier of the discriminating taste of the owner. Through its commodification, Mayan cloth is transformed into a status symbol for the wealthy, while Mayan connections with their own past are disrupted in the process.

La Esperanza

A small group of women from Xe'caj are reasserting control in a myriad ways over the production of cloth even as they are forced to sell under circumstances not of their own making. In so doing, they have created new kinds of relations with their neighbors as well as other village women. Most married women have little opportunity to socialize with nonkin women. As a result of the political violence, however, some widows have more freedom of movement and association within the confines of local institutions such as development projects, creating new possibilities. Several widows from a weaving project in Xe'caj decided to organize a local buying and selling group. The women pooled their money and bought thread together in large quantities in Guatemala City where the prices are cheaper. The women are making *tzutes* (carrying cloths), napkins, huipiles, and fajas in the old styles and colors, items that might be appealing to tourists as well as other Mayas locally. They are selling in the local market, by word of mouth, and at the entrance to the Mayan Kaqchikel ruins of Iximche. Although this strategy provides no more economic assistance than the weaving project does, it allows the women to exercise some control over their own circumstances.

In the process, these women are reshaping their ties to one another through their cloth. As the women work together they keep alive their vision of the world, mitigating in part the self-interest inherent in capitalist relations. Weaving too provides the women with some emotional relief. Women have often used strong colors to express their pain and sadness. "Se gita un poco mi tristeza" (my sadness is a little lessened), women would tell me. Thus, through their efforts, in small, undramatic ways that James Scott (1985) called "everyday resistances," some of the widows oppose the invisible violence of development on their lives. Through the process of weaving, some are reworking their sense of identity and community and finding emotional respite despite the disintegrating cultural effects of development aid on daily habits, family structures, and indigenous identity.

Contradictions Embedded in Weaving Projects

Most Mayan widows of Xe'caj were much in need of economic assistance in the aftermath of the civil war, yet the type of assistance offered to them by development interventions raises several important issues. First, projects that promoted weaving and to a lesser extent soap and candle making and raising small animals for sale did not ground their strategies in the social realities of women's lives. While petty commodity production has long been at the heart of women's economic practices, the income generated has been supplemental to the household cash economy. Cash earned by men through productive activities outside the household has been an integral factor for the economic well-being of the household. As is nearly always the case, female-headed households are the most impoverished. The money earned by widows from participation in these projects did create a cash flow, but it was far from adequate even to begin to address the loss of men in the household as milpa producers and generators of cash income. The projects not only reinforced existing values that restricted women's roles to domestic and child-bearing activities but overlooked feminist critiques of development projects that merely reinforce women's marginal status (Kabeer 1994).

Weaving projects designed to assist widows brought neither a significant reduction in poverty nor a substantial economic improvement in their lives. The participation in the projects did have consequences for the women, however. While they continued their activities as backstrap weavers, they did so under new socioeconomic arrangements that altered social relations of production, time, and the aesthetics of making cloth, undermining an important aspect of Mayan cultural production. Moreover, the projects bypassed local people's creativity and knowledge, which could have contributed to finding ways to solve their own problems.

Yet cloth and clothing continue to remain important symbolic expressions of Mayan cultural and gender identity, continually refashioning the past in the present. What is not clear is how these new arrangements may alter poor women's relationship with their cloth.[13] One unexpected benefit of the projects is that they have brought together nonkin women in new ways that have created spaces for different kinds of social bonds and networks of reciprocity.

FIGURE 7.1
Fundamentalist preacher at work. (*Sean Sprague*)

7. shifting affiliations: social exigencies and evangelicos

The imposition of a new religion in itself does not necessarily imply a change in ethnic identity or a rupture in cultural and historical continuity, as irrefutably demonstrated by the "spiritual conquest" of Mesoamerica.

—Guillermo Bonfil Batalla, *Mexico Profundo* (1996)

Most evenings in the villages and pueblos of Xe'caj, competing loudspeakers from the different sects of the evangelical churches broadcast familiar songs to the handful in attendance. Even in the smallest of villages, with no more than forty to fifty families, there may be five or six different congregations, such as the Church of God, New Jerusalem, the Prince of Peace.[1] In the small aldeas, these chapels are mostly rough-hewn, furnished with simple wooden benches and lit by candles. Here, the preachers may proclaim the Word of God using microphones hooked up to car batteries that serve as generators. Inside these small rooms, a few people gather nightly, at times only six or eight congregants, mostly women, to pray along with the local pastor in Kaqchikel. The pastor, among other things, admonishes them to forego *costumbre*—the rituals and practices of Mayan religiosity—and to obey the pastors, husbands, civil patrol heads, and military commanders with authority over them. Yet, in sharp contrast to this severe, fundamentalist discourse, group hand clapping, singing, shouting, and praying lends a hypnotic, rhythmic air to the *cultos* (worship services). And most congregants I know readily describe the cultos as "muy alegre" (a pleasurable experience).

Although Guatemala has been a Catholic country since the Conquest, mainstream Protestant missionaries have been proselytizing in the highlands for well over a century. The Presbyterians first came to the highlands in the late 1800s at the invitation of then-president Justo Rufino Barrios, the Liberal caudillo, with the intention of undermining the entrenched power of the Catholic Church.[2] Thirty years later, the first conservative Pentecostal missionaries—or the "tongue movements," as they were disparagingly known by their mainline, liberal counterparts—arrived in Guatemala. Despite this attention, on the whole the number of indigenous converts grew slowly and rather unremarkably until the 1980s, when the murder of dozens of Catholic priests and hundreds, perhaps thousands, of lay catechists and congregants by the state sent a large number of Catholics flocking to evangelical meetings as a haven from repression (Stoll 1993; Wilson 1995).[3] By the late 1980s evangelical leaders were claiming over 30 percent of the national population and predicting that, if growth rates remained high, Guatemala would become the first Protestant country in Latin America.

In this chapter, I address the question of what a shift to fundamentalism might mean specifically for some of the widows of Xe'caj who have abandoned their apparently exclusive allegiance to traditional or orthodox Catholicism. Does this turn away from Catholicism to Pentecostalism mean that people have simply been coerced? Or are the modernizing processes of dispossession, differentiation, and displacement accelerating the transformation so long predicted by anthropologists whereby Mayas are at last becoming ladinoized? I suggest that with the multiple, complex, and contradictory processes taking place in the highlands today, religious conversions need to be explored locally and historically within a context of religious pluralism and violence, recognizing a number of divergent trends in communities.

In the 1980s Protestant evangelism—particularly the fundamentalist and Pentecostal strains and to a lesser extent Catholic charismatics[4]—was uniquely situated to offer a social and religious alternative to people whose lives had been shaken by unimaginable atrocities as a result of political violence and whose communities had been fractured by years of privation and the increasingly disruptive effects of capitalist penetration. Today, when community members need each other perhaps more than ever before, the material and social bases of those connections are being eviscerated by structural and political violence.

Yet the assumption that conversion to Pentecostalism is inevitably a step toward loss of Mayan identity cannot be fully substantiated. Although there has been a dramatic and significant rise in the number of Pentecostal conversions in rural communities, the boundaries of religious affiliations are neither fixed nor static, and neither do the conversions themselves necessarily represent a rejection of a Mayan identity or Mayan epistemology. Some of these conversions may in fact be understood as survival tactics, not only in that they stem from a desire to seek refuge from political persecution, but also because they represent a search for an arena in which Mayas can express their notions of justice, dignity, and well-being based on a sense of community.

I must distinguish here between conversion, which implies a transformation in ideology or worldview, and affiliation, which indicates membership. In the cases I examine below, Christian religious affiliations among the widows of Xe'caj are tactics that emerge out of their recent lived experiences. I hope to convey the sense of pragmatism shared by the women I know: they are not dupes of false consciousness—although their lives are not without contradictions—fickle opportunists, or acting in bad faith; rather, they are subjects deeply involved in the shaping of their lives within the context of profound social upheaval. With much of their community-resource base destroyed, shifting religious affiliations is a practical, cultural, and emotional response to pressing social exigencies and their personal needs. Western explanations tend to interpret religious affiliation as an exclusive category signifying a particular ideological bent; in this case, however, mobility across religious institutional boundaries can be also understood as part of a set of social and cultural survival strategies (Gill 1996). Additionally, these shifting affiliations point to the ways in which people experience, construct, and contest their collective identities. Given the complex and multiple nature of this dynamic, new representations do not necessarily come to replace each other in an ascending continuum or obliterate old images of the past.

A Religion of Repression

We want to contribute to the building of a country different from the one we have now. This path has been and continues to be full of risks, but the construction of the Reign of God has risks and can only be built by those that have the strength to confront those risks.

—Bishop Juan Gerardi (1998)[5]

During the counterinsurgency war, it became politically dangerous to be identified as a Catholic in some areas of the altiplano. In the eyes of the Guatemalan military, Catholicism had become synonymous with subversion, especially in areas where the Christian base communities had flourished. As I noted earlier, by the late 1970s, any type of community organizing in the altiplano was interpreted by the Guatemalan state as dangerous to its fragile yet coercive rule. Although orthodox Catholicism rooted in Western capitalist values has never been deemed a threat to the status quo, the progressive wing of the church, with its explicit philosophy of social justice, has been marked by the state as insurrectionist.[6]

Most church workers, however, were not revolutionaries.[7] Although they had become convinced of the need for substantial social change to redress the institutionalized poverty and racism so evident in rural villages, their challenges were made through conventional means, such as leadership training, popular education, and small-scale development projects, methods utilized by both base communities and USAID alike.

In many of the aldeas of Xe'caj in the late 1970s, for example, Catholic lay workers from all over the Kaqchikel-speaking region began to organize CBCs to train local leaders to read the Bible based on an understanding of peace and justice formulated at the Latin American Bishops Conferences of Medallion.[8] With an explicit philosophy of solidarity with the poor through community service, these lay workers introduced a more radical development agenda. Utilizing a methodology promoted by earlier Catholic Action training—"to see, to reflect, to act"—the catechisms supported the community members involved in CBCs, encouraging them to identify and analyze the problems in their communities to find concrete solutions to mitigate their suffering. For example, catechists offered literacy classes and organized women's and youth groups in the villages that provided mechanisms for ordinary people not only to reflect on their daily experiences but also to redress those circumstances. The analyses and plans of action, in many cases, threatened entrenched local power structures because they sought to illuminate the very processes that gave rise to people's problems and sufferings.

In the wake of repression the CBCs were disbanded, and today in Xe'caj they no longer formally exist. One priest, Padre Juan, did speak out against local exploitation, however, and encouraged people not to give up their faith in justice, despite the climate of fear in which they lived. Like several of his predecessors in Xe'caj—by the early 1980s several of these catechists and a parish priest had been killed in Xe'caj, and another priest had been forced to abandon the area because of death threats, as had been a number of catechists, who went into hiding or exile—Padre Juan too had to abandon his parish in Xe'caj in 1991 because of death threats. Not surprisingly, in the aftermath of brutal repression some priests as well as congregants became convinced that the only way to redress the flagrant abuses was actively to join forces with the armed insurgency. Moreover, in some villages of Xe'caj, as elsewhere, large numbers of local people converted to Protestant fundamentalism.

The village of Ri Bay is a case in point. Although by 1981 there was one fundamentalist church in the village, the majority of the population of seven hundred identified themselves as Catholic. By 1983 the village was mostly deserted because of the army's scorched-earth sweeps. When three hundred people resettled the village in the mid-1980s, all but a few declared themselves to be Protestant evangelicos. Today there are seven evangelical congregations in Ri Bay alone.

Much of the academic literature as well as reports in the popular press on evangelical conversions in Latin America published in the 1980s focused on the connection between United States Christian missions and the conservative political regimes north and south of the Rio Grande.[9] The perception of a linkage between the coercive state apparatus and foreign fundamentalist missionaries in Guatemala was warranted in the wake of the brutal scorched-earth campaign of 1982–83 presided over by General Efrain Rios Montt, the born-again military dictator and an elder in the Eureka, California-based Gospel Outreach Mission, who ruled the country with the Bible and an iron fist (Bogenschild 1992).[10] And certainly there was cause for alarm among progressive academics and activists as they witnessed a shift from politically engaged struggles for social justice by means of base communities to a Christian fundamentalism that has been understood as "intensely conservative, that underscores submission to authority, erodes collective identity, and undercuts justification for social action" (Burdick 1993:7).

On closer inspection, while political repression in the altiplano is a crucial component in the phenomenally rapid growth of fundamentalism in Guatemala, it does not fully capture the tensions and contradictions embedded in this recent wave of conversions. While fear and intimidation have been important accelerators of membership growth, they cannot fully explain the ongoing local participation.[11] Simply categorizing fundamentalism as a religion of repression is insufficient to account for the ways in which people engage with and give meaning to their experiences. Moreover, a single explanatory model cannot explicate the multiple and complex meanings, discourses, and practices that individual people or groups give to seemingly similar religious experiences (Burdick 1993).

A Religion of Advancement

Widespread conversions to Protestantism in Catholic Latin America have also been tied to the intensification of capitalist productive relations in rural communities[12] (Martin 1990). Prior to the onslaught of the political repression in Guatemala in the 1970s, several anthropological studies examined Protestant conversions among the Mayas in highlands towns (Sexton 1978). Although these analyses pointed to the diverse economic, social, cultural, and political factors at work in this transformation, the conclusions often linked the rise of Protestantism to modernization and its attendant destruction of non-Western cultures.

More recently, Sheldon Annis (1987), in his neo-Weberian analysis of the Kaqchikel-speaking municipio of San Antonio Aguas Calientes, contended that Protestant conversion there is correlated with economic advancement. In his ethnography *God and Production in a Guatemalan Town*, Annis quantifies a positive association between the evangelicos and economic well-being among the town's people. Additionally, he notes that a campesino transition to Protestantism not only heralded a shift from an indigenous milpa-based agricultural economy to one grounded in cash cropping and commercial artisan production but also included a cultural logic as well. These new, so-called rational microentrepreneurs were simultaneously freed from both the economic backwardness of milpa production and the cultural remnants of an Indian identity expressed through their cofradia participation.

Furthermore, Annis argued, indigenous men who entered into commercial ventures such as trade and cash cropping found that the costs associated with cofradia participation were untenable. As these individuals advanced economically, the traditional cultural practices represented by cofradias no longer resonated with their lived experiences. Thus these Mayan men also reworked their ideas about proper behavior, placing an emphasis on individualism, competition, and success. In the town of Amolonga, Quetzaltenango, Liliana Goldin and Brent Metz (1991) found a number of "invisible converts," people who had not altered their public religious affiliations but who held some of the same values as their evangelical counterparts.

While these studies provide invaluable insights into how shifts in economic production have reshaped cultural practices and social organization in highland communities, implicit in these accounts is a unidirectional vision of social change, from folk Catholicism to a modern Christian fundamentalism, from peasant to microentrepreneur, from an explicit indigenous identity to tacit ladinoization. And while in some situations this indeed has been the case, still missing from these narratives are accounts of how historical contingencies and the multiple contradictions embedded in quotidian life simultaneously destabilize these processes.[13]

External factors and local-level internal struggles crosscut by violence operate in ways that both mitigate and accentuate the erosion of Mayan economic and cultural production but do not necessarily destroy them.[14] Guillermo Bonfil Batalla (1996) has argued that despite the cultural heterogeneity in the daily life of indigenous Mexicans, a "minimal cultural nexus" exists with its own distinctive identity that continues to give meaning and coherence to their subjective reality. In this way, people confront their domination through processes of resistance, appropriation, innovation, and accommodation.

The possibilities for Mayan social and economic advancement must be set in a context that underscores the very real limitations in Guatemalan society as it presently exits. Despite the fact that they are the majority of the population, Mayan people live under minority rule, and they are continually denied even their basic rights as citizens. Moreover, they have no choice but to participate in a modern capitalist economy that enfranchises only a few. As production practices and social relations in communities changed over the centuries, Mayas indeed refashioned their lives out of the available options, yet those spaces are circumscribed by a racist and oppressive state.

The reasons for conversion to evangelism are not easily generalizable across the Mayan landscape. A consideration of economic differentiation is integral to any understanding of religious change, but it does not fully account for the attraction of Protestantism or its relationship to ethnic identity. For example, Manning Nash (1958) found in his study of rural industrialization during the 1950s in the town of Cantel that few factory workers there were converting to evangelism, as would have been expected. Instead, Nash described those converting at the time as "marginal" to the community rather than representatives of the "proletariat." Artisans and "ladinoized" Indians converted because of their disapproval of personal behavior associated with cofradia participation. While Ricardo Falla (1980) in his study of San Antonio Illotenango observed that it was Catholic Action adherents, particularly those involved with commercial pursuits, who were most forcefully against the Catholic traditionalists. As these cases illustrate, the relationship of religion to politicoeconomic events perhaps is best understood dialectically rather than as direct cause and effect (Bloch 1986).

The choice to affiliate with Pentecostalism is not unique to the late twentieth century in rural Guatemala. The first conservative Pentecostal missionaries arrived in Guatemala around 1920 (Bogenschild 1992). In these early decades some Mayans abandoned their traditional forms of worship to adopt religious practices centered on the tenets of Protestantism. Recent scholarly work on the Presbyterian missionary efforts in the department of Quetzaltenango in the western highlands attribute the rapid rise in evangelical membership during this period to the disruptive effects of the coffee boom (Cambranes 1985). By 1923 these efforts were yielding a steady stream of converts in rural areas of Quetzaltenango, Retalhuleu, and Suchitepequez, which lie along the fertile coastal plain where land was confiscated for coffee plantations. A network of lay indigenous preachers offered cultos in local languages to residents of villages and fincas.

Thomas Bogenschild (1992) has argued that those prone to conversion were from communities most affected by the social and economic transformations of the period. Diaries and correspondence from one of the early mission workers documented poverty and despair among those seeking affiliation with the church. These papers reveal that impoverished Mayas were turning to Protestantism as a survival strategy. As indigenous campesinos were forced into debt by labor demands and loss of land, some abandoned their participation in the cofradia because of its prohibitive costs. In communities most affected by these processes, withdrawal from cofradia allegiance was another blow to already weakened indigenous social structures. In these circumstances, missionaries assumed some of the traditional social functions of community elders, such as resolving disputes over property rights, inheritance, and local feuds. Nevertheless, Bogenschild contends that "basic cosmological principles were not necessarily abandoned by Mayan converts even if traditional ritual forms of costumbre were dropped" (190).

After the Repression: Religious Pluralism in Xe'caj

In sharp contrast to the small evangelical chapels that have sprung up helter-skelter amid the cornfields, the imposing colonial-style Catholic churches dominate the town squares in the three pueblos of Xe'caj. Inside these churches, decorated altars and saints of the Catholic faith are cared for by the cofradias. In some cases, the saints are dressed in traje of the pueblo. In others, as Jean-Marie Simon has captured in her splendid photography in

Guatemala: Eternal Spring, Eternal Tyranny (1989), some saints in the Ixil Triangle were dressed as soldiers during the worst years of political repression.

Two Catholic priests are responsible for all three of the municipios of Xe'-caj. Padre Juan, who had responsibility for two of the three municipios in the late 1980s, celebrated mass daily in the two pueblos in his domain (one for the cofrades and the other for the Catholic Action members). Although there are small Catholic chapels in most villages, with only one priest to look after such a large population mass was rarely said in the aldeas. Padre Juan, however, traveled most days to some of the aldeas to hear confessions or simply to offer spiritual and social guidance to villagers.

People must walk to the town center, often over difficult terrain, to attend mass and receive the sacraments. Since the changes wrought by Vatican II, mass is said in Spanish rather than Latin, yet for the majority of the population, it remains unintelligible, leaving them alienated from the content of the service. Most priests in Guatemala are either foreign-born or ladinos who speak only Spanish.[15] During the 1970s in a nearby municipio in the department of Chimaltenango, however, several foreign priests did learn the indigenous language, and they, along with two Mayan Catholic priests, said at least one mass every Sunday in Kaqchikel, much to the consternation of local ladinos.[16] Yet even after five centuries of evangelization, few Mayas have become Catholic priests. To become a priest requires years of training, education, and resources often not available to rural Mayas. Carlos Berganza, a Dominican Catholic priest in Guatemala, has argued that Mayan seminarians face the added stress of being trained in Western philosophy and theology that seeks to obliterate their indigenous worldview (as cited in Cleary 1997).

In contrast, one can become an evangelical pastor in less than a year, with little formal training. And while evangelical churches also rant against Mayan ritual practices, the pastor is more likely than not to live in the village as a campesino. Moreover, evangelical pastors are usually local men who pray along with their congregants in Kaqchikel. And the cultos held nightly in the aldeas are highly participatory, with clapping, singing, group prayer, and supplication for daily needs. Although the prayers for salvation are to a Christian god, the prayers may also plead for active intervention in daily life, for rain for the milpa, a good harvest, protection, or assistance with illness and misfortune, much as Mayan prayers do. Following the formal liturgy, Catholics, on the other hand, tend to pray and petition a Christian god for salvation in the afterlife.

The Catholic Church in Xe'caj now comprises a number of different splinter groups: the traditionalist cofradias, orthodox Catholic Action, and the charismatic renewal. During his tenure, Padre Juan tried to maintain close ties with all the groups, Yet tensions, rivalries, and political divisions existed. And in some families, all three groups were represented, with all members claiming to be Catholic.

Few men, and those mostly older, participate in the cofradias in the pueblos. One mayodomo told me that it would cost him Q1000 to meet the responsibilities of honoring the saints that year.[17] Catholic Action adherents and charismatics, like their evangelical counterparts, are opposed to the excessive drinking and expenses that the cofradia imposes, sometimes causing people to go into debt or sell their land to finance these obligations.

The cofradias were once the repositories of power and authority in communities. Yet this folk Catholicism has been in decline in some communities for much of the twentieth century (Rojas Lima 1988). As I noted earlier, the reasons for this are multifold; the challenges came about as a result of both internal and external forces. Cofradias played important social, economic, political, moral, and ritual functions in communities: adjudicating local disputes, allocating use of communally held lands, organizing how political power worked, as well as providing an important space for ritual performance.

With land scarcity increasing exponentially in many communities, along with the loss of local political power as ladinos took office, the once-important social and political functions of the cofradia were seriously undermined. The cofradias, initially a Spanish-colonial imposition, also served as important sites of Mayan cultural production practices. Thus they were both sites of outside domination and spaces where Mayas were able to reshape the meaning of that domination. From the point of view of the colonial Catholic clergy, the cofradias structured religious devotion and provided priests with an income through tributes. Yet even as Mayan traditional rituals and customs were forbidden, public worship led by cofrades continued to be infused with Mayan moral and cultural principles (Farris 1984). Some Mayan communities were able to resist elements of their domination by inverting the traditionally understood notion of syncretism, that is, by reworking non-Mayan cultural features and making them their own. The saints and feast days, for examples, were often aligned with Mayan calendar practices of planting and harvesting corn.

Some scholars assumed that cofradia participation was a dominant factor in the construction of Mayan identity and pointed to its demise as an indication of assimilation into ladino society. Yet rituals themselves, as Bloch (1986) has noted, must be understood as historically situated phenomena. The dissolution of cofradias certainly produced cultural suffering among the Mayas, but it did not of necessity break Mayan ties with their culture. As Gerald Sider has suggested: "[There is] a way of conceptualizing culture that goes beyond the question of the *content* of culture (values, beliefs, symbols, rituals, etc.) and addresses the connection between culture and social relations. The core of culture is the form and manner in which people perceive, define, articulate, and express their mutual relations" (1988:120).

Internal challenges to the cofradia came about through the introduction of Catholic Action by foreign priests with an ideology of orthodox Catholicism that criticized the drinking, pagan rituals, idolatrous worship, and expense of cofradia participation. Nonetheless, many studies attribute the switch of allegiances from traditional Catholicism to Catholic Action to increasing factionalism, feuding, and divisions in communities.

More recently, charismatic groups have sprung up providing a Catholic alternative to fundamentalism. The charismatic members who attend mass and hold nightly cultos in Xe'caj often use the parish hall for their social events and sometimes hold larger prayer meetings. In several aldeas of Xe'caj, many Catholics who were once part of the progressive base communities have become charismatic adherents. While this group too is against the traditional ways of the cofradias, as well as marimba music, dancing, and alcohol consumption, many charismatics and evangelicals continue to honor a Mayan worldview in their daily practices in the milpa and their notions of illness.

In some important aspects, these fundamentalist groups correspond to Mayan notions of community, much as the CBCs did earlier. Membership in these evangelical groups allows people a space for collective expressions of their suffering through passion and emotion. Notwithstanding the fact that the basis of that suffering is now spiritual and mostly devoid of a material analysis, the enigma for analysts is how people who had been politicized previously have been able to put that consciousness aside and become evangelicos. Moreover, in some communities people worship alongside neighbors who were responsible for the deaths or disappearances of their family members. One former catechist theorized that many people who were active in CBCs have certainly changed the expression of their faith—a faith he claims is rooted in a Mayan sense of justice—but they have not forgotten their past. What may make evangelical groups attract so many Mayas is that their notions of faith are grounded in collective work and a sense of community.

Widows and Evangelicos

Cultos, the nightly services of the evangelical churches, allow women a safe haven to participate in communal activities. Most widows comment that the clapping, shouting, and praying integral such services provide a pleasurable diversion. The ritual of the nightly service offers women some emotional respite from the enormous pressures under which they live. The feeling of belonging to a community, being with their neighbors, gives them a sense of ease as they struggle with their grief over what has happened to them and their family members. Moreover, these groups not only provide the widows with emotional and psychological relief but refashion community in a material sense.

Evangelical church members help each other. They work together to build houses, plant and harvest corn, and do other tasks that have traditionally involved men and group efforts. This is a particularly important advantage for the many widows who lost more than just their husbands to the repression. Many also lost brothers, fathers, grandfathers, uncles during the political violence and to hostilities over religion and politics within families. Inside the evangelical congregations, women have opportunities to replace kin-related labor sharing through fictive kin ties with other church members, who often refer to each other as *hermano* (brother) or *hermana* (sister). Not all widows converted, of course. Many remained Catholic. Of those women who did become evangelicos, however, many have had a constant, steady affiliation with a particular denomination.

Shifting Affiliations

Some stories of individual widows will help to destabilize static ideas about how fear operates, the concept of fixed religious identity, and notions about the ways in which religious affiliation may be at odds with an imagined Mayan identity. Attention to their experiences offers new possibilities for understanding the multiplicity of apparently contradictory religious practices that must take into account an indigenous worldview.

One day I met with doña Martina and thirty-five other widows as they were waiting in front of the small Catholic chapel in the village of Be'cal for a relief group to arrive. Representatives of this small church-based project were to distribute beans, dry milk, and a liter of oil to each woman. Dressed in the colorful traje of Be'cal, the women knelt in the shade of a bougainvillea tree, talking in small groups while their children played. "Perhaps they aren't coming today," some began to murmur. They had been waiting for over an hour.

Martina said that not all the widows of Be'cal had agreed to participate in the Catholic project. "They don't want handouts," she said. At first she too was reluctant, until her daughter, also a widow, became so ill that she could no longer work.

Seven years before, Martina had become a member of the Prince of Peace, a church that believes in the power of the Holy Spirit, speaking in tongues, and faith healing. On the advice of neighbors, she joined Prince of Peace to help her son, Pedro, who was drinking heavily. The pastor prayed for him time after time, until he began to sober up. Now Pedro doesn't drink anymore. Martina said she was a Catholic before the violence, when her second husband was alive, but the church does not have specific prayers to help men stop drinking. A Catholic priest had told her simply to trust in God.

This story is not unique: many women in Xe'caj and elsewhere have benefited from the positive social effects resulting from evangelical affiliations. Most notable among these are a decline in alcohol abuse and domestic violence and an increase in the money available for household expenses (Nash 1960; Bossen 1984; Stacey 1990).

Martina was also preoccupied by the illness of her daughter, who had lost so much vitality that she was unable to walk, eat, or work. Believing her daughter to be suffering from susto, Martina went to a Mayan prayermaker for help. She was especially concerned because her first husband had died from susto some years before. Her second husband had been kidnapped in 1982, when heavily armed strangers in civilian dress came to the house and took him away. No one knows why. He never returned, joining the innumerable Guatemalans who have been disappeared by government-backed death squads.

Martina saw no contradiction in being a member of the Prince of Peace congregation, seeking out a Mayan healer for her daughter's suffering, and accepting relief aid from the Catholic Church. She knew that some people in her church criticized her superstitions as well as her lack of exclusive allegiance to the Prince of Peace Church. Martina responded to these allegations, however, with aplomb, merely stating that "cada cabeza tiene su propio mundo" (each person sees the world differently). Fear alone did not drive Martina to join the Pentecostal church; rather, it was a sense of peace, she said, that sustained her commitment.

I first met Elena in 1989, when she was twenty-five years old, five years after her husband, José, had been killed in front of her and her two children. She lives with her mother, Marcelina, and her sister-in-law, both also widows, in Ri Bay. All three women regularly attend the services of the Church of God. A year after we met, Elena asked my field assistant, Sophia, and me to help baptize her youngest child, only a few months old. At first I was bewildered. Why couldn't she make the arrangements herself? It turned out that Elena wanted to baptize the child in the Catholic Church, just as her two older children had been, to make her strong and healthy. The baptism was meant as a protective blessing for the child's well-being here and now; it was not about cleansing the soul of original sin for salvation in the next life. Yes, she said, there are baptisms in the Church of God, at the age of decision (around ten years old), but that is not what she wanted. Catholics bless children soon after birth, just as the young corn is blessed soon after harvest.

We set up the baptism for her, but not at the local parish. The priest there, Padre Juan, would not have objected—in fact he did not—but Elena knew some of her evangelical neighbors would protest. After the baptism, Elena, her two children, Sophia, and myself went to Sophia's house in another pueblo, where her mother and sisters had prepared a special lunch to celebrate. The next day, we returned to Ri Bay, where Elena continued to attend Church of God worship services.

While it is true that some widows go to services out of fear of local reprisals, this explanation does not sufficiently uncover the dilemmas that the women face as they try to make sense of their present circumstances. Elena, like doña Martina, drew on all the resources available to her in her struggles to survive with her children.

Unlike Martina and many of the other widows who are now practicing evangelicals, doña Alejandra was never a Catholic. She was raised in the Central American Mission Church in her pueblo; her father was one of the early converts to the CAM in the 1940s. Alejandra said she does not know why he converted, but for years her family was one of only a few in her village who were evangelical. Yet in 1987 Alejandra joined El Grupo, the Protestant base community described in chapter 5 that interprets the Bible in a radically different way from the CAM. The women who gather together weekly talk about their sufferings and sorrows, the underlying causes, and ways in which they might work together to change their situations. At one such meeting in November 1989 the widows formed a circle of prayer, holding hands and crying as they spoke of the tragedy of the six Jesuit priests, their housekeeper, and her daughter who had been killed by Salvadoran death squads and related it to their own stories.

Alejandra continued her membership in the CAM. She saw no contradiction between the two forms of Christianity. She said the widow's group sought ways to redress social injustices, while the church services "calma mi corazon"(relieve my heart). Since the day her husband was kidnapped, Alejandra said, she had been sad and her head ached with worry. Like her late husband, Alejandra's oldest son had a drinking problem and at times became violent toward her. She moved between the widows' group and the CAM seeking refuge and hope in a self-styled community.

Mayan Worldview

In 1992, while something known as the Salvation of the Americas was being celebrated, a Catholic priest arrived in a community located deep in the mountains of Chiapas.

Before mass, he held confession. In the Mayan language Tojolabal, the Indians recounted their sins to the priest. Carlos Lenkersdorf translated as best he could those confessions, one after the other, even though he knew full well that there was no way he was able to translate their mysteries.

He said that he had abandoned the corn, translated Carlos. He said the milpa was very sad. It had been many days since he had gone to the milpa.

She said that she had mistreated the fire. The flame was allowed to go out and now the fire didn't burn well. She suffers.

He said that he had profaned the path, while walking with his machete in hand he had cut everything around him without reason.

He said that he felled a tree and he had not explained to the tree why.

He said he had mistreated his bull.

The priest did not know what to do with these sins, sins that do not figure into the commandments of Moses.

—Eduardo Galeano, *The Sinners*

When I started my field work in Xe'caj, I asked people about their religious affiliations. When no one mentioned anything about Mayan religion, I asked them directly.[18] Most often the question was met by silence, but when people did respond they said that there were bone setters, calendar readers, prayermakers, or healers elsewhere, but none of these practitioners lived in Xe'caj. What I had not realized at the time is that my question was unanswerable for many people because they did not regard their perceptions of the world—about life, the universe, and fundamental human problems—as grounded in a Mayan religion per se. Yet their comprehension of how the world works and their own place in the universe, at least in part, continues to be rooted in a collective cultural legacy of the past. Even when some individuals have adopted the Catholic or evangelical faith, the cultural reality of their daily lives is circumscribed by a conception of the natural world and their place in it.[19] Over the course of my stay in Xe'caj, I encountered a number of people like doña Martina and her daughter, ill with susto, who were either Catholic or evangelical yet whose ideas regarding ill health and misfortune, for example, continued to express an indigenous reality.

While many individuals have indeed rejected an indigenous cosmovision (worldview) over the last five centuries, a Mayan worldview still persists, as evidenced by the daily practices of rural campesinos. And since 1992, when indigenous groups from all over the Americas met in Guatemala to protest a celebration of the Conquest,[20] an explicit Mayan religion and its attendant rituals have taken on a more public face alongside, and at times part of, a pan-Mayan movement (Fisher and Brown 1997).

More important for this discussion, however, is the ways in which a Mayan view of the world infuses the daily lives of many Mayan campesinos, and in this sense I argue that their religion is a living enterprise, as evidenced by their food, medicine, agricultural activities, weavings, and notions of time and community service. While Mayan beliefs and spiritual practices have clearly changed over time, subject to the influences of outside culture as well as socioeconomic factors, a Mayan spirituality has been maintained in quotidian life, theorized through a relationship between human beings and the natural and supernatural worlds, and lived through practices that encompass land, kinship, and community. These relationships are explicitly expressed in the sacred book of the Maya-K'iche, and while most rural Mayas today have never read the Popuh Vuh, the values and practices it espouses remain to some extent visible in Mayan rural communities. These ties to their history though practice have been crucial for Mayas in giving shape and meaning to their present world.

In a Mayan worldview, the natural world—the earth, mountains, trees, rivers, fire, plants—is not comprised of objects to be dominated but rather elements that exist in harmony with human beings. One's relationship to the natural world is expressed through work, such as growing corn and weaving cloth. The supernatural world and those forces beyond human control are embodied within the natural world. Many Mayas believe that only by respecting and honoring the gods and spirits that embody the natural world are they able to maintain a semblance of harmony and avert adversity in their lives. Today, many Mayas are struggling to find an arena to manifest their faith that often involves multiple expressions: Catholic, Protestant, and Mayan.

Debates in Mesoamerican anthropology about the nature of ethnicity and identity have for the most part centered on an either/or understanding of Mayan identity and tradition. Yet neither an essentialist nor relativist point of view alone captures fully the ways in which Mayas have maintained continuity with their past under the impact of violence, be it colonialism's or modernity's. Perhaps the cultural responses of some Mayan widows to the most recent political violence provide insights into how these processes may work.

Evangelical churches, although never dominant in rural Guatemala, have been present for decades. The fundamentalism they promote is neither a religion of repression, although initially it was for many, nor a religion of advancement, although it has been for a few. As a religion of survival and a refuge from suffering, it offers a space in which people, especially widows, are able to reclaim some personal and social control over their lives, however partial. Community social relations in Xe'caj have been severely fractured. The plethora of female-headed households, civil patrols, military garrisons, increasing lawlessness and immigration, alcoholism, factionalism among community leaders, and local as well as state violence all take their toll on familial and community social organization. Within these fissures evangelical churches have proliferated.

Although these churches may fill some of the social gaps resulting from the disarray of community structures, that fact that the women move back and forth between churches and denominations suggests that the various groups meet the women's needs only partially. The fluidity with which the women cross religious boundaries points to the pragmatic approach they have adopted as they struggle to survive. They see no particular epistemological contradiction in this mobility. They make their choices from available options, trying to recapture piecemeal elements of community—trust, cooperation, communalism, dignity, and justice—through permissible institutions in a militarized society.

For many of the widows in Xe'caj, affiliations with Western religious systems, be they Catholic or Protestant, are not necessarily at odds with a Mayan cultural reality or an indigenous identity. While Western ideological constructions of the world and one's place in it may theoretically contradict a Mayan approach, the processes I am describing here point to some Mayan widows as active agents in the reconstruction of their lives, drawing on both the remade past as well as undeniable influences of the present.

FIGURE 8.1
Women on Good Friday. (*Jonathan Moller*)

8. mutual betrayal and collective dignity

The primary preoccupation of this study has been to explicate the survival tactics utilized by Mayan widows in the aftermath of a brutal counterinsurgency war waged in Guatemala in the late 1970s and early 1980s. Yet by necessity this work encompasses something more. Its central enigma has been the simultaneity of mutual betrayal and collective dignity among Mayas in the villages of Xe'caj. An exploration of the complexities of the lived lives of some ordinary Mayan women whose husband were killed or disappeared during the repression—their consciousness, experiences, and feelings, processes that Raymond Williams has called "structures of feeling" (1977:132)—and the multiplicity of practices within which repression and terror operated reveals the subtle and not so subtle ways in which some people have responded to the heterogeneity of violence.

This story, however, does not have a neat conclusion. In fact, the tensions that exist in the narratives and in the lived realities of the women are in the end not easily resolvable, either theoretically or politically. The aim of the work has been to begin thinking dialectically about complex issues central to the anthropological enterprise, issues of culture, community, violence, suffering, and identity. As a political project, my ambition has been to give the reader a sense experience of Mayan widows, their being-in-the-world, that is partial in both senses of the word—"not whole" and "taking sides"—that contributes to possibilities of political engagement with suffering and with social justice.

On Contradictions

My initial understanding of the counterinsurgency war and repression that took place in Guatemala in the late 1970s and early 1980s was based on the numerous human rights reports as well as the few scholarly writings available at the time that documented the atrocities of that war. I went to Guatemala to capture the survival strategies of Mayan widows. Once I began my fieldwork, however, I was confronted with disturbing stories of how violence operated locally. Some of the widows told me that they knew who had denounced their husbands to the army as subversives. And then there was doña Tomasa, whose son was a member of the elite Kabile forces, self-proclaimed killing machines. And the case of ten-year-old Marcos, who spoke of the death of his father at the hands of civil patrollers from the community. One of the men responsible lived up the hill from him, and they often passed each other on village trails. Marcos remarked that although they were neighbors and greeted each other, they were not able to talk about what happened.

Within this nexus of victim-survivor-victimizer I have attempted to explicate the lived reality of some rural Mayan campesinos during the most recent brutal period in their history. Bertell Ollman's (1990:49) insight on contradiction—"a union of two or more internally related processes that are simultaneously supporting and undermining of one another"—is particularly useful in trying to discern this complicated story. The inextricable relationships between structural and political violence, between domination and resistance, between continuity and rupture are integral in thinking about how some Mayas were able to commit acts of violence and brutality against one another during the worst years of repression without talking about Mayas in a profoundly racist way, as the violent Other. In a related vein, I have tried to describe a collective dignity that is also palpable among people in Mayan communities without falling into the trap of romanticizing the Other, attempting to capture their dignity in a way that is not demeaning to them as human beings.

On Violence and Suffering

Community has always been an integral expression of Mayan culture, the space and place of their domination as well as the locus of struggle and contestation. Violence, in its myriad forms, has permeated Mayan social spaces, social relations, and social institutions for more than five centuries. While domination has remained a central facet of their lives, the forms and meaning of that domination have shifted profoundly over time. Although indigenous communities have been reshaped by differing structures of inequality since the Conquest, they continued to be rooted in kin-based social relations. The Mayas have refashioned those spaces in ways that allowed them to endure as a people and a culture. And in this penumbra one may begin to grapple with the historical implications of blood on people's hands.

Social suffering too took many forms. The suffering produced by poverty, hunger, disease, and death were readily observable. However, the ways in which the fragile, intricate bonds that held communities together were severed by violence, both structural and political, were not so easily discernible. Anthropologists for the most part have tended to report but not to analyze the effects and meanings of suffering on people's everyday lives, neglecting how racism, cultural imperialism, marginalization, exploitation, and powerlessness shape people's identities.

For much of the last five centuries Mayan principles of reciprocal aid and obligation to both the living and the dead, based on a relationship with land, continued to be expressed through practical activities of survival and cultural symbols such as corn production and consumption. Through work, whether weaving cloth or growing corn, Mayas have produced and re-created the bases of their material and cultural survival. And that survival was understood at least in part as a collective enterprise. By the turn of the twentieth century, with land becoming increasingly scarce, the interstitial tissue of communities—the bonds created, for example, by the cofradias and extended family networks—came under increasing strain. Land was the vital link both materially and culturally in forming community bonds. In many communities semi-subsistence production and processes of commodification led to the breakdown of local indigenous social organization such as the cofradias and extended family and kin networks. Although far from egalitarian in either class or gendered terms, the social relations that formed the basis of these institutions helped mediate between individual and community cooperation and opportunism. Their eventual breakdown created spaces in which internal political violence could operate. Contemporary Mayas are not a creation or a simple legacy of colonialism or a continuation of the preconquest period; rather, Mayan culture falls within the intersection of the vectors of difference and sameness, rupture and continuity. Some anthropologists have argued that Mayan practices such as planting corn and weaving cloth can be traced back to preconquest times, but in the late twentieth century the meanings people give to material and cultural production are different from those given in the early sixteenth. The increasing loss of ancestral lands—in the context of an ancestor-centered religious praxis—is just one of the complex ways in which meanings fracture and are reshaped through structural violence. In the last half of the twentieth century—particularly during the almost three decades of war—these processes have only intensified.

Throughout this book I have examined the innumerable contradictions that arise out of social-historical processes, for example, the profound effects on individuals and communities of what I have called the doubleness of racism, when it is internalized and thus lending itself to lethal consequences. As Raymond Williams so poignantly described it, "Right back inside the oppressed and deprived community there are reproduced elements of the thinking and the feeling of that dominating centre" (1989:117).

The widows themselves were simultaneously victims and survivors of the war. As victims they witnessed the brutal disappearances or deaths of their husbands and other loved ones. Much of the violence was gendered, in that many of those killed were men, but for the women and children who lived, survival is a complicated affair. The violence had a double edge to it: not only were people killed, but there was an attempt to kill the spirits of the people who remained alive. Some widows, however, have embodied the violence in their minds and bodies, in "*memorias de sangre*," blood memories that run through their veins and create a division felt in the body, a break in the continuum of their lives, a before and after, while keeping the past literally alive in the present. For other women, it is better to struggle to survive alone, as the effects of structural violence take their toll on relations between men and women.

Violence is embedded not only in the social landscape—the very communities that had been sites of refuge for many now shelter some of the perpetrators of terror: the soldiers, civil patrollers, and military commissioners—but also within the geographical landscape. There are estimated to be thousands of clandestine cemeteries dotting the altiplano. In Xe'caj some women claimed that under one of the football fields in a center of the pueblo is a large mass grave. The political violence was aimed at destroying community, the very fabric out of which Mayas have constructed their relations to each other.

On Dignity

What I have come to think of as dignity is not easily articulated but was palpable in the everyday life in the villages of Xe'caj, and its expressions took on a myriad of subtle forms. By dignity I mean a presence in the world and, in the particular instance of Mayan widows, a reassertion of boundaries of humanness under extraordinary circumstances. In their everyday lives many of the widows denied terror its power by expressing a caring and concern for one another and their neighbors, as well as for strangers, in the face of ongoing brutality and increasing misery. They established new kin networks that transcended the usual notions of family and community as a basis for a reemerging solidarity among them. Survival was not only about individuals per se but also about rebuilding a sense of community. The widows of Xe'caj spoke frequently not only about their economic needs but also about their right to be recognized as human beings with dignity. Within a climate of fear and militarization some widows reworked spaces to reaffirm social relations and cultural values in which they regarded survival as a collective enterprise, even as the development projects there to assist them ignored their knowledge and creativity. Some widows of Xe'caj constructed alternative forms of community in the midst of their suffering that speak powerfully to the resiliency of the human spirit. They used the space of development projects, their own bodies, and those of evangelical worship to reinvigorate community and kin networks by pushing the limits of permissible spaces in a militarized society. As such, Mayan widows have rewoven their "traditions"—their "Mayaness"—out of the fabric of violence.

On Impunity

The most recent brutal period of violence against the Mayas in Guatemala is neither an aberration nor a blip in the historical record. The dirty war in Guatemala is a piece of a whole that extends from the arrival of the Spanish conquistador Pedro de Alvarado in the early 1500s to the present period of so-called peace when the poor—Mayas and ladinos alike—are dying everyday from not only the hunger and misery produced by the ravages of capitalism but also the ongoing state repression in the twin guises of delinquent crime and death squad activity. Cheap labor remains vital to the well-being of the Guatemala elite much as it did for the survival of the colonialists, and violence in its myriad forms is the means that continues to be used to procure that labor.

A war continues in Guatemala today, even though it is a war called peace. The 1996 Peace Accords failed to address the fundamental problems in Guatemalan society, those of land and impunity. Poverty and hunger stalk the well-being of almost 90 percent of the population, and impunity reigns. There has been no accountability at the national level of the intellectual authors of the war and repression. Moreover, violence continues locally. In one community near Xe'caj in 1997 some poor campesinos were kidnapped out of their milpa. A Q5000 ransom was demanded and paid. Eventually the family was released. Yet a month after the incident they continued to be harassed and were afraid to work their milpas. They know who had done it: local men tied to the military barracks nearby.

Such violence and impunity have become deeply embedded in daily life. And those who do speak out against injustice, be they in positions of authority or campesino organizers, often meet the same fate as Bishop Gerardi, who was murdered two days after leading the public presentation of *Guatemala: Nunca mas* (Guatemala: Never again). Without accountability, violence thrives. In the communities of Xe'caj today, as elsewhere in Guatemala, fear remains a way of life.

notes

1. In the Aftermath of War

1. The altiplano (or the western highlands) is where the majority of the Mayan population live, and 90 percent of the population of the altiplano is Mayan Indian.

2. Counterinsurgency, or "dirty wars," involves campaigns of "state-sponsored terror and repression deliberately carried out against suspected civilian populations" (Nordstrom and Martin 1992:261) that in many but not all cases have been the base of support for guerrilla struggles. In Guatemala, for example, this far-reaching strategy includes not only the defeat of the armed insurgency and the destruction of its civilian support but also a program of pacification of the civilian population in general. Horror, fear, and spectacle, along with murder and brutality, are some of the weapons of control used against the population. Specifically in Guatemala these take the form of disappearances (see n. 3, below), large population displacements as a result of "scorched-earth campaigns" that burn and raze villages, massacres, local civil militias, and model villages that severely restrict population movement (see Barry 1986; Jordahl 1987).

3. "To disappear" literally means to vanish, and in Guatemala, where the usage was first converted into a participle, "to be disappeared" means to be kidnapped by the

security forces. In Xe'caj, people describe how heavily armed men wearing civilian clothes and masks would grab family members or neighbors whose mutilated, tortured bodies might later be found along a roadside or in a ravine. Most of the disappeared are never seen again, alive or dead, leaving the other family members in a liminal state between hope and despair. According to the Argentine Forensic Anthropology Team's biannual report, "More people have been forcibly disappeared in Guatemala during the past four decades than in any other Latin American country" (EAAF 1996:71).

Contrary to the more conservative figure I quote in the text, Suzanne Jonas (1991) contends that 200,000 dead and disappeared is a reasonable estimate based on available information. America's Watch and Amnesty International tend to shy away from quoting precise numbers, instead referring more generally to "untold numbers" of dead and disappeared. One reason for this vagueness is that no fully developed infrastructure exists for collecting such data. In addition, documentation of human rights violations continues to be risky business. For example, in July 1996 the coordinator of the Guatemalan Forensic Anthropology Team received several death threats and was forced into exile. The EAFG—its Spanish acronym—has been conducting exhumations of mass graves in the Guatemalan countryside. In April 1998 Bishop Juan Gerardi was assassinated just two days after the release of a human rights report from the Guatemalan Archdiocesan Office of Human Rights.

4. PAVYH was a special project mandated by the Guatemalan Congress in 1987 with an appropriation of 10 million quetzals (approximately US$3.5 million at 1987 exchange rates), administered through the Ministry of Special Affairs. A pilot program was started in the department of Chimaltenango in 1988; by 1989 the first phase of the project had been completed in all fourteen departments covered by the program. The project consisted of three phases: a census, a food distribution program, and the initiation of small-scale village projects.

5. The civil patrol system was created in 1982 and by 1985 constituted a rural militia of more than one million men, more than half the highland male population over fifteen years of age. The PACs, as they were known, functioned to augment military strength and intelligence in areas of conflict; their primary purpose, however, was to provide vigilance and control over the local population (America's Watch 1986; Stoll 1993). In 1990 the PACs were officially renamed Civil Self-Defense Patrols (CVDC). Although the Guatemalan constitution stated explicitly that the CVDCs were voluntary, failure to participate in them or opposition to their formation often led to being marked as a subversive, subjected to subsequent harassment, and, on some occasions, being killed. In the early 1990s the CVDCs comprised about 500,000 men. Members were unpaid, scantily armed, and poorly trained. Local men were required to patrol their communities for long shifts every four to fifteen days, depending on the size of the community and the degree of attention deemed necessary by the army. Members of the CVDC have been implicated in numerous rural human rights violations (Baranyi and Loughan 1995).

Military commissioners were local men, many of whom had been in the army. In villages they served as local recruiters and spies for the army as well as coordinators for the local civil militia. The program, instituted nationwide in the 1960s, was one of the initial steps in the militarization of rural areas (Adams 1970). The military commissioner position was officially discontinued in July 1995.

6. Recent notable works by anthropologists on suffering include Scheper-Hughes 1992, 1996; Farmer 1992; Kleinman, Das, and Lock 1997.

7. On peasant studies, in particular see de Janvry 1981; Mallon 1983; Roseberry 1983, 1989; Scott 1985; Shanin 1987; G. Smith 1989; Stavenhagen 1978; Wolf 1955, 1957, 1966, 1969, 1982; and Wolpe 1980. On households and reproduction, see in particular Beneria and Roldan 1987; Deere 1977, 1990; Dwyer and Bruce 1988; Folbre 1986; Guyer and Peters 1987; Hartmann 1981; and Young, Wolkowitz, and McCullagh 1981.

8. In 1989 to clear and plant three to four cuerdas in Xe'caj would take two men three to four days. The cost was Q5 per man per day, plus lunch, and often totaled Q30 to Q40 ($10 to $15). In 1989 the exchange rate was approximately $1 to Q3. A cuerda in Xe'caj is a twenty-by-twenty-feet plot of land. On average, the widows I interviewed earned Q10 to Q15 per week.

9. In 1989 a 100-pound bag of 20–20 fertilizer cost Q28 to Q30; 1996 prices were Q90 to Q100, with the exchange rate at around six quetzals to the U.S. dollar.

10. I draw extensively in the section from Diane Wolf's inspiring edited collection, *Feminist Dilemmas in Fieldwork* (1996).

11. The area of Xe'caj includes three *municipios* (townships) and their surrounding *aldeas* (villages) in Chimaltenango Department with a combined estimated population of 50,000.

12. The military authorities knew where I was working and with whom. On beginning my work, following the advice of an experienced ethnographer, I went to the army base in Chimaltenango to introduce myself and my work to the base commander, as well as to the governor of the department. I also periodically obtained written permission to work in the area of Xe'caj from the commandantes of the local garrison, a relationship I describe in more detail in chapter 3.

13. See Sherry Ortner's thoughtful essay "Resistance and the Problem of Ethnographic Refusal" (1995), in which she discusses the "ethnographic stance" and the problems of fieldwork and writing

14. See Clifford 1988; Clifford and Marcus 1986; Marcus and Fischer 1986; Fox 1991; for thoughtful critique, see McClintock 1994.

2. The Altiplano

1. The altiplano, or the western highlands, where 90 percent of the indigenous population lives, make up about a third of the national territory.

2. The four major ethnic groups in Guatemala are Maya, Xinca, Garifuna, and Ladino.

3. The departments are Chimaltenango, Quiche, Solala, Quetzaltenango, Totonicapan, Huehuetenango, Alta Vera Paz, and Baja Vera Paz.

4. Chronic malnutrition has serious short-term and long-term consequences for children under five in Guatemala. The two leading causes of death among children under five are respiratory infections and diarrheal disease. Repeated diarrheal episodes lead to a vicious cycle of malnutrition and morbidity that leaves young children susceptible to a host of other infectious diseases; additionally, many suffer long-term effects: immature physical, emotional, and cognitive development.

5. See Martinez Pelaez 1979.

6. The INGUAT (Guatemalan National Tourism Institute) *Bulletin* (1997) reports that the tourism sector ranks second to coffee in terms of national economic revenues generated, followed by sugar, bananas, cardamom, meat, and cotton, in that order.

7. Martinez Pelaez has noted that the first *mestizaje* (mixed-blood) unions were "biological unions based on profound human disunion and inequality" (1979:355–60, as cited in Smith 1995:732).

8. Most Guatemalan elites consider themselves biologically white (although this is unlikely) and culturally European.

9. See Jean-Marie Simon's exquisitely photographed book, *Guatemala: Land of Eternal Spring, Eternal Tyranny* (1989).

10. According to the human rights report issued by REMHI (the Interdiocesan Recuperation of the Historic Memory Project) in April 1998, three out of every four victims of the violence were Mayan Indians. At least 30 percent of the victims belonged to an organized civilian group, and 92 percent of the victims who participated in some organization were civilians. Half the victims who participated in an organization belonged to a religious group, and one in every five belonged to a community group.

11. An excerpt from an address by General Juan Jose Marroquin S. to a graduating class of Kaibiles on December 6, 1989, is revealing: "Kaibil officers are trained to forget all humanitarian principles and to become war machines, capable of enduring whatever sacrifices, because from now on they will be called Masters of War and Messengers of Death" (author translation, as reported in the Guatemalan daily newspaper, *La Hora*, December 7, 1989).

12. In the REMHI report (1998), rape is mentioned as a feature of one out of every six massacres analyzed. Rape even in the West is notoriously underreported by victims in part because of the shame and stigma attached. According to studies, only one out of every five rapes that occurs in the West is actually reported. Certainly, the same level of underreporting, perhaps more, could be assumed to be the case for women in rural Guatemala. Domestic violence is similarly underreported. There are no reliable statistics on its incidence, yet over the past decade Guatemalan women's groups have been somewhat successful in making the problem a public issue.

13. The settlers were called *criollos*, Spaniards born in the New World, and *peninsulares*, Spanish residents of the New World born in Spain (Hill 1992).

14. *Encomiendas* were tributes of Indian labor and payments in kind and cash granted by the Spanish Crown to colonists as a reward for services rendered. *Repartimiento* were labor drafts from Indian Towns for colonial agriculture. Both were subject to widespread abuse by the colonists. See Lovell 1992.

15. Even though the form of the state changed from colonial to post-colonial, Mayas continued to be denied full citizenship until well into the twentieth century.

16. The *latifundia/minifundia* land tenancy was the necessary backbone that allowed this exploitative labor system to function. The highland Mayas spent most of the year working their small subsistence farms, where they were able to provide for their own livelihoods, meager though these were, particularly as access to land diminished. The *finca* (plantation) owners were thus relieved of the necessity of paying a living wage to a full-time workforce. Mayas were pressed into service on the large plantations only at harvest time. Initially the lati/mini system allowed for extensive exploitation of cheap labor by the latifundistas because the Mayas could subsist on the production of their own plots. Later, with population pressures, most families had to supplement their corn harvests with wage labor. In time the wages earned from work on the fincas in fact financed subsistence corn production in the highlands (de Janvry 1981). Simultaneously, however, work on the coffee fincas had a devastating impact on traditional subsistence economy. Each year plantation work took large numbers of men away from their communities and subsistence plots, making it difficult for them to tend their land properly and thus leading to low yields. A vicious cycle ensued, whereby the low yields that made it more difficult to meet subsistence needs led workers to spend more time supplementing their production through outside labor, which in turn caused them to neglect their own farms even more.

17. The 1952 Agrarian Reform Law had a substantial impact on United Fruit Company lands on the south coast. Under the conditions of the reform almost 400,000 acres of United Fruit plantation lands were expropriated and redistributed to peasants. United Fruit protested on two counts: it needed fallow lands because of the high prevalence of tropical diseases and its self-declared tax evaluation was not adequate compensation for the land expropriated. Allen Dulles was head of the CIA at the time, while his brother, John Foster Dulles, was a board member of United Fruit. Political pressure was put on the Eisenhower administration from United Fruit. Soon after a plan called "Operation Success" was conceived to overthrow the reformist Arbenz administration; it was subsequently launched by the CIA (Handy 1984; Schlesinger and Kinzer 1982; Immerman 1982). Although it was not the sole reason for the United States' decision to join with domestic opposition in staging a coup against Arbenz—the U.S. concern with the presence of communists in the Arbenz government was another factor—United Fruit's influence added impetus for doing so. Gleijeses (1991) has argued that there is no single villain to blame; rather, the coup stemmed from a complex interplay of economic, social, and political forces, both domestic and international in scope.

18. See Rigoberta Menchu's testimony, *I, Rigoberta Menchu* (Burgos-Debray 1983), for an poignant description of a Mayan family's migratory experiences.

19. In 1994 ANACAFE—the National Association of Coffee Exporters of Guatemala—and labor signed an agreement whereby the owners of coffee plantations would raise wages by 30 percent, from US$1.96 per day to US$2.54, as well as improve the living and working conditions on the plantations.

20. Nontraditional agricultural export production actually began in the altiplano in the late 1970s. Recognizing the need for and the impossibility of land reform, USAID began promoting nontraditional, high-value exports for small rural farmers as a way to increase productivity on small plots of land. The village of Chimachoy, in San Andreas Itzapa, began export production in the 1970s and by the early 1980s was considered a success story. The village was also the site of intensive organizing by lay workers involved in forming base communities (CBCs). Both efforts, however, were cut short by a massacre during the same period. Land was the central issue in each case: with contract farming, there were major changes in relations of production and, in the case of CBCs focusing on social justice issues including land ownership, processes were under way that questioned relations of power.

21. According to Watts 1992, snow peas are "almost six time more labor-absorptive than cultivation of the local staple, maize (613 days per hectare as opposed to 119 days per hectare for maize)" (79).

22. Tax (1937) identified two distinct types of municipios; the "vacant town," "which had practically no permanent Indian residents" (427), and the "town-nucleus," "where practically all of the people live in the town"(431).

23. Lovell and Lutz (1992) note that today the Mayan population of Guatemala is more than twice what is was at the time of European contact, "a trajectory of survival experienced by no other Native American population" (1). From 1520 until 1640, however, there was a precipitous decline in the population—some estimates place the loss at as high as 90 percent of the pre-contact population—as a result of warfare, culture shock, slavery, exploitation, and the introduction of Old World diseases (Cook and Lovell 1992). Population recovery began during the first half of the seventeenth century.

24. McCreery (1994) notes that it was during this period that highland agriculture became less diverse as Mayas turned exclusively to growing the milpa crops that required less care.

25. President Ubico abolished debt peonage in 1934, replacing it with the Vagrancy Law. Even before its abolition, debt peonage had not been in effect for some period of time in terms of labor control. The law changed all that. If a campesino had four manzanas (approximately six acres) of corn under cultivation and two harvests per year, he was exempt from labor service. If not, the new vagrancy law required that those who planted ten or more cuerdas were required to work at least 100 days per year on fincas, while those with less than ten cuerdas were required to work 150 days per year. All agricultural workers were required to keep a passbook that noted the number of days worked per year and was signed by employers. If a man (women were exempt) was caught as a vagrant he was fined or jailed (McCreery 1994). Most campesinos did not have sufficient land for exemption.

26. Rossell asserted: "Today [the Indian population] is a tame and long suffering lamb, but it is very easy to turn it into a cruel wolf, or a ravenous lion, or a poisonous snake" (Rossell 1949, as cited in Warren 1978:89)

27. In later statements, particular after 1954, Rossell began to promote projects that would improve the local economic and social conditions of the rural poor without challenging the status quo (Handy 1984; Warren 1979)

28. In some cases community members joined the Peasant Unity Committee (CUC), which had at least an implicit link with the armed opposition. Others went to the mountains to become active members of the guerrilla forces.

29. See Deborah Levenson-Estrada's discussion of the formative role of Catholic Action in the subsequent politization of Coca Cola union leaders in Guatemala City in *Trade Unionists Against Terror* (1994).

30. By 1990 the exchange rate of Guatemalan currency had fallen to Q5 to US$1.

3. Living in a State of Fear

1. Connerton (1989:12) has defined social memory as "images of the past that commonly legitimate a present social order," created out of social activity of commemorative ceremonies and bodily practices. In Guatemala, fear inculcated into the social memory has engendered a forced acquiescence to the status quo on the part of many Mayas. At the same time, a distinctly Mayan (counter) social memory exists and is expressed through concepts of time and space, for example, the indigenous dances, especially the dance of the conquest, oral narratives, the relationship with the antepasados maintained through the planting of corn, the weaving of cloth, and religious ceremonies.

2. Fear of strangers is not a new phenomenon in Guatemala. In the late 1940s, Maude Oakes, in her study of Todos Santos (1951), reported that local people were reluctant to talk with the few strangers who came to the community. She too was treated with suspicion at the beginning of her fieldwork, and she never did develop a rapport of trust with some, a common experience for most fieldworkers. Since the last wave of violence, however, community loyalties have been divided, and a level of distrust previously unknown has permeated social life. A climate of suspiciousness prevails in many villages. Olivia Carrescia's two ethnographic films (1982, 1989), made before and after the violence in Todos Santos, document some of the profound changes wrought by systematic state terror.

3. For example, between 1969 and 1991, according to the Academic Records Section of the School of the Americas, there have been over 500 Guatemalan military officers trained at the School of the Americas (SOA) (Dept. of Defense 1992). According to the REMHI report (1998), SOA graduates were well represented in the presidential cabinets of Lucas Garcia (1978–1982) and Rios Montt (1982–1983). Additionally, SOA graduates were working in the Guatemalan Intelligence Agency (D2), which, according to the REMHI report, was responsible for systematic human rights viola-

tions such as extrajudicial executions and assassinations. SOA graduate Benedicto Lucas Garcia, minister of defense under his brother, then president Romero Lucas Garcia, created the civil patrol system, and SOA graduates have been implicated in several of high-profile human rights cases and the assassinations of Myrna Mack, Michael Devine, Mincho, and Bácama.

4. A partial list of countries where state terror has proliferated since the 1960s includes Argentina, Bangladesh, Brazil, Burundi, the Central African Republic, Chile, East Timor, El Salvador, Guatemala, Haiti, Indonesia, Kampuchea, the Philippines, South Africa, Uganda, and Uruguay.

5. See Scary's (1985:5) discussion on the inexpressibility of physical pain. While Scary contends that it is only physical pain that can be characterized with no "referential content, it is not of or for anything," I would argue differently. The power of terror of the sort that is endemic in Guatemala and in much of Latin America lies precisely in its subjectification and silence.

6. The presence of the civil patrols in communities has turned petty feuding into a conduit for vigilante justice, of which Paul and Demarest (1988) and Montejo (1987) provide exemplary descriptions. As Aguayo (1983:2) has pointed out, in Guatemala counterinsurgency does not stop at the killing of real or imagined enemies, it "obliges the peasant to violate the human rights of the other peasant, it seeks not only victims but accomplices."

7. When insurgents first appeared in the eastern part of Guatemala in the 1960s as a result of an unsuccessful military rebellion, a repressive state apparatus was already in place. Between 1966 and 1968 an estimated 6,000 to 8,000 peasants were killed in a government campaign against 500 insurgents. Subsequently, in an attempt to improve the relationship between the military and the rural population and to eliminate local support for the insurgency, a program of military and civil action was introduced into rural areas under the guidance of U.S. advisers. Many of these development projects in road building, health, and education were financed by USAID and were located in areas where social inequalities were particularly acute and support for the popular forces the strongest. In 1982 the army created a civic affairs department (S-5) to promote development. In an 1987 interview, Colonel Mario Enrique Morales, then head of the department, stated: "We now understand that we can gain more with civic action than with war. This represents a very profound change in the military mentality in the Guatemalan Army, and in this we are being original, we are not copying models. . . . We have done all of this by ourselves, without foreign advice" (AVANCSO 1988:53).

8. Ignacio Martin-Baro, along with five other Jesuit priests, their housekeeper, and her daughter, were assassinated by government soldiers in San Salvador, El Salvador, in November 1989. For an English volume of his work, see Adrianne Aron and Shawn Corne, eds., *Writings for a Liberation Psychology* (1994).

9. A notable example of this is CONAVIGUA (National Coordination of Guatemalan Widows), which was started initially by widows from several villages who made demands to the state for survival assistance: food, medicine, clothing, and

housing. The organization, composed mostly of rural Mayan widows, first publicly presented itself in September 1988 at the first National Assembly of Widowed Women, where a nine-member directorate was elected. Several of the directorate members had been members of socially active groups such as communidades bases—Christian base communities—in their communities prior to the violence (Schirmer 1993).

10. Mersky (1989) identified two major camps within the ruling coalition consisting of the army, the civilian bourgeoisie, and politicians, the traditionalists and the modernists, while Jonas (1991) described four sources of discord that divided the ruling coalition in the 1980s: who should pay for the wars and who was responsible for the failure of a clear victory; the need for a civilian government; disagreement over taxes to increase state revenue; and Guatemala's role in the region and its foreign policy stance of active neutrality toward the then ruling Sandinista government in Nicaragua.

11. According to the *Bulletin of the Guatemalan Human Rights Commission/USA* (1997), between June and December 1997 human rights workers, politicians, political activists, journalists, indigenous leaders, campesinos, union leaders, teachers, and students received death threats; some were abducted by unidentified armed men and disappeared, while some were killed execution style. The *Bulletin* reports approximately one hundred such incidents took place over this six-month period.

12. The investigation of the murder of Bishop Gerardi is the most recent case in point and all the more significant because it is taking place during the postwar period. Despite recent evidence suggesting military involvement, the Guatemalan government continues to assert that the killing was without a political motive, maintaining instead that it was a crime of passion. A priest and a dog have been arrested.

13. On April 15, 1997, the Geneva-based United Nations Human Rights Commission (UNHRC) voted not to renew the mandate of a UN Independent Human Rights expert to monitor Guatemala's human rights record on a yearly basis. The decision was made despite the objections of international and Guatemalan human rights organizations. On May 1, 1997, Guatemala was named a member of the UNHRC for the 1998–2000 session. As one of fifty-four other member states on the commission, Guatemala is responsible for passing judgment on the human rights performance of other countries. Thus, in a period of just two weeks, Guatemala went from being a country under observation to an observer nation.

14. Begun in 1984, the Argentine Forensic Anthropology Team (Spanish acronym, EAAF) has worked to investigate human rights abuses by using the scientific tools and analysis of forensic anthropology to provide legal evidence of violations, to assist relatives of victims to recover the remains of the disappeared, to collaborate in the formation of in-country teams where necessary, to conduct seminars on human rights where there is interest, and to contribute to the historical reconstruction of the recent past (EAAF 1996). Initially, the team worked in Argentina, but since 1986 EAAF has expanded its activities to many countries of the world that have experienced human rights violations. The team first began work in Guatemala, in the department of Quiche, in

1991 at the behest of GAM and CONAVIGUA. Subsequently, working in conjunction with the Guatemalan Forensic Anthropology Team (EGAF), it has directed several other exhumations in Guatemala. The most recent was in the department of Chimaltenango, in the municipio of San Martin Jilotepeque, in 1997. In most cases, the efforts to carry out exhumations are thwarted by death threats against relatives and those involved in the excavations. See Amnesty International (1998).

15. Rumors of foreigners and strangers eating children are not limited to the women of Xe'caj. Scheper-Hughes (1992) found similar concerns among the people of northeast Brazil and also noted the prevalence of Pishtaco myths among Andean Indians, who believed that Indian fat and in particular Indian children's fat was used to grease the machinery of the sugar mills. In the 1980s a biological anthropologist working among Andean people found his research stymied because of rumors that he was measuring fat folds in order to choose "the fattest for . . . nefarious cannibalistic purposes" (236–37).

16. At an earlier stage in my study, this event might have had disastrous consequences for my continued work in the village. I noticed no discernible changes in how I was treated, however, which I attributed to the fact that I had been working in this particular village for well over a year.

4. From Wives to Widows

1. See Paul and Paul 1963, Tax 1952, Bunzel 1952, and Oakes 1951

2. See, for example, Paul and Paul 1963.

3. Early monographs document a degree of variation in pedida customs among the Maya, depending on community and region. See, for example, Paul and Paul 1963, Tax 1953, Bunzel 1952, and Nash 1970.

4. Likewise variations on gift giving are common. See Nash 1970, Rosenbaum 1993, and Eber 1995 for southern Mexico and Bunzel 1952, Paul and Paul 1963, Bossen 1984, and Ehlers 1990 for Guatemala.

5. See Lancaster 1992 regarding how poor people in a barrio of Managua, Nicaragua, use fictive kin networks as effective survival tactics.

6. In Chiapas, Rosenbaum 1993, Nash 1970, and Eber 1995 note that the young man lives with the bride's family for a year before he and his wife move to his father's house. In Guatemala, Gross and Kendall 1983 reports for Santiago Atitlan that although this is not the desired choice, it can and does happen. See Paul and Paul 1963.

7. The Gini coefficient is a measure of the concentration of resources. When applied to land, the Gini coefficient is based on two variables: farm size and amount of land. The number of farms in each farm size category is compared to the land in each category. In a perfectly equal distribution the Gini coefficient would equal 0. The higher the coefficient (100 is the theoretical maximum), the greater the concentration of land in larger farms. In 1979 the Gini coefficient for Guatemala was 85, higher than

all but two Latin American countries, prereform (1961) Peru, where the coefficient was 93.3, and prereform (1964) Colombia, where it was 86.4 (USAID 1982:1).

8. Bossen 1984 argued that there is a striking difference in cash value for women's subsistence work (weaving) and men's (corn production) because the local market is flooded with cheap machine-produced textiles while there is a scarcity of land for corn production, which drives up the price. In the late 1990s the market is flooded with cheap corn and beans imported from the United States, which now drives down the value and price garnered for men's subsistence work as well.

9. See Maynard 1963 and Smith 1995 for discussions of married Mayan women's status in their communities. Maynard focuses on women's economic contributions to the households and the difference between Mayan and ladino women, while Smith has argued that Mayan women have been the bearers of identity in exchange for a degree of social protection and autonomy inside the community, although endogamy was a prerequisite of that protection.

10. The Guatemalan Army did illegally cross the Mexican border in pursuit of the refugees and entered some of the refugee camps situated along the border. Later many were moved into the interior of Chiapas, and some as far north as the Yucatan.

11. The exchange rate of the U.S. dollar to the Guatemalan quetzal was about 1 to 3.5.

12. Departments most affected by the violence were El Quiche, Huehuetenango, Solala, Chimaltenango, Alta Vera Paz, Baja Vera Paz, and El Peten.

5. The Embodiment of Violence

1. None of the women in El Grupo, which is discussed below, spoke directly about rape, although they did speak openly about domestic violence. When they talked about sexual violations, the victim was always just someone they knew: a neighbor, a friend, or someone they had heard about.

2. Recently some medical and psychological anthropologists have theorized about the cultural construction of emotion and illness that contextualizes the political, economic, and social realities of people's lives (see Scheper-Hughes 1992; Jenkins 1991; Suarez-Orozco 1990; Low 1994). Yet, as Jenkins and Valiente (1994:176) have argued, the understanding of emotions as culturally constructed has led some scholars to exclude the body, neglecting to treat it as "both cultural object and cultural subject."

3. Jean Jackson (1994:209) has argued in her study of chronic pain sufferers in the United States that in some cases of chronic pain, "phenomenologically one is pain: ones' selfhood and one's body combine with pain. . . . Pain is a major component of the new self, the new identity."

4. See Csordas 1994 and Kleinman, Das, and Lock 1997 for important correctives.

5. El Grupo was part of a mainline Protestant church's larger project for widows in the area, located in Chimaltenango, in which Mayas participated in both the hier-

archy of the church as well as congregants. The goals of El Grupo were to address the spiritual, social, cultural, and material problems of the widows and to help them find solutions to these problems.

6. In Talcott Parson's well-known formulation (1972), the role associated with sickness involves related exemptions from the obligations of daily social life. A sick person is not held morally accountable for the illness and is relieved of responsibility for usual activities;. however, the sick person is expected to try to facilitate his or her recovery. In this sense, sickness is regarded as a "conditionally legitimate deviance" (132).

7. See also Cominsky 1983, Logan 1973, Nash 1967, and Woods and Graves 1973. Cominsky (1983) has argued that the separation of medicine and religion was reinforced in Guatemala by modern-day Catholicism as disseminated by missionaries and Western medicine.

8. Most studies have shown that the major encounter with Western medicine in rural Guatemala is with the pharmacist or at the local store to buy patent medicines.

9. Suarez-Orozco (1990) and Jenkins (1991) have found similar symptoms of distress among Central America refugees in the United States. Likewise, Guatemalan refugees in camps in Mexico experienced similar health problems (Melville and Lykes 1992).

6. The Dialectics of Cloth

1. These prices in U.S. dollars are based on the 1989/90 level of exchange rates of dollars to quetzals, ranging from US$1:Q3.25–4.1.

2. According to Hill (1992), during the colonial period a *corregidor* (Crown official at the local level) would purchase raw cotton, distribute it among the Indians in his district, and then force women, under penalty of fines or other threats, to spin and weave it into cloth that he would resell locally at a substantial profit.

3. Laurel Bossen (1984) notes, for example, that in the late 1970s some women in T'oj Nam began a weaving cooperative whose membership ranged from between twenty-five to a hundred women. And other women were selling new and used textiles to tourists in the town center.

4. PAVA began working informally with the Berhorst Foundation in Chimaltenango in 1982 to conduct a survey of the communities in the department that had been affected by the violence. The survey was funded by FUNDAPI—the development arm of the El Verbo Church (Church of the Word)—a Christian fundamentalist church, one of whose elders is General Efrian Rios Montt, who in March 1982 was part of a successful coup d'état that led to his presidency. Rios Montt was later overthrown in another coup in 1984. In 1983 PAVA received discretionary funds from USAID. During the time of my fieldwork PAVA had several small projects in municipios in the department of Chimaltenango.

5. In 1983 the Guatemalan government declared it illegal for more than two people to meet in a group.

6. Laura Woodward, the weaving coordinator for the PAVA project, stated that one of her responsibilities was to develop markets for the weavings, but she was unable to be maintain market outlets because most buyers of handwoven cloth were unwilling to pay prices adequate to sustain the weavers (author interview).

7. Multilaterals (UNICEF), bilaterals (the InterAmerican Foundation), NGOs (PAVA, Aj Quen, church-based projects, and Pueblo to People) have all funded weaving projects for widows in the department of Chimaltenango.

8. There are a few towns in the altiplano where both men and women as well as children continue to wear traje. And in San Pedro Sacetepequez in the department of Quetzaltenango most women no longer use traje (Ehlers 1990).

9. In the pueblos and aldeas of Xe'caj the corte is no longer distinctive but purchased in the marketplace according to the tastes of the buyer. What remains particular to the community besides the huipil is the way in which a women wraps and belts her corte.

10. To an outsider the contrast was startling. The order and aesthetics of people's homes and dress deviated sharply from the real and looming brutality and disorder created by army repression.

11. A Xe'caj huipil made mostly from mercerized cotton thread costs between Q150–200, a corte in the local market costs Q100–150, and a faja Q20, thus one basic outfit for an adult woman costs Q300–350, about US$100. Adding a delantal and a perraje would increase that by Q100–130 (1990 prices).

12. In *Guatemala: Eternal Spring, Eternal Tyranny* Jean-Marie Simon (1989) photographed a cadet at the Escuela Politecnica Military Academy displaying a huipil as he explained to other soldiers the different patterns of traje. I met several *desplacadas* (displaced women) living in Guatemala City who no longer used traje because they were afraid to do so. This was also true of several Mayan widows I met selling goods in the streets of Mexico City. Their fears were different, though: they were in Mexico without papers and did not want to draw attention to themselves. Mayan women who live in exile in the United States often do not use traje on a daily basis and only in their homes or on special occasions.

13. There has been a revitalization of traje use by middle-class educated Mayan women in the pan-Mayan movement. They explicitly make a statement of pride in their indigenous identity. What is unclear is whether in the future class itself will determine who among the Mayan women can afford to make and use traje.

7. Shifting Affiliations

1. In Xe'caj in 1990 there were at least ten different fundamentalist churches, not counting small splinter groups that had broken off from larger congregations. I distinguish among the terms "evangelical," "fundamentalist," and "Pentecostal" by drawing on the typologies used by David Stoll (1990): "evangelical" refers to any non-

Catholic Christian; "fundamentalist" signifies any Protestant who cites Scripture as the ultimate source; "Pentecostal" refers to one who subscribes to mystical forms of Protestantism based on the belief in the power of the Holy Spirit.

2. The arrival of Protestant missionaries in the late nineteenth century heralded the beginning of a new Christian era in Guatemala. Although the first missionaries were few in number and exercised limited influence at the local level, they were the beneficiaries of substantial state support. The Liberals, who came to national power in 1871, were determined to wrench the country from its colonial past, and their policy included destroying the political and economic foundations of Catholic Church influence in state affairs. Church properties and investments were confiscated, foreign clergy were expelled, religious orders were disbanded, and priests were not allowed to hold public office. Protestantism was to be the new religious ideology, accompanied by the rise of capitalist productive relations and modernity at the national level.

3. Some evangelical pastors were also targeted by the repressive forces, and some were killed while others were forced into exile (see Esquivel 1984).

4. The Charismatic Renewal, or *la renovacion*, as it is known in Guatemala, is a wing of the Catholic Church and is led locally by lay leaders. Adherents continue to identify themselves as Catholic, but their practices and beliefs are strongly influenced by Protestant fundamentalism.

5. Remarks made on April 24, 1998, in the National Cathedral of Guatemala, during an official presentation of the archdiocesan human rights report: *Guatemala: Nunca Mas* (REMHI 1998). On April 26—a little more than forty-eight hours later—Bishop Gerardi was assassinated on the parish grounds of San Sebastian Church in Guatemala City. Gerardi was the coordinating bishop for the interdiocesan project "The Recuperation of Historical Memory," which produced the report. During the worst years of political violence he had been bishop of El Quiche. Because of the assassination of priests and catechists and the harassment of the church by the military, Bishop Gerardi closed the diocese in June 1980. In 1982 he was forced into exile and did not return to Guatemala until 1984.

6. The human rights report *Guatemala: Nunca Mas* (REMHI 1998) states that in their review of 55,021 testimonies about victims, three out of every four victim were Mayan Indians. Of those, at least 30 percent belonged to an organized civilian organization, and, of those, half belonged to some religious group, with one in five belonging to a community group.

7. Some priests, nuns, and catechisms did join the guerrillas openly; others were sympathetic to the goals and methods of the armed insurgency, aiding in less obvious ways, such as supporting the CUC, a peasant organization founded by, among others, Vicente Menchu, the father of Rigoberta Menchu (see Burgos-Debray 1984). Others whom I interviewed state that they had initially opposed armed violence altogether but changed their minds after witnessing repression close at hand.

8. The documents issued from the Medallion Bishops Conference shifted the commitment of many priests and bishops in Latin American Catholic Church to service and solidarity with the poor. This represented an epistemological break

with the more conservative notions of trickle-down development. See Whitfield 1994 for a lengthy discussion of the formation of the progressive church in Central America.

9. Examples include Davis 1983; Dominguez and Huntington 1984; "The Rise of the Religious Right" 1987; and Westropp 1983. Stoll 1990 and Martin 1990 are notable exceptions in recognizing the diversity among evangelical forms. Among anthropological works that add to an understanding of evangelical Christians are two noteworthy collections: Schneider and Lindenbaum 1990 and Dow and Stephen 1990.

10. See Stoll 1990 for a discussion of Operation International Lovelift in the Ixil Triangle and other development projects financed by FUNDAPI, the development arm of the Church of the Word, during the presidency of Rios Montt. *Guatemala: Nunca Mas* (REMHI 1998) in April 1998 documented 422 massacres, with 192 of them committed in 1982, and noted that 80 percent of the violations cited coincided with the presidency of Rios Montt (1982–1983).

11. See Gill 1996 and Stacey 1990 for discussions of women in very diverse locales turning to evangelical churches as a haven from the vagaries of modernity and its disruption of community and familial social structures.

12. See Nash 1960, Brintnall 1979, Paul 1987, Annis 1987, Warren 1978, and Falla 1980.

13. See David Stoll's (1993) discussion of the multiple reasons given by local people for evangelical conversion in the Ixil Triangle.

14. John Watanabe notes that in the Mam community of Santiago Chimaltenango, "beyond these few restrictions . . . converts [whether Catholic or evangelical] remain outwardly indistinguishable from other Chimaltecos. The new religions wear lightly in normal day to day affairs, and as in the past, the dictates of *naab'l*, one's 'soul' or normal 'morality' continue to gauge acceptable Chimalteco behavior" (1983:229).

15. There are some Mayan Catholic priests, and after Padre Juan left Xe'caj he was replaced by a Maya-Quiche priest. Interestingly, although indigenous, this priest could not communicate to people in Xe'caj in Kaqchikel. Several people described him to me as someone with a heart of stone ("su corazon es como piedra"), explaining that he neither traveled to the aldeas frequently nor was attentive to people's social needs, as Padre Juan had been.

16. Sebastian Quinac, pers. comm., 1992.

17. "Mayodomo" is the title given to one of the principal officeholders of the cofradia. Ideally, a mayodomo is a man who is older, with physical strength, respect of community members, of good conduct, and with access to some money. The mayodomo keeps the saints of the cofradia in his house during the year he is in office, where he must maintain their altars with fresh flowers and candles, keep his doors open for people to visit the saints, tell their stories, and preside over meetings with the cofradia members.

18. In 1987, well before the public revitalization of Mayan spiritual practices, the CIA Country Guide listed three religions in Guatemala: Catholic, Protestant, and Mayan.

19. As Evan Vogt noted in writing about the Mayas of Chiapas, Mexico, in the 1960s:

> All Mayas today consider themselves Catholic (except insignificant minorities here and there which have joined Protestant churches), but this certainly does not mean that their Catholicism has obliterated aboriginal cosmological ideas. We have found a number of ancient Mayan concepts about the nature of the universe and of the gods in nearly every community in which ethnographic research has been penetrating. The deification of important aspects of nature continues as a crucial feature of the religious symbolism: the sun, the moon, rain, and maize are all prominent in most contemporary Maya belief systems. (1969:599).

20. The 1992 celebration by Spain and Latin American governments, called "Los Encuentros" (The Encounter), attempted to efface the violence of the Conquest, characterizing it innocently as a meeting of two worlds. Indigenous peoples from all the Americas protested this reworking of their history. Moreover, indigenous leaders began publicly to describe the process as an invasion rather than a conquest, pointing to the fact while they had been subjugated as a people they were never conquered, as evidenced by their continued existence.

glossary

aire. wind
ajk'ik. Mayan priest
alcalde. mayor
aldea. village
alegre. pleasant diversion
ancianas. elders
antepasados. ancestors
ataques. attacks
atole. corn-based drink
campesino. peasant
cargos. burdens
cedalina. pearl silk
ceiba. native tree of Guatemala; fine-leaved silk-cotton tree
chinamit. pre-Conquest residential Mayan settlement
cofradia. religious brotherhood dedicated to a particular saint in the local Catholic church
commandante. military commander

compadrazgo. ritual kinship
compadre. a person with whom one shares a ritual kinship bond
corregidor. local Crown official
corte. wraparound skirt
costumbre. Mayan spiritual practice
criollos. Spaniards born in the New World
cuerda. a unit of land measurement, varying in size by locale; in the area of Xe'caj, a twenty-by-twenty-foot parcel of farmland
culto. nightly religious service in an evangelical church
curandero. healer
delantal. apron
destacamento. military encampment
ejidos. village common lands
faja. woven belt
feria. fair
finca. large farm; in Guatemala, usually a commercial plantation growing crops for the international market
finca de mozo. land in the highlands that owners of coastal plantations rent out to campesinos in exchange for labor at harvest time
guaro. locally made alcohol
herencia. inheritance
hermano, hermana. brother, sister
huipil. traditional handwoven blouse worn by Mayan women
indigena. Indian
indio, indito. Indian, little Indian (pejorative)
intendente governor
ladino. non-Indian
lamina. metal sheets for roofing
maquilas. export apparel assembly plants
mal de ojo. evil eye
masa. corn dough
milpa. maize land
mestizaje. mixed-blood
morral. shoulder bag, mostly used by men
mozo. day laborer
municipio: administrative and territorial unit consisting of a town center and outlying villages. For Mayas, the municipio has also been the site of ethnic allegiance, signaled by distinctive dress (see *traje*), dialect, and customs.
nervios. nerves
oreja. spy
parcialidade. see *chinamit*
pedida. traditional betrothal ritual

pena. pain, sorrow, grief
peninsulares. Spanish residents of the New World born in Spain
perraje. shawl
pueblo. town
sobrehuipil. ceremonial woven blouse worn by Mayan women
suegra. mother-in-law
susto. fright; in some cases refers to soul loss
tienda. local store
traje. traditional clothing, apparel
tranquila. calm, peaceful
tzute. carrying cloth
yerba. wild plant

bibliography

Adams, Richard. 1970. *Crucifixion by Power: Essays on Guatemalan National Social Structure, 1944–1966*. Austin: University of Texas Press.

Agoson, Marjorie. 1987. "A Visit to the Mothers of the Plaza de Mayo." *Human Rights Quarterly* 9:426–435.

Aguayo, Sergio. 1983. "Los posibilidades de fascismo guatemalteco." *Uno sumo*, March 21, 11–15.

Alavi, Haniza. 1973. "Peasants and Revolution." In K. Gough and H. Sharma, eds., *Imperialism and Revolution in South Asia*, pp. 291–337. New York: Monthly Review Press.

America's Watch. 1984. *Guatemala: A Nation of Prisoners*. America's Watch Report, June. New York: America's Watch.

——. 1986. *Civil Patrols in Guatemala*. America's Watch Report, August. New York: America's Watch.

——. 1990. *Messengers of Death: Human Rights in Guatemala*. America's Watch Report, November 1988–February 1990. New York: America's Watch.

Amnesty International. 1981. "Guatemala: A Government Program of Political Murder." *New York Review of Books*, March 19, pp. 38–40.

——. 1982 (July). *Guatemala: Massive Extrajudicial Executions in Rural Areas Under the Government of General Efrain Rios Montt*. Special Briefing. New York: Amnesty International.

——. 1987. *Guatemala: The Human Rights Record*. New York: Amnesty International.

——. 1998 (April). *Guatemala: All the Truth, Justice for All*. New York: Amnesty International.

Anderson, Kenneth, and Jean-Marie Simon. 1987. "Permanent Counterinsurgency in Guatemala." *Telos* 73(fall): 9–46.

Anderson, Marilyn. 1978. *Guatemalan Textiles Today*. New York: Watson-Guptil.

Anderson, Marilyn, and Jonathan Garlock. 1988. *Granddaughters of Corn: Portraits of Guatemalan Women*. Willimantic, Conn.: Curbstone.

Anderson, Perry. 1976. *Conditions of Western Marxism*. New York: Verso.

Annis, Sheldon. 1987. *God and Production in a Guatemalan Town*. Austin: University of Texas Press.

Anwalt, Patricia Rieff. 1981. *Indian Clothing Before Cortes*. Norman: University of Oklahoma Press.

Appadurai, Arjun. 1986. "Introduction: Commodities and the Politics of Value." In Arjun Appadurai, ed., *The Social Life of Things: Commodities in Cultural Perspective*. Cambridge: Cambridge University Press.

Arendt, Hannah. 1958. *The Human Condition*. Chicago: University of Chicago Press.

——. 1973. *Origins of Totalitarianism*. New York: Harvest.

Arias, Arturo. 1990. "Changing Indian Identity: Guatemala's Violent Transition to Modernity." In Carol Smith, ed., *Guatemalan Indians and the State, 1549–1988*. Austin: University of Texas Press.

Aron, Adrianne, and Shawn Corne, eds. 1994. *Writings for a Liberation Psychology: Ignacio Martin-Baro*. Cambridge: Harvard University Press.

Asturias, Linda de Barrios. 1985. *Comalapa: Native Dress and Its Significance*. Guatemala City: Ixchel Museum Publications.

——. 1991. "Women's Costume as a Code in Comalapa, Guatemala." In Margot Blum Schevill, Janet Berlo, and Edward Duyer, eds. *Textile Traditions of Mesoamerica and the Andes*. New York: Garland.

AVANCSO. 1988. *La politica de desarrollo del estado guatemalteco, 1986–1987*. Cuaderno No. 7. Guatemala City: Inforpress.

——. 1992. *Donde esta el futuro? Procesos de reintegracion en comunidades de retornados*. Cuaderno No. 8. Guatemala City: Inforpress.

——. 1994 (July). *Impacto Ecológico de los cultivos hortícolas no-tradicionales en el altiplano de Guatemala*. Texto para Debate No. 5. Guatemala City: Inforpress.

Baranyi, Stephen, and Sean Loughlin. 1995. "Guatemala at the Crossroads." *New York Times*, October 1, p. 14.

Barry, Tom. 1986. *Guatemala: The Politics of Counterinsurgency*. Albuquerque: Inter-Hemispheric Education Resource Center.

Beneria, Lourdes, and Martha Roldan 1987. *The Crossroads of Class and Gender: Industrial Homework in Mexico City*. Chicago: University of Chicago Press.

Benjamin, Walter. 1969. "Theses on the Philosophy of History." In Hannah Arendt, ed., *Illuminations*, pp. 253–264. New York: Schocken.

Berman, Marshall. 1984. *All That Is Solid Melts Into the Air: The Experience of Modernity*. New York: Penguin.

Berryman, Phillip. 1994. *Stubborn Hope: Religion, Politics, and Revolution in Central America*. New York: New.

Binford, Leigh. 1996. *The El Mozote Massacre: Anthropology and Human Rights*. Tuscon: University of Arizona Press.

Bloch, Maurice. 1977. "The Past and the Present in the Present." *Man* (August), 12(2): 278–292.

——. 1986. *From Blessing to Violence*. Cambridge: Cambridge University Press.

Boff, Leonardo. 1993. *The Path of Hope: Fragments from a Theologian's Journey*. Maryknoll, N.Y.: Orbis.

Bogenschild, Thomas E. 1991. "The Roots of Fundamentalism in Western Guatemala, 1890–1944." Paper presented at the Latin American Studies Association meeting, Crystal City, Va., 1992.

——. 1992. "The Roots of Fundamentalism in Liberal Guatemala: Missionary Ideologies and Local Responses, 1882–1944." Ph.D. dissertation, University of California, Berkeley.

Bolton, Ralph. 1981. "Susto, Hostility, and Hypoglycemia." *Ethnology* 20(4): 261–276.

Bonfil Batalla, Guillermo. 1996. *Mexico Profundo*. Austin: University of Texas Press.

Boserup. Esther. 1970. *Women's Roles in Economic Development*. London: Allen and Unwin.

Bossen, Laurel. 1983. "Sexual Stratification in Mesoamerica." In Carl Kendall, John Hawkins, and Laurel Bossen, eds., *Heritage of Conquest: Thirty Years Later*, pp. 35–72. Albuquerque: University of New Mexico Press.

——. 1984. *The Redivision of Labor: Women and Economic Change in Four Guatemalan Communities*. Albany: State University of New York Press.

Bourdieu, Pierre. 1977. *Outline of a Theory of Practice*. Richard Nice, trans. Cambridge: Cambridge University Press.

Boyarin, Jonathan, ed. 1994. *Remapping Memory: The Politics of Time and Space*. Minneapolis: University of Minnesota Press.

Brecht, Bertolt. 1976. "The Anxieties of the Regime." In R. Manheim and J. Willet, eds., *Bertolt Brecht: Poems, 1913–1945*. London: Methuen.

Brintnall, Douglas E. 1979. *Revolt Against the Dead: The Modernization of a Mayan Community in the Highlands of Guatemala*. New York: Gordon and Breach.

Bulletin of the Guatemalan Human Rights Commission/USA. 1997 (June–December). Washington, D.C.

Bunzel, Ruth. 1972. *The Pueblo Potter: A Study of the Creative Imagination in Primitive Art*. 1929. Reprint. New York: Dover.

——. 1952. *Chichicastenango: A Guatemalan Village*. Locust Valley, N.Y.: Augustin.

Burdick, John. 1993. *Looking for God in Brazil: The Progressive Catholic Church in Urban Brazil's Religious Arena*. Berkeley: University of California Press.

Burgos-Debray, Elizabeth, ed. 1984. *I, Rigoberta Menchu: An Indian Women in Guatemala*. London: Verso.

Burleigh, Elizabeth. 1986. "Patterns of Childhood Malnutrition in San José Poaquil, Guatemala." Ph.D. dissertation, University of California, Los Angeles.

Burnett, Virginia Garrard. 1990. "Positivismo, Liberalismo e Impulso Misionero: Misiones Protestantes en Guatemala, 1880–1920." *Mesoamerica* 19 (June): 13–31.

Cabrera, Maria Luisa Perez-Arminin. 1990. *Tradicion y Cambio de la Mujer Quiche*. Guatemala City: IDESAC.

Cambranes, Julio C. 1985. *Coffee and Peasants in Guatemala*. Guatemala City: University of San Carlos.

Camus, Albert. 1955. *The Myth of Sisyphus and Other Essays*. New York: Vintage.

Carlsen, Robert. 1993. "Discontinuous Warps: Textile Production and Ethnicity in Contemporary Highland Guatemala." In June Nash, ed., *Crafts in the World Market*, pp. 199–222. Albany: State University of New York Press.

Carlsen, Robert S., and David Wenger. 1991. "The Dyes Used in Guatemalan Textiles: A Diachronic Approach." In Margot Blum Schevill, Janet Berlo, and Edward Duyer, eds. *Textile Traditions of Mesoamerica and the Andes*. New York: Garland.

Carmack, Robert. 1989. "The State and Community in Nineteenth-Century Guatemala: The Momostenango Case." In Carol Smith, ed., *Guatemalan Indians and the State, 1540–1988*. Austin: University of Texas Press.

——. 1995. *Rebels of Highland Guatemala: The Quiche-Mayas of Momostenango*. Norman: University of Oklahoma Press.

——, ed. 1988. *Harvest of Violence: The Mayan Indians and the Guatemalan Crisis*. Norman: University of Oklahoma Press.

Carrescia, Olivia. 1982. *Todos Santos Cuchumatan: Report from a Guatemalan Village*. New York: First Run/ICARUS films.

——. 1989. *Todos Santos: The Survivors*. New York: First Run/ICARUS Films.

Carter, Michael, Bradford Barham, and Dina Mesbah. 1996. "Agricultural Export Booms and the Rural Poor in Chile, Guatemala, and Paraguay." *Latin American Research Review* 31(1): 7–32.

Chance, John K., and William B. Taylor. 1985. "Cofradias and Cargos: An Historical Perspective on the Mesoamerican Civil-Religious Hierarchy." *American Ethnologist* 12(1): 1–20.

Chinchilla, Norma. 1977. "Industrialization, Monopoly Capitalism, and Women's Work in Guatemala." *Signs* 3(1): 38–56.

Clay, S. A. 1996. *Follow-up Study of Girls and Mayan Participation in Guatemalan Primary Education*. Arlington, Va.: USAID.

Cleary, Edward. 1997. "Birth of Latin American Indigenous Theology." In Guillermo Cook Leiden, ed., *Crosscurrents in Indigenous Spirituality: Interface of Maya, Catholic, and Protestant Worlds*, pp. 171–189. New York: Brill.

Clendinnen, Inga. 1987. *Ambivalent Conquests: Maya and Spaniard in the Yucatan, 1517–1570*. New York: Cambridge University Press.

Clifford, James. 1985. "Objects and Selves." In George Stocking, ed., *Objects and Other Essays on Museums and Material Culture*. Madison: University of Wisconsin Press.

——. 1988. *The Predicament of Culture: Twentieth-Century Ethnography, Literature, and Art*. Cambridge: Harvard University Press.

Clifford, James, and George Marcus. 1986. *Writing Culture: The Poetics and Politics of Ethnography*. Cambridge: Harvard University Press.

Cohen, Anthony. 1982. *The Symbolic Construction of Community*. London: Tavistock.

Cohn, Carol. 1987. "Sex and Death in the Rational World of Defense Intellectuals." *Signs* 12(4): 687–718.

Colby, B. N., and L. Colby. 1981. *The Daykeeper: The Life and Discourse of an Ixil Diviner*. Cambridge: Harvard University Press.

Comaroff, Jean. 1985. *Body of Power, Spirit of Resistance: The Culture and History of South African People*. Chicago: University of Chicago Press.

Cominsky, Sheila. 1972. *Decision Making and Medical Care in a Guatemalan Indian Community*. Ph.D. dissertation, Brandeis University, Waltham, Mass.

——. 1977. "The Impact of Methods in the Analysis of Illness Concepts in Guatemalan Commentary." *Social Science and Medicine* 11:325–332.

——. 1983. "Medical Pluralism in Mesoamerica." In Carl Kendall, John Hawkins, and Laurel Bossen, eds., *Heritage of Conquest: Thirty Years Later*, pp. 159–174. Albuquerque: University of New Mexico Press.

Connerton, Paul. 1989. *How Societies Remember*. Cambridge: Cambridge University Press.

Conroy, Michael, Douglas Murray, and Peter Rosset. 1996. *A Cautionary Tale: Failed U.S. Development Policy in Central America*. Boulder, Colo.: Lynne Reinner.

Cook, Noble David, and W. George Lovell, eds. 1992. *"Secret Judgments of God": Old World Disease in Colonial Spanish America*. Norman: University of Oklahoma Press.

Cook, Scott. 1984. *Peasant Capitalist Industry*. New York: University Press of America.

Coronil, Fernando, and Julie Skurski. 1991. "Dismembering and Remembering the Nation: The Semantics of Political Violence in Venezuela." *CSSH* 33(2): 288–337.

Csordas, Thomas. 1990. "Embodiment as Paradigm for Anthropology." *Ethos* 18(1): 5–47.

——, ed. 1994. *Embodiment and Experience: The Existential Ground of Culture and Self*. New York: Cambridge University Press.

Culbert, T. Patrick. 1974. *The Lost Civilization: The Story of the Classic Maya*. New York: Harper and Row.

Daniel, Valentine. 1996. *Charred Lullabies: Chapters in an Anthropology of Violence*. Princeton: Princeton University Press.

Das, Veena. 1997. "Language and Body: Transactions in the Construction of Pain." In Arthur Kleinman, Veena Das, and Margaret Lock, eds. *Social Suffering*, pp. 67–92. Berkeley: University of California Press.

Davis, Sheldon. 1983. "Guatemala: The Evangelical Holy War." *Global Reporter* 1(1): 9–10.

Davis, Sheldon, and Julie Hodson. 1982. *Witness to Political Violence in Central America.* Boston: Oxfam America.

Deere, Carmen Diana. 1977. "Changing Social Relations of Production and Peruvian Peasant Women's Work." *Latin American Perspectives* 4(12–13): 58–69.

——. 1990. *Household and Class Relations: Peasants and Landlords in Northern Peru.* Berkeley: University of California Press.

Deere, Carmen Diana, and Magdalena Leon, eds. 1987. *Rural Women and State Policy: Feminist Perspectives on Latin American Agricultural Development.* Boulder, Colo.: Westview.

de Janvry, Alain. 1981. *The Agrarian Question and Reformism in Latin America.* Baltimore: Johns Hopkins University Press.

de Leon Carpio, Ramiro, qtd. in "De Leon Carpio propone la tesis de la amnistia el dialogo." 1991. *La Hora* (Guatemala City), December 27, p. 2.

Deleuze, Gilles, and Félix Guattari. 1977. *Anti-Oedipus: Capitalism and Schizophrenia.* New York: Routledge.

Department of Defense, United States Army. 1992. The Academic Records Section of the School of the Americas FOIA: Archive No. 920985ARM035. Washington, D.C.: United States Army School of the Americas.

Diprose, Rosalyn. 1995. "The Body Biomedical Ethics Forgets." In Paul Komesaroff, ed., *Troubled Bodies: Critical Perspectives on Postmodernism, Medical Ethics, and the Body*, pp. 202–212. Durham: University of North Carolina Press.

Dominguez, Enrique, and Deborah Huntington. 1984. "The Salvation Brokers: Evangelicals in Central America." *NACLA Report on the Americas* 18(1): 2–36.

Doughty, Paul. 1988. "Crossroad for Anthropology: Human Rights in Latin America." In Theodore E. Downing and Gilbert Kushner, eds., *Human Rights and Anthropology*, pp. 43–72. Human Rights and Anthropology Report 24. Cambridge, Mass. : Cultural Survival.

Dow, James, and Lynn Stephen, eds. 1990. *Class, Politics, and Popular Religion in Mexico and Central America.* Society for Latin American Anthropology Publication Series, vol. 10. Washington, D.C.: Society for Latin American Anthropology, American Anthropological Association.

Downing, Theodore E., and Gilbert Kushner, eds. 1988. *Human Rights and Anthropology.* Human Rights and Anthropology Report 24. Cambridge, Mass.: Cultural Survival.

Dunkerley, James. 1988. *Power in the Isthmus: A Political History of Modern Central America.* London: Verso.

Dwyer, Daisy, and Judith Bruce, eds. 1988. *A Home Divided: Women and Income in the Third World.* Stanford: Stanford University Press.

EAAF (Equipo Antropologo Argentina Forense [Argentine Forensic Anthropology Team]). 1996. *Biannual Report 1994–1995.* Buenos Aires: EAAF.

Eber, Christine. 1995. *Women and Alcohol in a Highland Maya Town: Water of Hope, Water of Sorrow.* Austin: University of Texas Press.

Ehlers, Tracy Bachrach. 1990. *Silent Looms: Women and Production in a Guatemalan Town*. Boulder, Colo.: Westview.

——. 1993. "Belts, Business, and Bloomingdale's: An Alternative Model for Guatemalan Artisan Development." In June Nash, ed., *Crafts in the World Market*, pp. 181–196. Albany: State University of New York Press.

——. 1996. "Revisiting San Pedro Sacatepequez: W. R. Smith and the Entrepreneurial Woman." Paper presented at the annual meeting of the American Anthropological Association. San Francisco, November 18–22.

Enloe, Cynthia. 1993. *The Morning After: Sexual Politics at the End of the Cold War*. Berkeley: University of California Press.

——. 1996. "Women After Wars: Puzzles and Warnings." In Kathleen Barry, ed., *Vietnam's Women in Transition*, pp. 299–315. London: St. Martin's Press.

EPOCA (Environmental Project on Central America). 1990. "Guatemala: A Political Ecology." Green Paper No. 5. San Francisco: Earth Island Institute.

Escobar, Arturo. 1988. "Power and Visibility: Development and the Invention and Management of the Third World." *Cultural Anthropology* 13(4): 428–443.

——. 1991. "Anthropology and the Development Encounter: The Making and Marketing of Development Anthropology." *American Ethnologist* 18(4): 658–682.

Esquivel, Julia. 1984. "On the Persecution of Christians and the Church in Guatemala." In Suzanne Jonas, Ed McCaughlin, and Elizabeth Martinez, eds., *Guatemala Tyranny on Trial*. San Francisco: Synthesis.

Etienne, Mona. 1980. "Women and Men, Cloth, and Colonialization: The Transformation of Production and Distribution Relations Among the Baule (Ivory Coast)." In Mona Etienne and Eleanor Leacock, eds., *Women and Colonialization: Anthropological Perspectives*, pp. 214–238. New York: Praeger.

Fabian, Johannes. 1983. *Time and the Other: How Anthropology Makes Its Object*. New York: Columbia University Press.

Falla, Ricardo. 1980. *Quiche Rebelde*. Guatemala City: Editorial Universitaria de Guatemala.

——. 1983. "The Massacre at the Rural Estate of San Francisco," July 1982. *Cultural Survival Quarterly* 7(1): 37–42.

——. 1992. *Masacres de la Selva, Ixcan, Guatemala, 1975–1982*. Guatemala: Universidad de San Carlos de Guatemala.

Farmer, Paul. 1992. *AIDS and Accusation: Haiti and the Geography of Blame*. Berkeley: University of California Press.

——. 1997. "On Suffering and Structural Violence: A View from Below." In Arthur Kleinman, Veena Das, and Margaret Lock, eds. *Social Suffering*, pp. 261–284. Berkeley: University of California Press.

Farriss, Nancy. 1984. *Maya Society Under Colonial Rule: The Collective Enterprise of Survival*. Princeton: Princeton University Press.

Feldman, Alan. 1991. *Formations of Violence: The Narrative of the Body and Political Terror in Northern Ireland*. Chicago: University of Chicago Press.

Fergusson, Edna. 1930. *Guatemala*. New York: Knopf.

Firth, Raymond. 1979. *Art and Life in New Guinea*. 1936. Reprint. New York: AMS Press.

Fisher, Edward, and R. McKenna Brown, eds. 1997. *Maya Cultural Activism in Guatemala*. Austin: University of Texas Press.

——. 1981. "Engagement and Detachment: Reflections on Applying Social Anthropology to Social Affairs." *Human Organization* 40(3): 193–201.

Folbre, Nancy. 1986. "Cleaning House: New Perspectives on Households and Economic Development." *Journal of Development Economics* 22(1): 5–40.

Forche, Carolyn. 1994. *The Angel of History*. New York: HarperCollins.

Forester, Cindy. 1992. "A Conscript's Testimony: Inside the Guatemalan Army." *Report on Guatemala* 13(2): 6, 14.

Foster, George. 1960. *Culture and Conquest: America's Spanish Heritage*. Chicago: Quadrangle.

——. 1961. "The Dyadic Contract: A Model for the Social Structure of a Mexican Peasant Village." *American Anthropologist* 63(6):1173–1192.

——. 1965. "Peasant Society and the Image of Limited Good." *American Anthropologist* 67(2): 293–315.

——. 1976. "Disease Etiologies in Non-Western Medical Systems." *American Anthropologist* 78(4): 773–782.

Foucault, Michel. 1977. *Discipline and Punish: The Birth of the Prison*. Alan Sheridan, trans. New York: Pantheon.

Fox, Richard, ed. 1991. *Recapturing Anthropology: Working in the Present*. Santa Fe, N.M.: School of American Research Press.

Franco, Jean. 1985. "Killing Priests, Nuns, Women, and Children." In Marshall Blouskey, ed., *On Signs*, pp. 414–442. Baltimore: Johns Hopkins University Press.

Fried, Morton H. 1967. *The Evolution of Political Society: An Essay in Political Anthropology*. New York: Random House.

Friedlander, Judith. 1975. *Being Indian in Hueyapan: A Study of Forced Identity in Contemporary Mexico*. New York: St. Martin's Press.

Galeano, Eduardo. 1967. Pais Ocupado . Mexico: Nuestro Tiempo.

Garcia, Ana Isabel, and Enrique Gomariz. 1989. *Mujeres Centroamericanas: Ante La Crisis, La Guerra, y El Proceso de Paz*. Vol. 1. San José, Costa Rica: Flacso.

Garcia Canclini, Nestor. 1993. *Transforming Modernity: Popular Culture in Mexico*. Lidia Lozano, trans. Austin: University of Texas Press.

Garst, Rachel, and Tom Barry. 1990. *Feeding the Crisis*. Lincoln: University of Nebraska Press.

Ghosh, Amitov. 1995. "The Ghost of Mrs. Gandhi." *New Yorker*, July 17, pp. 34–37.

Giddens, Anthony. 1990. *The Consequences of Modernity*. Stanford: Stanford University Press.

Gill, Lesley. 1990. "Like a Veil to Cover Them: Women and the Pentecostal Movement in La Paz." *American Ethnologist* 17(5): 708–721.

——. 1996. *Precarious Dependencies: Gender, Class, and Domestic Service in Bolivia*. New York: Columbia University Press.

Gleijeses, Pierto. 1991. *Shattered Hope*. Princeton: Princeton University Press.

Goldin, Liliana, and Brent Metz. 1991. "Expression of Cultural Change: Invisible Converts to Protestantism Among Highland Guatemala Maya." *Ethnology* 30(4): 325–338

Gossen, Gary. 1996. "Maya Zapatistas Move to the Ancient Future." *American Anthropologist* 98(3): 528–538.

Gough, Kathleen. 1968. "New Proposals for Anthropologists." Social Responsibility Symposium. *Current Anthropology* 9(5): 403–407.

Graburn, Nelson H. H. 1976. Introduction to Nelson H. H. Graburn, ed., *Ethnic Tourist Arts: Expression from the Fourth World*, pp. 1–32. Berkeley: University of California Press.

"Graduacion de escueal politecnica." 1989. *La Hora* (Guatemala City), December 7, p. 17.

Gramsci, Antonio. 1971. *Selections from the Prison Notebooks*. Quintin Hoare and Geoffrey Nowell, trans. and eds. New York: International.

Green, Linda. 1989. "Consensus and Coercion: Primary Health Care and the Guatemalan State." *Medical Anthropology Quarterly* 3(3): 246–257.

——. 1997a. "Broccoli, Brussel Sprouts, and *la violencia*: Social Relations of Power in Rural Guatemala." Paper presented at the annual meeting of the America Anthropological Association, Washington, D.C., November 19–23.

——. 1997b. "The Localization of the Global: Contemporary Production Practices in a Mayan Community." In Lynne Phillips, ed., *The Third Wave of Modernization in Latin America*, pp. 51–64. Wilmington, Del.: Jaguar.

——, ed. 1998. "The Embodiment of Violence." Special Issue. *Medical Anthropology Quarterly* 11(2).

Gross, Joseph, and Carl Kendall. 1983. "The Analysis of Domestic Organization in Mesoamerica: The Case of Postmarital Residence in Santiago Atitlán, Guatemala." In Carl Kendall, John Hawkins, and Laurel Bossen, eds., *Heritage of Conquest: Thirty Years Later*, pp. 201–228. Albuquerque: University of New Mexico Press.

Guyer, Jane, and Pauline Peters, eds. 1987. "Special Issue: Conceptualizing the Household." *Development and Change* 18(2).

Guzman Bochler, Carlos, and Jean Loup Herbert. 1970. *Guatemala: Una interpretation historico-social*. Mexico City: Siglo Ventiuno.

Hall, Stuart. 1994. "Cultural Identity and Diaspora." In Patrick Williams and Laura Chrisman, eds., *Colonial Discourse and Post-Colonial Theory: A Reader*, pp. 392–403. New York: Columbia University Press.

Hallowell, A. Irving. 1955. "The Self in Its Behavioral Environment." In *Culture And Experience*, pp. 75–100. Philadelphia: University of Pennsylvania Press.

Hammerschlag, Kari. 1991. "Indigenous Women's Crafts Groups in the Guatemalan Highlands: Opportunities and Constraints for Engagement through Organization." M.A. thesis, Latin American Studies, University of California, Berkeley.

Handy, Jim. 1984. *Gift of the Devil: A History of Guatemala.* Boston: South End.

——. 1990. "The Corporate Community, Campesino Organizations, and Agrarian Reform: 1950–1954." In Carol Smith, ed., *Guatemalan Indians and the State, 1540–1988.* Austin: University of Texas Press.

——. 1992. "Guatemala: A Tenacious Despotism." *Report on the Americas* 25(3): 31–37.

——. 1994. *Revolution in the Countryside: Rural Conflict and Agrarian Reform in Guatemala, 1944–1954.* Chapel Hill: University of North Carolina Press.

Hartmann, Heidi. 1981. "The Family as the Locus of Gender, Class, and Political Struggle." *Signs* 6(3): 366–394.

Harvey, David. 1989. *Conditions of Postmodernity.* Cambridge, Mass.: Blackwell.

——. 1996. *Justice, Nature, and the Geography of Difference.* Cambridge, Mass.: Blackwell.

Hastrup, Kristen. 1994. "Anthropological Knowledge Incorporated: A Discussion." In Kristin Hastrup and Peter Hervik, eds., *Social Experience and Anthropological Experience,* pp. 224–237. London: Routledge.

Hawkins, John. 1984. *Inverse Images: The Meaning of Culture, Ethnicity, and Family in Post-Colonial Guatemala.* Albuquerque: University of New Mexico Press.

Hendrickson, Carol. 1995. *Weaving Identities: Construction of Dress and Self in a Highland Guatemala Town.* Austin: University of Texas Press.

Herman, Judith. 1992. *Trauma and Recovery: The Aftermath of Violence from Domestic Abuse to Political Terror.* New York: Basic.

Hertz, Robert. 1960. "Contribution to the Study of the Collective Representation of Death." In *Death and the Right Hand,* pp. 29–88. London: Cohen and West.

Hill, Robert. 1992. *Colonial Cakchiquels: Highland Maya Adaptations to Spanish Rule, 1600–1700.* Fort Worth: Harcourt Brace College Publishers.

Hill, Robert, and John Monaghan. 1987. *Continuities in Highland Maya Social Organization: Ethnohistory in Sacapulas, Guatemala.* Philadelphia: University of Pennsylvania Press.

Holiday, David. 1997. "Guatemala's Long Road to Peace." *Current History* (February):68–74.

Hooks, Margaret. 1991. *Guatemalan Women Speak.* London: Catholic Institute for International Relations.

Hunter, Monica. 1936. *Reaction to Conquest: Effects of Contact with Europeans on the Pondo of South Africa.* London: Oxford University Press.

Hymes, Dell, ed. 1969. *Reinventing Anthropology.* New York: Pantheon.

Immerman, Richard. 1982. *The CIA in Guatemala: The Foreign Policy of Intervention.* Austin: University of Texas Press.

INGUAT (Guatemalan National Tourism Institute). 1997. *Tourism 1996.* Bulletin No. 25 (May). Guatemala City: INGUAT.

Inter-Hemispheric Education Resource Center. 1988. *Guatemala: Private Organizations with U.S. Connections in Guatemala*. Albuquerque: Inter-Hemispheric Education Resource Center.

Jackson, Jean. 1994. "Chronic Pain and the Tension Between the Body as Subject and Object." In Thomas Csordas, ed., *Embodiment and Experience: The Existential Ground of Culture and Self*, pp. 201–228. New York: Cambridge University Press.

Jameson, Fredric. 1989. "Postmodernism; or, The Cultural Logic of Late Capitalism." *New Left Review* 10(176): 31–45.

Jenkins, Janis. 1991. "The State Construction of Affect: Political Ethos and Mental Health Among Salvadoran Refugees." *Culture, Medicine, and Psychiatry* 15:139–165.

Jenkins, Janis, and Martha Valiente. 1994. "Bodily Transactions of the Passions" Et Calor Among Salvadoran Women Refugees." In Thomas Csordas, ed., *Embodiment and Experience: The Existential Ground of Culture and Self*, pp. 163–182. New York: Cambridge University Press.

Jonas, Susanne. 1991. *The Battle for Guatemala: Rebels. Death Squads, and U.S. Power*. Boulder, Colo.: Westview.

——. 1997. "The Peace Accords: An End and a Beginning." *Report on the Americas, New York: North American Congress on Latin America (NACLA)* 30(6): 6–10.

Jordahl, Mikkel. 1987. "Counterinsurgency and Development in the Altiplano: The Role of Model Villages and the Poles of Development in the Pacification of Guatemala's Indigenous Highlands." Washington, D.C.: Guatemalan Human Rights Commission.

Kabeer, Naila. 1994. *Reversed Realities and Gender Hierarchies in Development Thinking*. New York: Verso.

Katz, Cindi. 1992. "All the World Is Staged: Intellectuals and the Projects of Ethnography." *Society and Space* 10:495–510.

Kessing, Roger. 1987. "Anthropology as Interpretive Quest." *Current Anthropology* 28(2): 161–176.

Kleinman, Arthur, and Joan Kleinman. 1997. "The Appeal of Experience, The Dismay of Images: Cultural Appropriations of Suffering in Our Times." In Arthur Kleinman, Veena Das, and Margaret Lock, eds., *Social Suffering*, pp. 1–24. Berkeley: University of California Press.

Kleinman, Arthur, Veena Das, and Margaret Lock, eds. 1997. *Social Suffering*. Berkeley: University of California Press.

Krueger, Chris, and Kjell Enge. 1985. *Security and Development: Conditions in the Guatemalan Highlands*. Washington, D.C.: Washington Office on Latin America.

Kuper, Hilda Beemer. 1947. *An African Aristocracy: Rank Among the Swazi of Bechwanaland*. London: Oxford University Press.

La Farge, Oliver. 1947. *Santa Eulalia: The Religion of a Cuchumatan Town*. Chicago: University of Chicago Press.

Lancaster, Roger N. 1988. *Thanks to God and the Revolution*. New York: Columbia University Press.

——. 1992. *Life Is Hard: Machismo, Danger, and the Intimacy of Power in Nicaragua.* Berkeley: University of California Press.

Lefebvre, Henri. 1991. *Critique of Everyday Life.* 1947. John Moore, trans. London: Verso.

Lesser, Alexander. 1933. *The Pawnee Ghost Dance Hand Game: A Study of Cultural Change.* Columbia University Contributions to Anthropology 16. New York: Columbia University Press.

Levenson-Estrada, Deborah. 1994. *Trade Unionists Against Terror: Guatemala City, 1954–1985.* Chapel Hill: University of North Carolina Press.

Lincoln, Stephen J. 1942. *The Maya Calender of the Ixil of Guatemala.* Washington, D.C.: Carnegie Institution.

Lira, Elizabeth, and Maria Isabel Castillo. 1991. *Psicologia de la Amenaza Politica y del Miedo.* Santiago, Chile: Ediciones Chile America, CESOC.

Lock, Margaret. 1993. "Cultivating the Body: Anthropology and Epistemologies of Bodily Practice and Knowledge." *Annual Review of Anthropology* 22:133–155.

Logan, Michael H. 1973. "Humoral Medicine in Guatemala and Peasant Acceptance of Modern Medicine." *Human Organization* 32(4): 385–395.

——. 1979. "Variations Regarding Susto Causality Among the Cakchiquel of Guatemala." *Culture, Medicine, and Psychiatry* 3:153–166.

Lovell, W. George. 1988. "Surviving Conquest: The Maya of Guatemala in Historical Perspective." *Latin America Research Review* 23(2): 25–57.

——. 1992. *Conquest and Survival in Colonial Guatemala.* Kingston, Ontario: Queens University Press.

Lovell, W. George, and Christopher Lutz. 1992. "Conquest and Population: Maya Demography in Historical Perspective." Paper presented at the Latin American Studies Association meeting, Los Angeles, September 21–24.

Low, Setha. 1994. "Embodied Metaphors: Nerves as Lived Experience." In Thomas Csordas, ed., *Embodiment and Experience : The Existential Ground of Culture and Self,* pp. 139–162. New York: Cambridge University Press.

Mallon, Florencia. 1983. *The Defense of Community in Peru's Central Highlands: Peasant Struggle and Capitalist Transitions, 1860–1940.* Princeton: Princeton University Press.

——. 1995. *Peasant and Nation: The Making of Postcolonial Mexico and Peru.* Berkeley: University of California Press.

Manz, Beatriz. 1988. *Refugees of a Hidden War: The Aftermath of Counterinsurgency in Guatemala.* Albany: State University of New York Press.

Marcus, George, and Michael Fischer. 1986. *Anthropology as Cultural Critique: An Experimental Moment in the Human Sciences.* Chicago: University of Chicago Press.

Martin, David. 1990. *Tongues of Fire: The Explosion of Protestantism in Latin America.* Oxford: Blackwell.

Martin-Baro, Ignacio. 1989. "La institucionalizacion de la guerra." Conferencia prenunciada en el XXII Congreso International Psicologia. Buenos Aires, June 25–30.

——. 1990. "La violencia en Centroamerica: Una vision psicosocial." *Revista de Psicologia de El Salvador* 9(35): 123–146.

Martinez Pelaez, Severo. 1979. *La patria del criollo: Ensayo de interpretacion de la realidad colonial quatemalteca*. San José, Costa Rica: Editorial Universitaria Centroamerica.

Mason, J. W. 1973. "A Historical View of the Stress Field." *Journal of Stress Research* (June):22–36.

Maynard, Eileen. 1963. "The Women of Palin: A Comparative Study of Indian and Ladino Women in a Guatemalan Village." Ph.D. dissertation, Cornell University, Ithaca, N.Y.

McClintock, Cynthia. 1994. "The Angel of Progress: The Pitfalls of the Term 'Post-Colonialism.' " In Patrick Williams and Laura Chrisman, eds., *Colonial Discourse and Post-Colonial Theory*, pp. 291–305. New York: Columbia University Press.

McCreery, David. 1976. "Coffee and Class: The Structure of Development in Liberal Guatemala." *Hispanic American Historical Review* 56:438–460.

——. 1990. "State Power, Indigenous Communities, and Land in Nineteenth-Century Guatemala." In Carol Smith, ed., *Guatemalan Indians and the State, 1540–1988*, pp. 96–115. Austin: University of Texas Press.

——. 1994. *Rural Guatemala, 1760–1940*. Stanford: Stanford University Press.

Melville, Margarita, and W. Brinton Lykes. 1992. "Guatemalan Indian Children and the Socio-Cultural Effects of Government-Sponsored Terrorism." *Social Science and Medicine* 34(5): 533–548.

Melville, Marjorie, and Tom Melville. 1971. *Guatemala: The Politics of Land Ownership*. New York: Free.

Merleau-Ponty, Maurice. 1962. *The Phenomenology of Perception*. Colin Smith, trans. 1945. Reprint. London: Routledge and Kegan Paul.

Mersky, Marcie. 1989. "Empresarios y transcion politica en Guatemala." Unpublished manuscript.

Messick, Brinkley. 1987. "Subordinate Discourse: Women, Weaving, and Gender Relations in North Africa." *American Ethnologist* 14(2): 210–225.

Mintz, Sidney, and Eric Wolf. 1950. "An Analysis of Ritual Co- Parenthood (*Conpadrazgo*)." *Southwestern Journal of Anthropology* 6(4): 341–368.

Mohanty, Chandra. 1994. "Under Western Eyes: Feminist Scholarship and Colonial Discourse." In Patrick Williams and Laura Chrisman, eds., *Colonial Discourse and Post-Colonial Theory*, pp. 196–220. New York: Columbia University Press.

Montejo, Victor. 1987. *Testimony: Death of a Guatemalan Village*. Willimantic, Conn.: Curbstone.

Morris, Walter, Jr., and Jeffrey Jay Foxx. 1987. *The Living Maya*. New York: Abrams.

Nandy, Ashis, ed. 1988. *Science, Hegemony, and Violence: A Requiem for Modernity*. Delhi: Oxford University Press.

Nash, June. 1960. "Protestantism in an Indian Village in the Western Highlands of Guatemala." *Alpha Kappa Deltan* (winter):49–53.

——. 1967. "Death as a Way of Life: The Increasing Resort to Homicide in a Mayan Indian Community." *American Anthropologist* 69(5): 455–470.

——. 1970. *In the Eyes of the Ancestors: Belief and Behavior in a Maya Community*. New Haven: Yale University Press.

——. 1980. "Aztec Women: The Transition from Status to Class in Empire and Colony." In Mona Etienne and Eleanor Leacock, eds., *Women and Colonization: Anthropological Perspectives*. New York: Praeger.

——. 1995. "The Reassertion of Indigenous Identity: Mayan Responses to State Intervention in Chiapas." *Latin American Research Review* 30(5): 7–42.

——, ed. 1993. *Crafts and the World Market*. Albany: State University of New York Press.

Nash, June, and Helen Safa, eds. 1986. *Women and Change in Latin America*. South Hadley, Mass.: Bergin and Garvey.

Nash, Manning. 1958. *Machine Age Maya: The Industrialization of a Guatemalan Community*. Chicago: University of Chicago Press.

Nelson, Diane. 1996. "Maya Hackers and the Cyberspacialized Nation-State: Modernity, Ethnostalgia, and a Lizard Queen in Guatemala." *Cultural Anthropology* 11(3): 287–308.

Nordstrom, Carolyn. 1997. *A Different Kind of War Story*. Philadelphia: University of Pennsylvania Press.

Nordstrom, Carolyn, and JoAnn Martin, eds. 1992. *The Paths to Domination, Resistance, and Terror*. Berkeley: University of California Press.

Nordstrom, Carolyn, and Antonius C. G. M. Robben, eds. 1995. *Fieldwork Under Fire: Contemporary Studies of Violence and Survival*. Berkeley: University of California Press.

Oakes, Maude. 1951. *Two Crosses of Todos Santos*. Princeton: Princeton University Press.

Ollman, Bertell. 1990. "Putting Dialectics to Work: The Process of Abstraction in Marx's Method." *Rethinking Marxism* 3(1): 26–74.

——. 1993. *Dialectical Investigations*. New York: Routledge.

O'Neale, Lila M. 1945. *Textiles of Highland Guatemala*. Washington, D.C.: Carnegie Institute.

O'Nell, Carl W., and Henry A. Selby. 1968. "Sex Difference in the Incidence of Susto in Two Zapotec Pueblos: An Analysis of the Relationship Between Sex Role Expectations and Folk Illness. *Ethnology* 7:95–105.

Opazo Berneles, Andres. 1990. "El movimiento protestante Centroamerica: Una aproximacion cuantitativa." In Luis E. Sasande, ed., *Protestantismos y procesos sociales en Centroamerica*, pp. 13–37. San José, Costa Rica: EDUCA.

Orellana, Sandra L. 1987. *Indian Medicine in Highland Guatemala: The Pre-Hispanic and Colonial Periods*. Albuquerque: University of New Mexico Press.

Ortner, Sherry. 1995. "Resistance and the Problem of Ethnographic Refusal." *Journal of Comparative Studies of Society and History* 37(1): 173–193.

Osbourne, Lily de Jongh. 1935. *Guatemalan Textiles*. New Orleans: Tulane University Press.

Otzoy, Irma. 1991. "Maya Clothing and Identity." Paper presented at the annual meeting of the American Anthropological Association, Chicago, November 18–22.

Pages Larraya, F. 1967. *La esquizofrenia en tierra Ayamaras y Quechuas*. Buenos Aires: Drusa.

PAHO (Pan American Health Organization). 1994. *Health Conditions in the Americas*. No. 549 (II). Washington, D.C.: PAHO.

Parsons, Talcott. 1972. "Definition of Health and Illness in the Light of American Values and Social Structure." In E. Gartly Jaco, ed., *Patients, Physicians, and Illness*, pp. 107–127. Glencoe, Ill.: Free.

Paul, Benjamin D. 1987. "Fifty Years of Religious Change in San Pedro La Laguna, a Mayan Community in Highland Guatemala." Paper presented at the annual meeting of the American Anthropological Association, Chicago, November 22–26.

Paul, Benjamin, and William Demarest. 1988. "The Operation of a Death Squad in San Pedro, La Laguna." In R. Carmack, ed., *Harvest of Violence*. Norman: University of Oklahoma Press.

Paul, Lois, and Benjamin D. Paul. 1963. "Changing Marriage Patterns in a Highland Guatemalan Community." *Southwestern Journal of Anthropology* 19:131–148.

Perelli, Carina. 1994. "Memorias de Sangre: Fear, Hope, and Disenchantment in Argentina." In Jonathan Boyarin, ed., *Remapping Memory: The Politics of Time and Space*, pp. 39–66. Minneapolis: University of Minnesota Press.

Peteet, Julie. 1991. *Gender in Crisis: Women and the Palestinian Resistance Movement*. New York: Columbia University Press.

Peterson, Kurt. 1992. *The Maquiladora Revolution in Guatemala*. Occasional Paper 2. New Haven: Yale Law School.

Poole, Deborah, ed. 1994. *Unruly Order: Violence, Power, and Cultural Identity in the High Provinces of Southern Peru*. Boulder, Colo.: Westview.

Popkin, Margaret. 1997. "Guatemala's National Reconciliation Law: Combating Impunity or Continuing It?" *Revista IIDH* (Instituto Interamericana de los Derechos Humanos), no. 24 (July–December 1996): 173–184.

Prechtel, Martin, and Robert Carlsen. 1988. "Weaving and Cosmos Amongst the Tzutujil Maya of Guatemala." *Res* 15 (spring): 122–132.

Price, Sally. 1989. *Primitive Art in Civilized Places*. Chicago: University of Chicago Press.

Recinos, Adrian, and Della Goetz, trans. 1953. *Annals of the Cakchikels*. Norman: University of Oklahoma Press.

Redfield, Robert. 1930. *Tepoztlan: A Mexican Village*. Chicago: University of Chicago Press.

——. 1941. *The Folk Culture of Yucatan*. Chicago: University of Chicago Press.

Redfield, Robert, and Alfonso Villa Rojas. 1934. *Chan Kom: A Maya Village*. Publication 448. Washington, D.C.: Carnegie Institute.

REMHI (Recuperation of Historical Memory Report). 1998 (April). *Guatemala: Nunca Mas*. Guatemala City: Archdiocese of Guatemala.

"The Rise of the Religious Right in Central America." 1987. *Resource Center Bulletin* (Albuquerque), no. 10 (summer/fall).

Robert F. Kennedy Center for Human Rights. 1993. *Persecution by Proxy: The Civil Patrols in Guatemala*. New York: Robert F. Kennedy Center for Human Rights.

Rojas, Flavio Lima. 1988. *La Cofradia: Reducto Cultural Indigena. Guatemala: Seminario de Integracion Social.*

Rosaldo, Michelle. 1984. "Toward an Anthropology of Self and Feeling." In R. Shweder and R. Levine, eds., Culture Theory. Cambridge: Cambridge University Press.

Roseberry, William. 1983. *Coffee and Capitalism in the Venezuelan Andes*. Austin: University of Texas Press.

——. 1989. *Anthropologies and Histories: Essays in Culture, History, and Political Economy*. New Brunswick, N.J.: Rutgers University Press.

Rosenbaum, Brenda. 1993. *With Our Heads Bowed: The Dynamics of Gender in a Mayan Community*. Albany: Institute for Mesoamerican Studies, SUNY Albany; distributed by University of Texas Press.

Rossell Arellana, Mariano. 1949. "Discurso del arzobispo con motivo de la benedicion de nuevo local del instituto indigena de Nuestro Senor de Socorro." *Verbum* (Guatemala City), January 30, p. 1.

Rosset, Peter. 1991. "Non-traditional Export Agriculture in Central America: Impact on Peasant Farmers." Working Paper #20. Santa Cruz: University of California.

Rowe, Ann Pollard. 1981. *A Century of Change in Guatemalan Textiles*. New York: Center of Inter-American Relations.

Rubel, Arthur. 1964. "The Epidemiology of a Folk Illness: Susto in Hispanic America." *Ethnology* 3:268–283.

Rubel, Arthur J., Carl W. O'Nell, and Rolando Collado-Ardon. 1991. *Susto, a Folk Illness*. Berkeley: University of California Press.

Sahlins, Marshall, and Elman Service, eds. 1960. *Evolution and Culture*. Ann Arbor: University of Michigan Press.

Said, Edward, 1978. *Orientalism*. London: Routledge.

Salovesh, Michael. 1983. "Person and Polity in Mexican Cultures: Another View of Social Organization." In Carl Kendall, John Hawkins, and Laurel Bossen, eds., *Heritage of Conquest: Thirty Years Later*, pp. 175–200. Albuquerque: University of New Mexico Press.

Sanford, Victoria. 1993. "Victim as Victimizer: Indigenous Childhood and Adolescence in Guatemala's Culture of Terror." Master's thesis, San Francisco State University.

Saqb'ichil-COPMAGUA. 1995. "Acuerdo sobre identida y derechos de los pueblos indigenas Puento 3 del acerdo de Laz Firme and Duradura 31 March 1995." Guatemala City: Saqb'ichil-COPMAGUA.

Sayer, Chole. 1985. *Costumes of Mexico*. Austin: University of Texas Press.

Scary, Elaine. 1985. *The Body in Pain: The Making and Unmaking of the World*. Oxford: Oxford University Press.

Scheper-Hughes, Nancy. 1992. *Death Without Weeping: The Violence of Everyday Life in Brazil*. Berkeley: University of California Press.

——. 1996. "Small Wars and Invisible Genocides." *Social Science and Medicine* 43(5): 889–900.

Scheper-Hughes, Nancy, and Margaret Lock. 1987. "The Mindful Body: A Prolegomenon to Future Work in Medical Anthropology." *Medical Anthropology Quarterly* 1(1): 6–41.

Schevill, Margot Blum. 1985. *Evolution in Textile Design from the Highlands of Guatemala*. Occasional Papers No. 1. Berkeley: Lowie Museum of Anthropology, University of California.

——. 1986. *Costume as Communication*. Studies in Anthropology and Material Culture, vol. 4. Bristol, R.I.: Haffenreffer Museum of Anthropology, Brown University.

——. 1990 "Guatemalan Maya Dress and Its Creation; Gender and Ambiguity." Paper presented at the annual meeting of the American Anthropological Association, New Orleans, December 2–6.

Schirmer, Jennifer. 1993. "The Seeking of Truth and the Gendering of Consciousness: The Comadres of El Salvador and the CONAVIGUA Widows of Guatemala." In Sarah Radcliffe and Sallie Westwood, eds., *Viva: Women and Popular Protest in Latin America*, pp. 30–64. New York: Routledge.

——.*The Guatemalan Military Project: A Violence Called Democracy*. 1998. Philadelphia: University of Pennsylvania Press.

Schlesinger, Stephen, and Stephen Kinzer. 1982. *Bitter Fruit: The Untold Story of the American Coup in Guatemala*. New York: Anchor.

Schneider, Jane. 1987. "Anthropology and Cloth." *American Review of Anthropology* 16:409–448.

Schneider, Jane, and Shirley Lindenbaum, eds. 1990. "Frontiers of Christian Evangelicals." *American Ethnologist* 14(1).

Scott, James. 1985. *Weapons of the Weak: Everyday Forms of Peasant Resistance*. New Haven: Yale University Press.

Sen, Gita, and Caren Grown. 1987. *Development, Crises and Alternative Visions: Third World Women's Perspectives*. New York: Monthly Review Press.

Seremetakis, C. Nadia. 1991. *Women, Death, and Divination in Inner Mari*. Chicago: University of Chicago Press.

Service, Elman. 1962. *Primitive Social Organization: An Evolutionary Perspective*. New York: Random House.

Sexton, James. 1978. "Protestantism and Modernization in Two Guatemalan Towns." *American Ethnologist* 5(2): 280–302.

Shaefer, Stacy. 1990. "Huichol Weavers: Design Keepers of Sacred Knowledge." Paper presented at the annual meeting of the American Anthropological Association, New Orleans, December 2–6.

Shanin, Teodore, ed. 1987. *Peasants and Peasant Societies*. 2d ed. Oxford: Blackwell.

Sherman, William. 1979. *Forced Native Labor in Sixteenth-Century Central America*. Lincoln: University of Nebraska Press.

Sider, Gerald. 1988. *Culture and Class in Anthropology and History: A Newfoundland Illustration*. New York: Cambridge University Press.

——. 1989. "A Delicate People and Their Dogs: The Cultural Economy of Subsistence Production—A Critique of Chayanov and Meillassoux." *Journal of Historical Sociology* 2(1): 14–40.

——. 1996. "The Making of Peculiar Local Culture: Producing and Surviving History in Peasant and Tribal Societies." In Alf Luedtke, ed., *Was bleibt van marxistischen Perspekitven in der Geshichtsforschung?* pp. 101–148. Göttingen, Germany: Vendenhoeck und Ruprecht.

Simon, Jean-Marie. 1989. *Guatemala: Land of Eternal Spring, Eternal Tyranny*. New York: Norton.

Sluka, Jeffrey. 1992. "The Anthropology of Conflict." In C. Nordstrom and J. Martin, eds., *The Paths to Domination, Resistance, and Terror*. Berkeley: University of California Press.

Smith, Carol A. 1987. "Culture and Community: The Language of Class in Guatemala." In Mike Davis, Manning Murable, Fred Pfeil, and Michael Sprinkler, eds., *The Year Left: An American Socialist Yearbook*, 2:197–217. London: Verso.

——. 1990a. "Class Formation and Class Consciousness in an Indian Community: Totonicapan in the 1970s. In Carol Smith, ed., *Guatemalan Indians and the State, 1540—1988*. Austin: University of Texas Press.

——. 1990b. "The Militarization of Civil Society in Guatemala: Economic Reorganization as a Continuation of War." *Latin America Perspectives* 67(4): 8–41.

——. 1995. "Race-Class-Gender Ideology in Guatemala: Modern and Anti-Modern Forms." *Journal of Comparative Study of Society and History* 37(4): 723–749.

Smith, Gavin. 1989. *Livelihood and Resistance: Peasants and the Politics of Land in Peru*. Berkeley: University of California Press.

Smith-Ayala, Emilie. 1991. *The Granddaughters of Ixmucane Guatemalan Women Speak*. Toronto: Women's Press.

Sontag, Susan. 1977. *Illness as Metaphor*. New York: Vintage.

Stacey, Judith. 1990. *The Brave New Families*. New York: Basic.

Stavenhagen, Rodolfo. 1968. "Classes, Colonialism, and Acculturation." In Joseph A. Kahl, ed., *Comparative Perspectives on Stratification: Mexico, Great Britain, Japan*, pp. 31–63. Boston: Little Brown.

——. 1978. "Capitalism and the Peasantry in Mexico." *Latin American Perspectives* 5(3): 27–37.

Stephen, Lynn. 1991a. *Zapotec Women*. Austin: University of Texas Press.

——. 1991b. "Export Markets and Their Effects on Indigenous Craft Production: The Case of the Weavers of Teotitlan del Valle, Mexico." In *Textile Traditions of Mesoamerica and the Andes*, pp. 381–402. New York: Garland.

Stohl, Michael. 1984. "International Dimensions of State Terrorism." In M. Stohl and

G. A. Lopez, eds., *Terrible Beyond Endurance? International Dimensions of State Terrorism*, pp. 1–9. Westport, Conn.: Greenwood.

Stoll, David. 1990. *Is Latin America Turning Protestant?* Berkeley: University of California Press.

——. 1993. *Between Two Armies: In the Ixil Towns of Guatemala* . New York: Columbia University Press.

Suarez-Orozco, Marcelo. 1990. "Speaking of the Unspeakable: Toward a Psycho-Social Understanding of Responses to Terror." *Ethos* 18(3): 353–383.

——. 1992. "A Grammar of Terror: Psychological Responses to State Terrorism in the Dirty War and Post Dirty Argentina." In C. Nordstrom and J. Martin, eds., *The Paths to Domination, Resistance, and Terror*, pp. 219–259. Berkeley: University of California Press.

Tax, Sol. 1937. "The Municipios of the Midwestern Highlands of Guatemala." *American Anthropologist* 39(3): 423–444.

——. 1941. "Worldview and Social Relations in Guatemala." *American Anthropologist* 43(1) : 27–42.

——. 1952. "Economy and Technology." In Sol Tax, ed., *Heritage of Conquest: The Ethnology of MIddle America*, pp. 20–34. Glencoe, Ill.: Free.

——. 1953. *Penny Capitalism: A Guatemalan Indian Economy*. Smithsonian Institution, Institute of Social Anthropology Publication No. 16. Washington, D.C.: Smithsonian Institution.

Tedlock, Barbara. 1982. *Time and the Highland Maya*. Albuquerque: University of New Mexico Press.

Tedlock, Barbara, and Dennis Tedlock. 1985. "Text and Textiles: Language and Technology in the Arts of the Quiche Maya." *Journal of Anthropological Research* 41(2): 121–146.

Thompson, E. P. 1972. "Time, Work Discipline, and Industrial Capitalism." *Past and Present* 20:56–97.

Tousignant, Michael. 1979. "Espanto: A Dialogue with the Gods." *Culture, Medicine, and Psychiatry* 3:347–361.

Turner, Terrance. 1994. "Bodies and Anti-bodies: Flesh and Fetish in Contemporary Social Theory." In Thomas Csordas, ed., *Embodiment and Experience : The Existential Ground of Culture and Self*, pp. 27–47. New York: Cambridge University Press.

Turton, Andrew. 1986. "Patrolling the Middle Ground: Methodological Perspectives on Everyday Peasant Resistance." *Journal of Peasant Studies* 13(2): 36–48.

USAID (United States Agency for International Development). 1982. *Land and Labor in Guatemala: An Assessment*. Washington, D.C.: GPO.

Uvin, Peter. 1998. *Aiding Violence: The Development Enterprise in Rwanda*. West Hartford, Conn.: Kumarian.

Uzzell, Douglas. 1974. "Susto Revisted: Illness as Strategic Role." *American Ethnologist* 1(2): 369–378.

Vilas, Carlos. 1995. *Between Earthquakes and Volcanoes: Market, State, and Revolutions in Central America*. Ted Kuster, trans. New York: Monthly Review Press.

Vincent, Joan. 1990. *Anthropology and Politics*. Tucson: University of Arizona Press.

Vogt, Evon. 1969. *Zinacatan: A Maya Community in the Highlands of Chiapas*. Cambridge: Harvard University Press.

Wagley, Charles. 1941. *Economics of a Guatemalan Village*. Memoirs of the American Anthropological Association. Menasha, Wisc.: American Anthropological Association.

Warren, Kay. 1978. *Symbolism of Subordination: Indian Identity in a Guatemalan Town*. Austin: University of Texas Press.

——. ed. 1993. *The Violence Within: Cultural and Political Opposition in Divided Nations*. Boulder, Colo.: Westview.

Watanabe, John. 1983. "In the World of the Sun: A Cognitive Model of Mayan Cosmology." *Man* 18(4): 710–768.

——. 1992. *Maya Saints and Souls in a Changing World*. Austin: University of Texas Press.

Watts, Michael. 1992. "Living Under Contract: Work, Production Politics, and the Manufacture of Discontent in a Peasant Society." In Alan Pred and Michael Watts, *Reworking Modernity Capitalisms and Symbolic Discontent*, pp. 65–105. New Brunswick, N.J.: Rutgers University Press.

Weiner, Annette, and Jane Schneider, eds. 1989. *Cloth and the Human Experience*. Washington, D.C.: Smithsonian Institution Press.

Weschler, Lawrence. 1990. *A Miracle, a Universe: Settling Accounts with Torturers*. New York: Penguin.

Westropp, Mary. 1983. "Christian Counterinsurgency." *Cultural Survival Quarterly* 7(3): 28–31.

Whitfield, Teresa. 1994. *Paying the Price: Ignacio Ellacuria and the Murdered Jesuits of El Salvador*. Philadelphia: Temple University Press.

Wickham-Crowley, Timothy. 1990. "Terror and Guerrilla Warfare in Latin America." *Journal of Comparative Studies in Society and History* 32(2): 201–216.

Williams, Raymond. 1977. *Marxism and Literature*. Oxford: Oxford University Press.

——. 1983. *Keywords*. New York: Oxford University Press.

——. 1989. *People of Black Mountain*. London: Chatto and Windus.

Williams, Robert. 1986. *Export Agriculture and the Crisis in Central America*. Chapel Hill: University of North Carolina Press.

Wilson, Richard. 1991. "Machine Guns and Mountin Spirits: The Cultural Effects of State Repression Among the Q'eqchi of Guatemala." *Critique of Anthropology* 11(1): 33–61.

——. 1995. *Maya Resurgence in Guatemala Q'eqchi's Experiences*. Norman: University of Oklahoma Press.

——. ed. 1997. *Human Rights, Culture, and Context: Anthropological Perspectives*. London: Pluto.

Wolf, Diane. 1992. *Factory Daughters: Gender, Household Dynamics, and Rural Industrialization in Java*. Berkeley: University of California Press.

——. ed. 1996. *Feminist Dilemmas in Fieldwork*. Boulder, Colo.: Westview.

Wolf, Eric. 1955. "Types of Latin American Peasantry: A Preliminary Discussion." *American Anthropologist* 57(3): 452–471.

——. 1957. "Closed Corporate Peasant Communities in Mesoamerica and Java." *Southwestern Journal of Anthropology* 13(1): 1–18.

——. 1966. *Peasants*. Englewood Cliffs, N.J.: Prentice-Hall.

——. 1969. *Peasant Wars of the Twentieth Century*. New York: Harper and Row.

——. 1982. *Europe and the People Without History*. Berkeley: University of California Press.

——. 1986. "The Vicissitudes of the Closed Corporate Peasant Community." *American Ethnologist* 13(2): 325–329.

——. 1994. "Perilous Ideas: Race, Culture, People." *Current Anthropology* 35(1): 1–12.

Wolpe, Harold, ed. 1980. *The Articulation of Modes of Production: Essays from "Economy and Society."* London: Routledge and Kegan Paul

Woods, Clyde, and Theodore Graves. 1973. *The Proces of Medical Changes in a Highland Guatemalan Town*. Latin American Studies Series, vol. 21. Los Angeles: University of California Latin American Center.

Young, Allen. 1995. *The Harmony of Illusions: Inventing Post-Traumatic Stress Disorder*. Princeton: Princeton University Press.

Young, Iris. 1990. *Justice and the Politics of Difference*. Princeton: Princeton University Press.

Young, Kate, Carol Wolkowitz, and Roslyn McCullagh, eds. 1981. *Of Marriage and the Market*. London: Routledge and Kegan Paul.

Zingg, R. 1938. *Primitive Artists: The Huichols*. Denver: University of Denver Contributions to Ethnology.

index